Y0-BZW-573

Financial Reporting & Analysis:
Using Financial Accounting Information

8th Edition

Charles H. Gibson

The University of Toledo

SOUTH-WESTERN
™
THOMSON LEARNING

Australia · Canada · Mexico · Singapore · Spain · United Kingdom · United States

Study Guide and Forms for *Financial Accounting: A Bridge to Decision Making, 4/e*, by Robert W. Ingram and Bruce A. Baldwin

Team Director: David L. Shaut
Acquisitions Editor: Sharon Oblinger
Sr. Developmental Editor: Sara E. Wilson
Production Editor: Deanna Quinn
Marketing Manager: Larry Qualls
Manufacturing Coordinator: Doug Wilke
Printer: Globus Printing

Printed in the United States of America
1 2 3 4 5   03 02 01 00

For more information contact South-Western, 5101 Madison Road, Cincinnati, Ohio, 45227 or find us on the Internet at http://www.swcollege.com

For permission to use material from this text or product, contact us by
• **telephone: 1-800-730-2214**
• **fax: 1-800-730-2215**
• **web: http://www.thomsonrights.com**

ISBN 0-324-02459-2

This book is printed on acid-free paper.

TABLE OF CONTENTS

SECTION F1: THE ACCOUNTING INFORMATION SYSTEM

CHAPTER F1: ACCOUNTING AND ORGANIZATIONS

Introductory Note to Students: As you begin your study of accounting, please consider the following ideas:

- Accounting makes important contributions to all phases of the transformation process that converts resources into goods and services. This major theme along with related concepts and techniques can assist individuals in many different situations.

- The introductory study of accounting is not just calculations. The authors of both the textbook and ***Study Guide*** integrate underlying concepts, important vocabulary, and specific quantitative analysis to provide an introductory view appropriate for a wide variety of students.

- *Active learning* should be a big part of your overall study plan. Answering self-study questions in the text; working homework problems; researching, discussing, and presenting projects; and completing the questions and exercises in the ***Study Guide*** reinforce the learning that begins with reading and listening.

- This ***Study Guide*** reviews major concepts of each chapter and provides exercises for practice. Each chapter of the ***Study Guide*** includes a chapter focus; a chapter outline; review questions, exercises, and short essays; and suggested answers. In this introductory chapter shaded boxes provide explanations of these components.

Chapter Focus

The ***Chapter Focus*** contains the major theme, important elements, and specific learning objectives for the chapter. This is a key section that describes important vocabulary, skills, and concepts you should know when you finish studying the chapter. This section can be used as both a preview (to see what's coming up) and a final checklist (to be sure you have covered everything).

Major Theme: Accounting is a system that provides information for making decisions about organizations.

Important Elements: As you study the chapter, look for the following major topics:

> An illustration of the accounting process
> The purposes and functions of organizations
> Decisions made in organizations
> The role of accounting in making decisions about organizations

Learning Objectives: After studying this chapter, you should be able to:

Identify:	How accounting information helps decision makers.
	Financing activities and the types of decisions they require.
	Investing activities and the types of decisions they require.
	Operating activities and the types of decisions they require.
Explain:	Why accounting is an information system.
	Why owners invest in businesses.
	Why accounting information is useful to investors.
Compare and Explain:	Major types of organizations and their purpose.
Describe:	The steps in an organization's transformation process.
Define:	Accounting.

Chapter Review

The ***Chapter Review*** presents important concepts in a sentence outline form. This section reviews the chapter and places the vocabulary and ideas in an organized pattern.

Introduction. Accounting is a system that produces information useful in making decisions about organizations. This chapter establishes fundamental vocabulary and concepts that serve as foundations for further study. Major topics include the role of information in decisions, the accounting process, the purpose of organizations, decisions in organizations, a summary of the transformation process, and a definition of accounting.

1. **Information for Decisions**. Various forms of information such as facts, ideas, and concepts assist in understanding situations. More specifically, accounting information assists decision makers in evaluating economic choices.

    A. Virtually all components of accounting information are measurable in monetary terms.

        1. In many cases, decision makers use accounting information to assess the level of risk or uncertainty involved in a specific course of action.

        2. Decision makers also use accounting information to measure an organizations' profit.

    B. Overall, accounting provides a model of a business by measuring business activities in monetary terms.

2. **The Accounting Process**. Economic decisions involve choices about resource allocation, and the accounting process helps managers and investors understand the possible consequences of economic decisions.

    A. In general, the accounting process provides basic financial information about economic activities.

        1. Accounting records provide detailed information about specific economic events. (A check register for a personal checking account is a good example of a basic accounting record.)

        2. Summary reports group specific accounting records and provide an overall view for decision makers. (A checking account report that displays a beginning balance, total deposits, total withdrawals, and an ending balance is an example of an accounting report.)

    B. An accounting system includes several steps that process information from accounting records and provide summary reports.

1.   An <u>account</u> is an accounting record designed to track increases or decreases in a specific type of activity. For example, a cash account would track all cash increases and decreases while a land account would track all the purchases and sales of land.

2.   A <u>transaction</u> is an economic event that changes various account balances. For example, the purchase of land for cash is an economic event, or transaction, that effects both the cash and land accounts.

[Important Note: *Transactions* are events or activities in the life of an individual or organization. These transactions affect accounting records, or *accounts,* that track the financial impact of activities.]

3.   By providing a mechanism for recording, summarizing, and reporting economic information, an <u>accounting system</u> serves decision makers.

C.   Broadly speaking, <u>organizations</u> are groups of people who develop, produce, and/or distribute goods or services. Many <u>stakeholder</u> groups of any organization can and should use accounting information. Owners, creditors, employees, suppliers, customers, communities, and governmental may all have a direct or indirect economic interest in an organization.

3.   **The Purpose of Organizations**. Organizations may be categorized using several different criteria.

A.   One important criterion is profit objectives. <u>Business organizations</u> sell their goods and services with the expectation of earning a profit. Alternatively, <u>governmental and nonprofit organizations</u> provide goods or services without the profit expectation.

B.   A second criterion is the specific nature of activities. <u>Merchandising organizations</u> purchase finished products and resell them to other organizations or individuals. <u>Manufacturing organizations</u> purchase raw materials and produce finished goods. <u>Service organizations</u> do not sell goods at all; they provide needed services such as financial, legal, public safety, or educational services to other organizations and individuals.

C.   To be successful, all organizations must create value by transforming resources from their most basic form to a different form which society considers more valuable. This transformation process involves transactions in markets. An accounting measure for the increased value an organization provides is the difference between the total price of goods and service sold by an organizations and the organization's cost for resources used in the transformation process.

D.   The difference between the resources created and the resources consumed represents profit. In equation form, this relationship is:

Resources Created - Resources Consumed = Profit.

1.   Owners invest in a business in order to receive a return on their investment in the form of profit. Return on investment is:

Profit ÷ Amount Invested = Return on Investment

This calculation provides a percentage measure of an organization's profitability. Profits may be distributed to owners or kept in the business. Either way, the owners benefit.

2.   Distributed profits are paid to owners for their personal use. Undistributed profits are retained or reinvested in the business to enhance the opportunities for greater profitability.

E.   Decisions about initial investments or reinvesting undistributed profits involve risk about the return that might be achieved.

F.   Effective businesses successfully provide goods and services demanded by the public. Efficient businesses provide those goods and services at a low enough cost to assure profits. Accounting information helps investors assess both the effectiveness and efficiency of a firm.

4.   **Decisions in Organizations**. Stakeholders make decisions about three general types of organizational activities: financing activities, investing activities, and operating activities.

A.   <u>Financing activities</u> include decisions and transactions designed to obtain and manage financial resources. Financial resources may be provided by either owners or creditors (or in many cases both).

    1.   The specific process of financing through owners depends upon the legal form of organization.

        a.   A <u>corporation</u> is a legal entity independent from any of its owners. Investors purchase <u>shares of stock</u> or shares of ownership in a corporation. These shares allow shareholders to vote on major decisions and share in any profit of the corporation.

        b.   <u>Proprietorships</u> or <u>partnerships</u> do not have legal status separate from the owners of these organizations. Owners still contribute resources to these organizations and have a stake in organizational decisions and financial success.

        c.   Corporations have several specific advantages over proprietorships or partnerships.

            (1)   They have <u>continuous lives</u>, <u>limited liability</u>, <u>professional management</u>, and <u>the ability to raise large amounts of capital</u>.

            (2)   In addition, shareholders need not be concerned with <u>mutual agency</u> -- the right of a partner to enter into contracts that bind all the other partners.

        d.   Corporations also have disadvantages when compared with proprietorships or partnerships.

            (1)   They <u>pay taxes on their incomes</u>, <u>comply with costly regulations</u>, and <u>make audited financial disclosures</u>.

            (2)   Corporations may be <u>difficult to manage</u> due to their large size.

            (3)   Shareholders do not usually have access to the same level and detail of information as those individuals who actually manage the firm.

(a)   This creates a <u>moral hazard</u> situation. Moral hazards are conditions where <u>agents</u> -- the managers -- may use their superior information to benefit themselves more than the <u>principals</u> -- the shareholders.

(b)   To control this moral hazard, managers are required to make frequent reports to shareholders.

2.   Financing from creditors, or lenders, comes in the form of loans or other forms of debt. Creditors expect to receive both the repayment of the amount loaned and interest payments.

3.   Financing decisions involve managerial choices about the amount of resources required as well as the specific sources of financing and the resulting obligations of the organization.

B.   <u>Investing activities</u> include the selection and management of specific long-term resources that assist in the development, production, and sales of goods and services. These resources include land, buildings, equipment, and legal rights such as patents. Investing decisions involve the amounts of specific resources that will be acquired and their control.

C.   <u>Operating activities</u> include the use of resources to develop, produce, and distribute goods and services. These day-to-day operating activities include research and development, design and engineering, purchasing, human resource management, production, distribution, marketing and selling, and providing customer service.

[Important Note: The nature of financing, investing, and operating activities is a major theme running throughout this introduction. Remember that managers within an organization must be engaged in all three phases:

Financing Activities: Acquiring financial capital.
Investing Activities: Using the financial capital to
**   acquire various types of long-term resources.**
Operating Activities: Using the resources to develop
**   produce, and distribute products and services.]**

5.   **Summarizing the Transformation Process.** Each organization performs some type of transformation process which includes the acquisition of capital (financing activities), the acquisition of equipment and other resources (investing activities), and the use of these various resources to develop, produce, and distribute goods and services (operating decisions).

6.   **Definition of Accounting**. Accounting is an information system that assists managers as they make financing, investing, and operating decisions within an organization's transformation process. Specifically, accounting measures and reports the various transactions that form the transformation process.

7.   **Accounting as a Profession**. The accounting profession includes accountants who work in businesses, public accounting firms, governmental and nonprofit organizations, and educational institutions.

      A.   Management accountants provide all accounting functions within business organizations. These activities include accounting systems development and management, financial reporting, financial planning and analysis, cost accounting and cost management, and internal auditing.

      B.   Public accountants provide independent auditing, tax advisory, and consulting services to businesses, nonprofit organizations, and individuals. Independent audit services may only be performed by a Certified Public Accountant (CPA).

      C.   Accountants in governmental and nonprofit organizations provide services such as accounting systems support and the preparation and interpretation of financial reports for their organizations.

      D.   Accounting educators engage in both teaching and research activities related to accounting.

Review Questions, Exercises, and Short Essays

The *Review Questions, Exercises, and Short Essays* section presents questions and exercises for practice. Success in the multiple-choice questions, exercises, and short essays is an important indication of mastery of the content of the chapter. Suggested answers appear at the end of the chapter.

<u>Multiple Choice Questions</u>: These questions reinforce vocabulary and basic concepts from the chapter. In each case, select the answer you believe to be the *best*.

1.   The purpose of accounting is to help people make decisions about:
    a.   Profit-seeking businesses only.
    b.   Economic activities in general.
    c.   Risk of investments.
    d.   Investment returns to shareholders.

2.   Financial accounting systems measure activities in terms of:
    a.   Local currency.
    b.   Metric units.
    c.   Various quantities.
    d.   When they happen.

3.   Return on investment is a term that refers to:
    a.   The dollar amount that is paid to investors.
    b.   Another expression for interest.
    c.   The returning of an investors funds when an investment matures.
    d.   A measure that provides information about the profitability of an investment.

4.   Risk, in financial decisions, refers to:
    a.   The *possibility* that an investment will not earn a return.
    b.   The *likelihood* that an investment will not earn a return.
    c.   Uncertainty about an outcome.
    d.   Any investment, because they are all risky.

5.   An information system can be broadly described as:
    a.   A set of computers and computer terminals used to provide information.
    b.   A set of interrelated activities that are coordinated to record, summarize, and report information.
    c.   An organizational unit that provides reports to those asking for information.
    d.   A completed set of financial reports.

6. The basic information unit in an accounting system is:
   a.   An account.
   b.   A transaction.
   c.   A company.
   d.   An operating department within any organization.

7. Those who have an economic interest in an organization and who are affected by the activities of the organization are known as:
   a.   Stockholders.
   b.   Stakeholders.
   c.   Employees.
   d.   Owners.

8. Organizations create value by:
   a.   Transforming less desirable resources into more desirable resources.
   b.   Selling goods and services only.
   c.   Using labor to produce goods and services.
   d.   Researching customer preferences.

9. A disadvantage of the corporate form of organization is:
   a.   Moral hazard.
   b.   Limited liability.
   c.   Unlimited life.
   d.   Separation of management and ownership.

10. Markets can be classified by the types of goods and service exchanged. Important market types are:
   a.   Financial markets.
   b.   Supplier markets.
   c.   Product markets.
   d.   All of the above.

11. Price is regarded as an important piece of information in a market economy because:
   a.   It describes inflation.
   b.   The higher that prices are, the less people will buy.
   c.   It represents the value agreed to between a willing buyer and willing seller at a particular point in time.
   d.   It measures business profit.

12. An accounting measure of the value resulting from transformations is:
    a. Price of resources.
    b. Cost of resources.
    c. Selling price of resources produced minus the cost of resources used.
    d. Cash Received.

13. *Revenues* are:
    a. Sales prices of goods and services.
    b. Cash collected from customers.
    c. The amount of profit earned.
    d. Investments by owners.

14. *Financing decisions* are choices made about alternative:
    a. Sources of financial resources.
    b. Types of business organizations.
    c. Resources that will be used in the transformation process.
    d. Nonfinancial resources that will be required by the business.

15. *Operating activities* may include:
    a. Borrowing money for a new transportation facility.
    b. Human resource management.
    c. Issuing new shares of stock and selling them to investors.
    d. Acquiring a building.

<u>Exercises</u>: These questions require the analysis of economic situations and application of accounting concepts.

1.   <u>Calculating Profit</u>. Ann James invested $20,000 in a business selling in-line skates and accessories. She opened a bank account in her business' name and began to look for a location and inventory to sell. During her first month, she engaged in the following transactions:

   a.   Rented space in a downtown building and paid $1,500 for the first month's rent.

   b.   Purchased inventory for $5,000 and sold this merchandise for $8,000.

   c.   Paid a sales assistant $400 for two weeks of work.

   d.   Paid an electric bill of $250 for the month.

   e.   Paid taxes of $560 for the month.

   f.   Paid for $250 of supplies that were used.

   What is Ann's profit for the month? (Hint: Prepare a statement of profit earned similar to text Exhibit 9.) Do you think she has been successful? Why or why not?

2. <u>Identifying Financing, Investing, and Operating Decisions</u>. Tom Robinson, an avid kayaker and fly-fisher has decided that he will turn his hobbies into a career by opening a kayak and fly-fishing business in the San Juan Islands. He realizes that he will need a business plan and that he will need to make a number of decisions:

a. For tax and legal reasons, Tom plans to incorporate the business. He will deposit $10,000 of his own money in a checking account in the name of the business and will be the sole shareholder.

b. He develops a detailed list of equipment and estimates that it will cost $20,000.

c. Tom has approached a local banker who has indicated a willingness to lend another $10,000 to the business.

d. Tom feels that he will need another $5,000 for supplies and cash on hand for unforeseen events. He will take a loan from a credit union in his own name and lend the money to his business with the intention that the business will repay the loan with interest.

e. Tom will need some clerical assistance. He plans to hire a part-time bookkeeper.

Identify each of Tom's decisions as a financing, investing, or operating decision.

3.   <u>Describing Specific Transformation Processes and Exchange Transactions</u>. Organizations in a variety of service, merchandising, and manufacturing activities participate in various transformation processes and exchange transactions.

   a.   Describe how the following organizations engage in a process that transforms resources and creates value:

   The Boeing Company.

   Microsoft Corporation.

   American Van Lines.

   YMCA.

   b.   Can the following organizations be seen as engaging in exchange transactions? How do these exchanges differ? What is exchanged?

   The New York Times.

   The Limited.

   The Salvation Army.

   US National Park Service.

Short Essays: The following short essay questions not only reinforce important concepts but also give you a chance to practice writing skills. Answer these questions in complete sentences.

1. Summarizing the Transformation Process. Briefly summarize the transformation cycle in you own words.

2. Describing Operating Activities. Describe briefly some of the functions involved in operating activities and give examples.

3.   <u>Describing Investing Activities</u>. Describe briefly some of the functions involved in investing activities and give examples.

4.   <u>Describing Financing Activities</u>. Describe briefly some of the functions involved in financing activities and give examples.

5.   <u>Discussing Accounting Careers</u>. How does the work of management accountants differ from the work of public accountants?

Suggested Answers to Review Questions, Exercises, and Short Essays

Suggested Answers for both the review questions and exercises allow you to check your work immediately. The most benefit comes completing all the questions or exercises in a specific section prior to checking the answers.

Multiple Choice Questions:

1. (b) Accounting is a process of measuring and reporting economic activities to assist in the decisions that must be made in *all* organizations -- not just business organizations. Risk and return are economic characteristics of events and activities that are objects of the measurement process, not a purpose of measurement.

2. (a) The measurement unit in financial accounting is the local currency. In the US, accounting systems report the measurements of activities in dollars; in Mexico, it would be pesos; in Japan, yen. Since the purpose is to measure economic activities, it makes sense to measure in monetary units. Consistency in the measurement units is important. Time is a factor only in determining when to report the measurements to decision makers.

3. (d) Return *on* investment (ROI) is a measure of profitability. It measures how much an investor (who can be an individual, a group, or a corporation) has earned from an investment. Because investments can be of different amounts, it is convenient to express it as a percentage of the original investment. Choice (a) is incorrect because a return on investment can consist of the increase in the value of an investment, not just payments to investors; (b) is incorrect because a return can be earned in many forms, not just interest. Finally, (c) is incorrect because a return represents what an investor has earned, not what is returned from the original investment.

4. (c) Risk is used, in a financial context, somewhat more broadly but also more precisely than in ordinary language. It refers to our uncertainty about the outcome of events. Thus an investor may be uncertain about the exact return on an investment or the profit that will be earned in a given period. All of these represent risk. Choices (a) and (b) are incorrect because the concept of risk includes all possible outcomes, and a zero return is only one outcome. Choice (d) is incorrect because risk is only one characteristic of all investments.

5. (b) A system is a set of interrelated activities that are coordinated to achieve some goal. If the goal is to provide information, the system is an information system. Parts of the system may be represented by entire organizational units, such as the accounting department, and the system may use computers and terminals, but the system as a whole will be much greater than any one of these components.

6. (a) The basic information unit is the account. All information that is collected by an accounting system is summarized and represented by an account total called the *account balance*. Transactions are events that increase or decrease balances. The set of all accounts represents a financial picture of the organization.

7. (b) Stockholders are owners of a company. However, there are others that have an economic interest (for example, employees, suppliers, creditors, and possibly

governments). Thus, the term stakeholders is used to represent a wider constituency for organizations.

8.   (a) Value is created by converting resources into more desirable forms. A transformation may be effected without an exchange -- a sale -- and it will usually involve not just labor but also capital as, for example, in a highly automated process that functions without human intervention.

9.   (a) Limitation of the liability of owners and an unlimited life are clearly advantages of corporations. The separation of management and ownership is also usually seen as an advantage because corporations can be managed professionally and owners can diversify their investments into many corporations. However, the separation can create a problem called moral hazard because managers may have incentives to make decisions not in the best interests of the owners.

10.   (d) All of these are types of markets, classified by the nature of the goods and services exchanged.

11.   (c) The price agreed to between a willing buyer and willing seller is the best available measure of the value of the goods exchanged. So, in a market economy, price is an aggregate measure of the value people put on an item. Inflation is a *general increase* in prices of goods and services rather than a change in the price of any specific good. Also it is true that price increases may be accompanied by a reduction in the amount people will buy, but that is a response to prices and not an important characteristic of prices. In addition, price is only one component of a firm's profit.

12.   (c) Since resources are usually obtained in exchange transactions, their cost represent their value. When the product of the transformation process is sold, the price paid is a measure of the value of the transformed good. The difference between the price paid for the materials and other beginning resources (cost) and the price received for the transformed resources (selling price) measures the value that was added by the transformation.

13.   (a) Revenues represent a total of the sales prices of goods and services. It is not necessarily the same as cash collected from customers, and it is neither a measure of profit or investment.

14.   (a) Financing decisions represent choices about financing activities. As explained in the text, financing activities are the methods an organization uses to obtain financial resources and how it manages these resources. Choices among financial resources can determine the type of business organization, determine whether an organization borrows money, repays debt, or issues stock.

15.   (b) Human resource management is an operating activity because it involves resources that design, produce, distribute, and market goods and services. Choices (a) and (c) are financing activities. Choice (d) is an investing activity.

Exercises:

1.   Calculating Profit.

A statement of profit earned similar to text Exhibit 9 summarizes Ann's transactions by organizing her revenues and expenses.

Statement of Profit Earned		
Resources Created		$8,000
Resources Consumed:		
Rent	$1,500	
Merchandise sold	5,000	
Sales assistant's salary	400	
Electricity	250	
Taxes	560	
Supplies used	250	
Total Resources Consumed		7,960
Profit		$40

Ann has been successful in the limited sense that she has earned a profit, but other factors must be considered. If she worked an average of 50 hours per week, she would have earned $40/200 hours or $0.20 per hour in her first month. Does this change your perspective? Also, had she invested her $20,000 in a certificate of deposit at a bank earning 6% per year, she would have earned $100 [($20,000 x .06)/12 months = $100]. With the certificate of deposit, she also would not have had to work and there would have been little or no risk of losing the money. So, profit by itself doesn't tell the whole story.

2.   Identifying Financing, Investing, and Operating Decisions.

a.   The decision to invest $10,000 of his own money in the business is a *financing* decision. It involves the selection of a source of financial resources.

b.   The decision to acquire $20,000 of equipment is an *investing* decision. It involves a decision about the use of financial resources to acquire other long-term resources (equipment).

c.   The decision or borrow another $10,000 from the bank is a *financing* decision; an acquisition of financial resources.

d.   The decision to borrow money and lend the funds to the business is a *financing* decision, also. [Note: Tom is now both a creditor and an owner of the business.]

e.   The decision to hire a bookkeeper is an *operating* decision. The information provided by the bookkeeper will help Tom plan and control the operations of his business.

3.   Describing Specific Transformation Processes and Exchange Transactions.

a.   Transformation Processes:

Boeing, among other things, turns aircraft parts into aircraft. An assembled airplane is considerably more useful than a pile of unassembled parts. So, a less useful resource (parts) is transformed into a more useful form (airplanes).

Microsoft's business is the creation of instructions for computers. It takes the knowledge possessed by software engineers about computer instructions and creates a more useful form of knowledge -- computer programs desired by computer users around the world

American Van Lines moves goods from one location, which is less useful to its customers to another, which is more useful.

The *YMCA* is a social service organization. Unlike the other three organizations, the "Y" is not a profit-making organization. However, it nonetheless takes resources, financial and physical, and transforms them into services such as housing and recreational programs for clients.

b.   Exchange Transactions:

The *New York Times* provides news and entertainment for readers and an audience for advertisers. It exchanges its news stories, opinion pieces and entertainment articles for cash from readers, and it exchanges space in its publications for cash from advertisers.

The Limited exchanges clothing and accessories for cash from retail customers.

The *Salvation Army* provides food and shelter for the needy. In this organization, however, no direct monetary exchange exists between those receiving services and the organization providing the services. As a result, while assigning a value for the service or goods to the customers of the Times and The Limited is easy, establishing a value in the case of the Salvation Army is difficult. No price exists to provide information about the value of the good to the recipient.

The *US National Park Service* provides an example similar to that of the Salvation Army. The Service creates value by providing access to and protection for the National Parks and Monuments. However, user fees are set by legislation and are not prices determined by negotiation between buyer and seller. These fees, therefore, do not express the value that is created by the Service.

Short Essays:

1. Summarizing the Transformation Process.

    The transformation cycle begins with the acquisition of resources (capital) from owners and creditors. Capital is invested in equipment, buildings, supplies, inventory, and other resources to develop, produce, and distribute goods and services. The sale of goods and services brings new resources into the organization, which enables the cycle to continue.

2. Describing Operating Activities.

    Operating activities are those activities that result in the design, production, distribution, and marketing of goods and services. Research and development generally involves the creation and design of products. Production involves the physical creation of goods and services as well as various supporting functions. Distribution involves the movement of goods to market, and marketing involves the specific techniques that are used to sell and/or service goods and services.

3. Describing Investing Activities.

    Investing activities result in the exchange of financial resources for nonfinancial resources that will be used to support all of the organization's functions. Some examples are the building of a new plant, the acquisition of land, natural resources, legal rights and equipment.

4. Describing Financing Activities.

    Financing activities involve the acquisition of financial resources from financial markets and the management of those resources. Sale of stock and bonds to investors and borrowing of money from banks are common examples.

5. Discussing Accounting Careers.

    Management accountants perform all accounting functions within business organizations. They develop and manage accounting information systems, prepare financial statements and other reports, plan and analyze financial position, and perform internal audits. Public accountants work independently of the businesses or individuals they serve. Public accountants provide tax advice, management consulting services, and -- if they are CPAs -- independent audit services.

Chapter Notes

CHAPTER F2: INFORMATION IN ORGANIZATIONS

Chapter Focus

Major Theme: Accounting is an information system that is used by decision makers to measure, summarize, and report the economic consequences of an organization's transformation process.

Important Elements: As you study the chapter, look for the following topics:

Information needs of external and internal decision makers
Primary functions of information systems
Components of an accounting information system
Processing information in an accounting system

Learning Objectives: After studying this chapter, you should be able to:

Explain:	Why contracts affect the needs for information about organizations.
	Why risk and return are important to investors and how financing decisions affect risk and return.
Identify:	The uses of information by an organization's stakeholders.
	The purpose of generally accepted accounting principles and audits.
	The purpose and activities in an accounting information system.
Compare and Contrast:	Financial accounting and managerial accounting.
Describe:	The type of accounts in an accounting information system and their relationships to financial statements.

Chapter Review

Introduction. Accounting information measures, summarizes, and reports the economic consequences of the transformation process. Information needs arise from relationships among various stakeholder groups such as managers, investors, suppliers, employees, customers, and governmental agencies.

1. **Information for Decision Makers.** As stakeholders interact, contracts -- legal agreements for the exchange of resources -- establish the rights and responsibilities of various individuals and groups. Accounting information assists decision makers in establishing and evaluating these contracts.

    A. Contracts identify rights and responsibilities that establish the distribution of risk and returns among the stakeholders. In general, the potential for higher returns should be associated with greater risk.

    B. Accounting information assists various stakeholder groups in evaluating contracts and exchanges.

        1. Investors (owners and creditors) use accounting information to assess the risk and potential returns associated with their investment.

            a. Creditors provide debt financing to an organization in exchange for interest payments and principal repayment.

            b. Owners provide equity financing to an organization in exchange for the opportunity to earn profits.

            c. An organization's mix of debt and equity financing affects its risk and return relationships.

        2. Managers use accounting information to make investing and operating decisions that concern the acquisition and use of resources. Accounting information also assists both managers and owners as they negotiate managers' compensation.

        3. Employees use accounting information to assess the risk and return of their employment contracts. In addition, managers use accounting information to evaluate the performance of employees or other managers.

      4.   <u>Suppliers</u> use accounting information to evaluate a buyer's ability to pay for specified purchases.

      5.   <u>Customers</u> use accounting information to evaluate a supplier's ability to fulfill the terms of a contract by delivering resources, goods, or services in a timely manner.

      6.   <u>Governmental agencies</u> use accounting information to make taxation and regulatory decisions.

  C.   <u>Financial accounting</u> is the process of preparing, reporting, and interpreting accounting information provided primarily for external decision makers.

      1.   Financial accounting information is presented in accordance with <u>generally accepted accounting principles (GAAP)</u> -- specific standards that identify appropriate accounting and reporting.

      2.   <u>Certified Public Accountants (CPAs)</u> perform detailed examinations or <u>audits</u> of an organization's financial reports to assure conformance with GAAP.

      3.   Through legislation, local, state, and national governments modify GAAP requirements for tax purposes. Thus, a business organization usually files several different tax reports using different regulations.

  D.   Managerial accounting is the process of preparing, reporting, and interpreting accounting information for use by an organization's internal decision makers as they evaluate financing, investing, and operating choices.

      1.   At times, managers and other decision makers focus on <u>planning</u> -- the identification of goals and strategies.

      2.   In other situations, managers focus on <u>control</u> -- the evaluation of accomplishments.

2. **Information Systems.** An information system assembles data from transformation activities and converts these data into information useful in decision-making.

  A.   A <u>management information system (MIS)</u> provides managers with information on all phases and components of the transformation process. Organizational components that provide information on the transformation process include <u>sales and distribution</u>, <u>human resources</u>, <u>materials management</u>, and <u>production</u>.

B.   The <u>accounting information system (AIS)</u> -- a subsystem of the management information system -- provides managers with very specific information. This system identifies the resources of the organization, tracking the transformation of resources into goods and services, determining the costs of resources, and reporting information about these activities to both internal and external users.

    1.   An AIS relies on three categories of input data: the <u>costs</u> of resources acquired and used, the <u>prices</u> of goods and services sold to customers, and management <u>policies</u>.

    2.   The source of information for the AIS is the organization's transformation process: financing activities, investing activities, and operating activities. These activities are <u>measured</u> and <u>reported</u> to decision makers.

3.   **Processing Accounting Information.** As described in Chapter 1, an <u>account</u> is the basic unit for recording accounting data. Five broad categories of accounts capture transformation process activities: assets, liabilities, owners' equity, revenues, and expenses.

A.   Assets, liabilities, and owner's equity accounts describe transformation activities involved in operating, investing, and financing.

    1.   <u>Assets</u> are resources acquired by an organization or available for its use. Examples of specific asset accounts include Cash, Accounts Receivable, Merchandise Inventory, Equipment, Buildings, Land, Natural Resources, Patents, and Trademarks.

    2.   <u>Liabilities</u> are obligations owed by an organization to creditors. Examples of specific liability accounts include Accounts Payable, Notes Payable, Bonds Payable, Wages Payable, and Taxes Payable. (Each of these accounts measures an obligation that must be met by an organization.)

3.   <u>Owners' Equity</u> accounts describe the investment made by the owners of the business and the profit retained in the business.

   a.   For proprietorships or partnerships, the owners' equity account is titled Proprietor's Capital or Partners' Capital. This includes the investment by the owners as well as the retained profits.

   b.   For corporations, the owners' equity accounts would be Capital Stock (or Common Stock), which reflects the investments by owners through the purchase of shares of stock. In addition, a Retained Earnings account contains profits earned by the corporation that have not been distributed to the owners as dividends. The undistributed profits become part of the owners' investment in the business.

4.   A summary report, the <u>Balance Sheet</u>, describes the relationships among assets, liabilities, and owners' equity. The Balance Sheet reflects an important relationship:

Assets = Liabilities + Owners' Equity

[Important Note: This equation must always balance since the value of resources must equal the value of the financing used to acquire the resources.]

B.   Revenue and expense accounts accumulate the results of operating activities.

1.   <u>Revenues</u> are the result of selling goods and/or services that are the primary operating activities of an organization. Revenues will either increase assets (resource inflows) or decrease liabilities (reductions in obligations).

2.   <u>Expenses</u> are the result of developing, producing, or delivering goods and/or services that are the primary operating activities of an organization. Expenses will decrease assets (resource outflows) or increase liabilities (increases in obligations).

3.   To report the results of operations, revenues and expenses are displayed on an <u>Income Statement</u> that reflects the following equation:

Revenues - Expenses = Net Income (Profit)

This equation captures the return for a given operating period since the revenues received minus the expenses incurred equals the profit that is a return on the owners' investment. (Recall that in Chapter 1, revenues were described as resources created and expenses were described as resources consumed.)

4.   Since profit is a return on the owners' investment, it becomes part of Retained Earnings (or Proprietor's/ Partners' Capital) if it is not distributed to owners in the form of Dividends (or Withdrawals).

C.   Because Net Income and Retained Earnings are related, the accounting equations may take several forms:

1.   If net income has not yet been transferred to Retained Earnings, the accounting equation is:

Assets = Liabilities + Owners' Equity + (Revenues - Expenses)

Since profit is transferred to Retained Earnings at the end of an operating period, this equation captures the organization's resources, obligations, owners' investment as well as any recent changes in resources or obligations.

2.   If net income has already been transferred to Retained Earnings:

Assets = Liabilities + Owners' Equity

Since profits (the results of revenues minus expenses) have already been transferred to Retained Earnings, this equation shows the balancing relationships among resources, obligations, and owners' investment

4.   **Preparation for an Accounting Career**. To prepare for an accounting career, a student should focus on a variety of courses and skills.

A.   Technical accounting concepts and procedures in courses that focus on the preparation and analysis of financial accounting information, managerial and cost accounting, accounting information systems, taxation, and auditing.

B.   Courses in finance, marketing, management, operations, and strategy provide important business concepts and skills.

C.   Skills in communication, group behavior, problem solving, and logical reasoning are valuable to accounting professionals.

D.   Integrity, ethical behavior, and the reputation for fairness are important foundations of the accounting profession.

Review Questions, Exercises, and Short Essays

<u>Multiple Choice Questions</u>: These questions reinforce vocabulary and basic concepts from the chapter. In each case, select the answer you believe to be the *best*.

1.   A contract in which one party cannot determine whether the other party is abiding by the contract terms is:
   a.   Unfair.
   b.   Illegal.
   c.   Unenforceable.
   d.   Routine.

2.   The term *investors* may refer to:
   a.   Owners.
   b.   Creditors.
   c.   Both owners and creditors.
   d.   All stakeholders.

3.   The amount borrowed by a debtor is called the:
   a.   Principal.
   b.   Dividend.
   c.   Interest.
   d.   Investment.

4.   Accounting information may be used to:
   a.   Identify the location and types of an organization's resources.
   b.   Estimate and compare companies' risks and returns.
   c.   Assess the risk of buying from certain companies.
   d.   All of the above.

5.   *GAAP* provide:
    a.   Accounting and reporting standards that have wide professional acceptance.
    b.   Minimum qualifications for incorporation.
    c.   Detailed discussion of the relationship between risks and returns.
    d.   Requirements for business contracts.

6.   An audit is an examination of an organization's accounts intended to establish:
    a.   The accuracy of accounting reports.
    b.   Whether accounting reports fairly present economic activities.
    c.   Whether employees have stolen resources from the organization.
    d.   The effectiveness of management.

7.   Companies whose stock is traded publicly in the United States must submit financial reports to which government organization?
    a.   Securities and Exchange Commission (SEC).
    b.   New York Stock Exchange (NYSE).
    c.   Federal Trade Commission (FTC).
    d.   U.S. Department of Commerce.

8.   The primary source of data for the accounting information system is:
    a.   Records of checks received and cash disbursed.
    b.   The organization's transformation process.
    c.   Accounting data bases.
    d.   Inventory and payroll records.

9.   A management information system usually tracks which of the following activities:
    a.   Sales and distribution activities.
    b.   Human resources activities.
    c.   Production activities.
    d.   All of the above activities..

10.   An accounting information system is composed of:
    a.   Accounting data stored in data bases.
    b.   Reporting rules.
    c.   The technology used to store, retrieve, and report information.
    d.   All of the above.

11. Accounting reporting rules specify:
    a. How data is to be stored.
    b. How information is to be reported.
    c. Which government department receives the reports.
    d. What managers should do with financial information.

12. The categories of accounts used in a business include all *except*:
    a. Profit accounts.
    b. Revenue accounts.
    c. Liabilities accounts.
    d. Expense accounts.

13. Asset accounts include all of the following *except*:
    a. Amounts of cash to be received in the future from credit sales to customers.
    b. Amounts of cash to be paid in the future for credit purchases from suppliers.
    c. Amounts representing valuable legal rights.
    d. Physical resources such as merchandise inventory or buildings.

14. Liability accounts include:
    a. Amounts of cash to be received in the future from credit sales to customers.
    b. Amounts of cash to be paid in the future for credit purchases from suppliers.
    c. Retained earnings.
    d. Costs incurred in carrying on normal business activities.

15. The relationship among assets, liabilities, and owners' equity can be expressed as:
    a. Liabilities = assets - owners' equity.
    b. Assets = liabilities + owners' equity.
    c. Owners' equity = assets - liabilities.
    d. All these relationships are correct.

Exercises: These questions require the analysis of economic situations and the applications of accounting concepts.

1.   Using the Accounting Equation. The accounting equation (Assets = Liabilities + Owners' Equity) may be used to analyze the following business situations.

a.   The Coral Gables Mining and Fishing Company has the following accounts in its accounting data base:

Account	Balance
Cash	$500
Accounts Receivable	100
Equipment	1,600
Patent	1,000
Accounts Payable	500
Common Stock	1,000
Retained Earnings	1,700

(1)   Show that the company's balance sheet will balance (i.e. that Assets = Liabilities + Owners' Equity).

(2)   Is Coral Gables a sole proprietorship, a partnership, or a corporation? What is the conclusive evidence?

b.   The Glacier Development Partnership has the following accounts in its accounting data base:

Account	Balance
Cash	$200
Notes Payable	3,100
Mineral Rights	50,000
Supplies	1,000
Accounts Payable	500

What is the Partners' Capital?

2.   <u>Calculating Liabilities and Owners' Equity</u>. The following business situations require the calculation of liabilities or owners' equity.

a.   At the end of the year, Mom and Pop's Grocery Store has total assets of $250,000. Mom and Pop have equity of $210,000. What is the amount that the store owes to creditors?

b.   At the end of the last reporting period, the Blooming Tulip Flower Shop had owners' equity of $43,000. During this reporting period, the business sold $175,000 of flowers and arrangements. The merchandise sold cost $50,000, and flowers costing $7,000 spoiled before they could be sold. Salaries and wages totaled $90,000, and utilities used cost $12,000.

If the owners took no money out of the business during this period, what is the owners' equity at the end of the current reporting period? (Hint: first, determine net income and then determine the impact on owners' equity.)

3.   <u>Identifying and Summarizing Transactions</u>. Noting the apparent popularity of ethnic restaurants in shopping mall food courts, you decide to open a *Lutefisk & Chips* restaurant in a mall near your home. You begin your business by transferring your life savings of $20,000 to a bank account in the name of the corporation on January 2nd.

The same day you pay the mall owners $500 which equals the first month's rent. In addition, you order merchandise of lutefisk and frozen, prepared potatoes, drinks, and various dessert items costing a total of $5,000. The vendors will bill you when the goods are delivered.

On January 3rd, you go to a restaurant supply dealer and buy the restaurant equipment needed. The used equipment costs $12,000, and you arrange to pay half the amount in cash (a down payment) and half to be paid in 90 days. By January 15th all of your merchandise has been received, and the vendors' invoices totaling $5,000 must be paid in 30 days.

You're now ready for business! The first day's business is a bit disappointing. The remainder of the month seems little better, and by month's end your sales total $2,000. The food and drinks sold cost $700, and $1,000 worth of food spoiled when your refrigerator developed a coolant leak. The repair cost $250.

a.   List the transactions that will have an impact on the expanded accounting equation.

(Exercise 3 continues on the next page.)

b. Fit these transactions into the following expanded accounting equation framework. (The first transaction -- investing $20,000 in the Lutefisk and Chips restaurant -- serves as an example.)

	Account	Balance Sheet				Income Statement	
		Cash	+ Other Assets	= Liabilities	+ Equity	+ Revenues	- Expenses
1	Cash Common Stock	20,000			20,000		

Short Essays: The following short essay questions not only reinforce important concepts but also give you a chance to practice writing skills. Answer these questions in complete sentences.

1.   Linking Returns and Risk. In recent years, the "Junk Bond" market has developed to provide debt financing for companies regarded as risky borrowers. How would you expect the interest rate these borrowers pay to compare to the interest rate paid by companies that are not regarded as risky borrowers? Please support your answer with financial concepts.

2.   Comparing Financial and Managerial Accounting. Specifically, how is managerial accounting different from financial accounting? How do decision makers use managerial accounting?

3.   <u>Discussing Measurement Rules and Reporting Rules</u>. Describe both
      measurement rules and *reporting* rules and discuss how they differ?

4.   <u>Linking Net Income and Retained Earnings</u>. How are net income and
      retained earnings related?

5.   <u>Preparing for an Accounting Career</u>. Describe four specific areas of
      preparation that are important for a successful career in accounting.

Suggested Answers to Review Questions, Exercises, and Short Essays

<u>Multiple Choice</u>:

1.   (c) A contract in which the performance of one party is not observable is not an enforceable contract. Each of the parties must know whether the other parties have complied with the requirements of the contract. While such "unobservable" contracts are not routine, they are not necessarily illegal or unfair if both parties enter into the agreement willingly.

2.   (c) An investor is someone who furnishes financial resources in exchange for future returns. The resources may be lent or given in exchange for ownership rights.

3.   (a) The amount of a loan is called the *principal*. A dividend is a distribution of profit to the stockholders. Interest is the charge that is made for the use of the borrowed principal, and an investment is made by an owner rather than a creditor.

4.   (d) The answer is all of the above. Accounting information is used to establish custody (location and types of resources); measure income, expenses, assets, and liabilities; and evaluate the risk and return of investments. In addition, accounting can be used to assess the likelihood that a supplier may be forced out of business.

5.   (a) Generally Accepted Accounting Principles (GAAP) provide standards for accounting and disclosure of financial information by non-governmental organizations. GAAP does not include qualifications for incorporation, requirements for business contracts, or discussion of the risk / return relationship.

6.   (b) Primarily, an audit establishes whether or not the financial statements of an organization fairly represent economic activities. Because of the complexity and the judgments that must be made in financial reporting, references to accuracy are not meaningful. Often, more than a single method of reporting a series of economic events exists. As a result, the auditing profession speaks of "fair presentation." Finally, the purpose of a financial statement audit is not to detect theft or to comment on management's effectiveness.

7.   (a) Under US securities laws, companies selling securities to the public must file periodic financial reports with the SEC. The NYSE is not a governmental organization, and neither the US Commerce Department nor the FTC regulates financial reporting.

8.   (b) Accounting information is collected at every stage of the transformation process. Information concerning only cash receipts and disbursements misses much important economic information. For example, an accounting system that only tracked cash movements would not capture the amount of inventory that had been used. It would measure only what cash had been paid for inventory items. Alternatively, this system would not measure the amount of labor that had been used, only the amount of cash that had been paid for labor.

9.   (d) A management information system provides information for managers to use in decision making. These systems capture information on sales and distribution, human resources, and production as well as other activities.

10. (d) An accounting information system includes stored data, rules governing how the data is assembled and reported, and the technical tools used to store, retrieve and report the data in a meaningful way.

11. (b) Reporting rules describe how data is assembled and reported to provide meaningful information to users. Although they specify the content and format of reports, these rules do not involve the mechanics of storage. Reports for governments generally follow the rules outlined by the specific government department requesting the information. Reporting rules do not dictate the use of accounting information by managers.

12. (a) Accounting systems in businesses use five categories of accounts: assets, liabilities, owners' equity, revenues, and expenses. Profits are determined by calculation from these account types; therefore, no separate profit account is needed.

13. (b) Assets are resources controlled by an organization and available for its future use. Future payments owed by customers for credit sales are an example of a resource that will result in future cash receipts for the organizations' use. The same is true of legal rights such as patents and copyrights. Cash owed to suppliers, however, is a liability and will require the use of future resources for payment.

14. (b) Liability accounts represent obligations for which resources will be needed in the future. Future payments to be received from customers are assets. Retained Earnings is an account that maintains a total of all undistributed net income earned by the company. Costs incurred should be classified as expenses.

15. (d) The relationship between assets, liabilities and owners' equity can be expressed as Assets = Liabilities + Owners' Equity. This equation can be rearranged algebraically to form the other equivalent relationships.

Exercises:

1. Using the Accounting Equation.

   a. Coral Gables Mining and Fishing:

      (1) The balance sheet for Coral Gables Mining and Fishing balances in the following manner:

         Assets = $500 + 100 + 1,600 + 1,000 = $3,200
         Liabilities = $500
         Owners' Equity = $1,000 + $1,700 = $2,700

         Assets = Liabilities + Owners' Equity
         $3,200 = $500 + $2,700

      (2) The firm is a corporation. The owners' equity accounts are titled Common Stock and Retained Earnings, and these accounts are characteristic of corporations.

b.   Glacier Development Partnership: The equation Assets = Liabilities + Owners'
Equity is the key to determining owners' equity.

Assets = $200 + $50,000 + $1,000 = $51,200
Liabilities = $3,100 + $500 = $3,600

Assets = Liabilities + Owners' Equity
$51,200 = $3,600 + Owners' Equity
Owners' Equity = $47,600

2.   Calculating Liabilities and Owners' Equity.

a.   Mom and Pop's Grocery Store: The equation Assets = Liabilities + Owners'
Equity is the key to determining liabilities.

Assets = $250,000
Owners' Equity = $210,000
Assets = Liabilities + Owners' Equity
$250,000 = Liabilities + $210,000
Liabilities = $40,000

b.   Blooming Tulip Flower Shop: The determination of ending owner's equity for the
period begins with the calculation of net income. Net income = Revenue -
Expenses can be determined in the following manner:

Revenues:		
Sales		$175,000
Expenses:		
Cost of merchandise sold	50,000	
Salaries and wages	90,000	
Utilities	12,000	
Spoilage	7,000	
Total expenses		159,000
Net income		$ 16,000

Net income increases owners' equity if it is not distributed to the owners. Since
no distributions were made during the period, the ending owner's equity can be
determined in the following manner:

With no distributions to owners,

Beginning Owners' Equity + Net Income = Ending Owners' Equity
$43,000 + 16,000 = $59,000

3. Identifying and Summarizing Transactions.

a. The transactions that have an impact on the accounting equation are:

The original investment.

The payment of rent.

The acquisition of equipment.

The receipt of inventory from vendors.

The sale of food and drinks for the month.

The use of inventory to provide food and drinks to customers.

The spoilage of inventory.

The repair of equipment.

b. These transactions would have the following impact on the expanded accounting equation framework:

	Account	Balance Sheet				Income Statement	
		Cash	+ Other Assets	= Liabilities	+ Equity	+ Revenues	- Expenses
	Beginning Balance	0	0	0	0	0	0
1	Cash Common Stock	20,000			20,000		
2	Cash Rent Expense	-500					-500
3	Cash Notes Payable Equipment	-6,000	12,000	6,000			
4	Merchandise Accounts Payable		5,000	5,000			
5	Cash Sales	2,000				2,000	
6	Merchandise Cost of Goods Sold		-700				-700
7	Merchandise Spoilage Expense		-1,000				-1,000
8	Cash Repair Expense	-250					-250
	Ending Balance	15,250	15,300	11,000	20,000	2,000	-2,450

Short Essays:

1. Linking Returns and Risk.

Lenders to risky borrowers -- such as those firms issuing junk bonds -- expect higher returns for the increased risk. Alternatively, borrowers in this market would expect to pay higher interest rates. One of the functions performed by markets for financial resources is to assess and price risk through differences and adjustments in interest   rates. Riskier borrowers are charged higher interest rates (a higher price) for the financial resources. The additional interest paid induces lenders to accept the additional risk.

2.   Comparing Financial and Managerial Accounting.

Managerial accounting produces information for internal decision makers. While managers regularly use financial accounting information, they may also need more detailed information at certain times. Managerial accounting information is used for planning (setting goals, strategies, and policies) as well as control (performance evaluation) in organizations.

3.   Discussing Measurement Rules and Reporting Rules.

Measurement rules determine the attributes of transactions that are captured and recorded in the accounting information system. Typically, these rules govern the accounts affected and financial amounts recorded during the transformation process. Reporting rules determine the content and format of information that will be reported by the accounting information system. For example, reporting rules permit the summary impact of transactions on a specific account to be reported rather than the detailed impact of every transaction.

4.   Linking Net Income and Retained Earnings.

Retained earnings represents the sum of all undistributed net income earned by a corporation since it began. The account title is drawn from *earnings* that have been *retained* by the organization. Many novice readers of financial statements mistakenly assume that retained earnings is cash. Retained earnings is not an asset; it is a part of owners' equity. Since the owners' equity provides financing for many different types of resources, retained earnings is an important source of financing for resources already listed among the firm's assets. Retained earnings can be viewed as the owners' reinvestment of the earnings in the firm.

5.   Preparing for an Accounting Career.

Preparing for an accounting career includes courses and experience in four distinct areas. Courses in technical accounting concepts and procedures along with courses in other business subjects provide important background and skills. in addition skills in communication and logical reasoning must be combined with integrity and the reputation for fairness.

CHAPTER F3: ACCOUNTING MEASUREMENT

Chapter Focus

Major Theme: Fundamental concepts of accounting measurement guide both the development of specific measurement rules within accounting information systems and the recording of information from economic events within the transformation process.

Important Elements: As you study the chapter, look for the following topics:

    Accounting measurement of the transformation process
    The importance of time in accounting measurement
    The relationship between accrual and cash measurements
    The purpose of accrual basis accounts

Learning Objectives: After studying this chapter, you should be able to:

Demonstrate:	The use of an accounting system to record financing, investing, and operating activities.
Explain:	The implications of the going concern principle and periodic measurement for the transformation process. Why change in cash is not a complete measure of an organization's performance for a period. The articulation of the three primary financial statements in an accrual accounting system.
Distinguish and Explain:	The accrual basis of accounting from the cash basis and why the accrual basis is used.
Identify:	Information reported by an accrual basis accounting system.

Chapter Review

Introduction. The accounting information system records, summarizes, and reports the economic impact of an organization's financing, investing, and operating activities. To establish fundamental measurement rules, this chapter examines typical transactions in the transformation process and evaluates both the cash basis and accrual basis measurement options.

1. **Accounting for the Transformation Process**. As presented at the end of Chapter 2, one of several possible forms of the <u>accounting equation</u> can be used to summarize the economic impact of a transformation process.

    A. <u>If revenue and expense account balances have already been transferred to Retained Earnings</u>, the equation may be expressed as:

    Assets = Liabilities + Owners' Equity

    B. <u>If revenue and expense account balances have not yet been transferred to Retained Earnings</u>, the equation may be expressed as:

    Assets = Liabilities + Owners' Equity + (Revenues – Expenses)

    C. These equations must be balanced at all times during the transformation process.

2. **Accounting for Incomplete Transformations**. For transformation processes that extend over some period of time, additional measurement concepts clarify some important recording, summarizing, or reporting issues.

    A. <u>Going concern</u> refers to the understanding that the indefinite life of many organizations will be long enough to complete any currently incomplete transformations.

    B. <u>Periodic measurement</u> expresses the need to report results of an organization's performance on a periodic basis with timely information.

    C. Accounting practices derived from both the going concern and periodic measurement concepts govern the recording, summarizing, and reporting of transformation processes that are incomplete at the time of periodic reporting.

3. **Time and Accounting Measurement**. Recording the sale of goods and services and the consumption of resources are both major decisions that significantly affect an organization's periodic performance. Alternative approaches exist for this recognition process: cash basis (either all cash flows or operating cash flows) and accrual basis.

    A. The cash basis alternative focuses on the cash inflows (the amount of cash received) and cash outflows (the amount of cash paid).

        1. The all cash flows approach evaluates performance based on the increase or decrease in cash during the operating period.

            a) This approach is severely limited since the all cash flow performance measure does not separate cash flows into three types of activities -- financing, investing, and operating.

            b) Without this separation, poor operating cash flows could be masked by increased financing cash flows to report a positive cash flow performance.

        2. The operating cash flows approach evaluates performance on the basis of cash flows from operating activities during the period.

            a) This approach is also limited since receipts and payments of cash may take place during a period that is different from the operating period when the goods are sold or resources used.

            b) An organization that sells goods at the end of one reporting period may receive the cash payment early in the next reporting period. Using operating cash flows as a performance measure, the activity will be counted in the second reporting period when, in fact, the transformation took place in the first reporting period.

                [Important Note: Cash flows are an important dimension of organizational performance, but

they do not effectively report the results of operating activities.]

B.   The <u>accrual basis</u> of performance measurement recognizes revenues when they are earned (resources created) and expenses when they are incurred (resources consumed).

1.   In most cases, <u>revenue</u> is recognized when goods and services are sold. A Sales account recognizes the revenue while the Cost of Goods Sold account recognizes the underlying cost of the merchandise sold.

2.   Sales may be made as either cash sales (an immediate cash inflow) or credit sales that create Accounts Receivable (an asset) that will later be paid in cash by customers

3.   <u>Expenses</u> (such as Wages Expense or Interest Expense) may be paid for in cash when they are incurred (an immediate cash outflow) or paid at a later date. Paying expenses at a later date creates a liability (such as Wages Payable or Interest Payable) until the obligation is paid.

4.   Certain asset accounts (such as Building and Equipment accounts) require periodic adjustment under the accrual basis.

a)   While the cash basis approach would only change these account balances when assets were acquired or sold, they must be adjusted periodically on the accrual basis to recognize a portion of their cost as an expense during each period of their useful lives.

b)   Since an organization derives benefits from these asset accounts each period even though they are not acquired anew each period, <u>Depreciation Expense</u> recognizes a portion of the asset's cost as an expense during each reporting period. The total of all depreciation expense taken on an asset is recorded as <u>Accumulated Depreciation</u>.

(1)   Accumulated Depreciation -- a <u>contra account</u> -- reduces the value of the asset it accompanies.

(2) A <u>contra account</u> is any account that reduces or offsets the amount of another account.

c) The periodic charge for Depreciation Expense is an estimate and can be adjusted over time to better reflect underlying conditions in the transformation process.

5. Accrual accounting attempts to <u>match revenues and expenses</u>. Expenses are associated, or recognized, with the revenues generated by the same operating activities.

a) <u>Product costs</u> are costs most directly associated with goods or services. For example, Cost of Goods Sold is a product cost.

b) <u>Period costs</u> are costs closely associated with a reporting period. For example, Interest Expense is usually considered a period cost.

4. **Reconciling Accrual and Cash Measurements**. To use accounting information effectively, managers must understand the relationship between cash flow and accrual information.

A. Cash flow information measures and reports the results of cash inflows and outflows from past, present, or future decisions that are received or disbursed during a given reporting period.

B. Accrual information measures and reports the economic consequences of operating activities during the reporting period in which they occur regardless of the timing of cash flows.

[Important Note: This relationship between cash flow and accrual information is displayed in text Exhibit 9. The two sides of the diagram capture distinctly different views of the organization's activity.]

5. **Measuring the Transformation Process**. Three financial reports (or financial statements) are necessary to describe the various results of the transformation process for a given reporting period.

A. The <u>income statement</u> expresses the economic results of operating activities for a given reporting period by reporting revenues, expenses, and profit measured on an accrual basis.

B.   The <u>balance sheet</u> describes the status of resources (assets), obligations (liabilities), and owners' investment (owners' equity) including recent operating activities at the end of a given reporting period.

C.   The <u>statement of cash flows</u> displays cash inflows and outflows from operating, investing, and financing activities that take place during a given reporting period.

[Important Note: These three perspectives of the transformation process are presented in text Exhibit 10. Each report describes a specific aspect of performance or organizational status.]

6.   **Accrual Basis Financial Statements**. Each of the three primary financial statements provides different information about accounts and balances that help managers understand information on the other two statements. This relationship is known as <u>articulation</u>.

A.   An income statement provides information on revenues and expenses.

1.   These revenues and expenses represent either past or future cash flows.

2.   Information on the timing of these cash flows is presented on the statement of cash flows.

B.   The statement of cash flows presents the cash inflows and outflows from operating, investing, and financing activities.

1.   Operating cash flows represent the cash inflows and outflows that result from the revenues and expenses reported on the current or prior income statements.

2.   Investing and financing cash flows represent the inflows and outflows associated with changes in the long-term asset, long-term liability, and equity accounts on the balance sheet.

C.   The balance sheet displays the current balances of asset, liability, and owners' equity accounts on a specific date.

1.   In general, assets represent the results of operating and investing activities.

a) Assets like Accounts Receivable and Merchandise Inventory represent the results of operating activities.

b) Assets like Equipment and Buildings represent the results of investing activities.

c) The asset Cash is a special case in that it represents the net impact of all operating, investing, and financing cash inflows and outflows up to the balance sheet date.

2. Liabilities represent the results of operating and financing activities.

a) Liabilities like Bonds Payable and Notes Payable result from financing activities.

b) Liabilities like Accounts Payable and Wages Payable result from operating activities.

c) Liabilities classified as Unearned Revenues represent obligations to provide goods and services in the future.

3. Owners' equity accounts represent the total invested by owners and Retained Earnings. Investments by owners are financing activities while Retained Earnings are the results of operating activities.

[Important Note: A <u>balance sheet</u> reports resources, obligations, and owners' investment <u>on a specific date</u>. An <u>income statement</u> reports resources generated or consumed <u>during a reporting period</u>. A <u>statement of cash flows</u> reports cash inflows and outflows <u>during a reporting period</u>.]

7. **The Historical Development of Accounting.** Although accounting has existed for thousands of years, specific events in the 19th and 20th centuries have influenced its modern development. The industrial revolution, the development of the New York Stock Exchange, income taxation, and the growth of federal securities regulation during the 1930's all influenced the development of modern accounting concepts and principles.

Review Questions, Exercises, and Short Essays

<u>Multiple Choice Questions</u>: These questions reinforce vocabulary and basic concepts from the chapter. In each case, select the answer you believe to be the *best*.

1.   When an organization pays for a good or service *before* receiving it, the payment should be recorded as a decrease in Cash and an increase in:
    a.   An expense.
    b.   An asset.
    c.   An owners' equity account.
    d.   A liability.

2.   At the end of an accounting period, the equation Assets = Liabilities + Owners' Equity does not necessarily balance. Which of the following actions balances the equation?
    a.   Add the difference between revenues and expenses to owners' equity.
    b.   Add revenues and subtract expenses from assets.
    c.   Subtract revenues and add expenses to owners' equity.
    d.   Subtract revenues from owners' equity and add expenses to assets.

3.   When a customer buys services on credit, the contract is regarded as complete when:
    a.   The services are rendered.
    b.   The bill is presented.
    c.   The cash payment is received.
    d.   On the date specified in the contract.

4.   The term *going concern* refers to:
    a.   A very profitable business.
    b.   An organization with on-going problems.
    c.   An organization with an indefinite, but sufficiently long life to complete existing transformation processes.
    d.   Any organization that is at least one year old.

5.   The phrase *periodic measurement* refers to:
    a.   Quality control measures in an accounting system.
    b.   Accounting measurement of performance during a particular period.
    c.   Accounting reporting of performance during a particular period.
    d.   A process for measuring the length of an operating period.

6. The amount of cash received or paid during a period is not an adequate measure of the economic consequences of an organization's activities because:
   a. Many activities may not involve the use of cash.
   b. Cash inflows may represent the result of activities completed in a previous period.
   c. Cash outflows may precede or follow the activities with which they are associated.
   d. All of the above reasons are correct.

7. The accrual basis of accounting:
   a. Recognizes revenues when products are produced as part of operating activities.
   b. Recognizes expenses when resources are consumed as part of operating activities.
   c. Recognizes revenues when cash is received.
   d. Recognizes expenses when cash is paid.

8. A sale of merchandise on credit represents an exchange of goods for a promise of future payment. This promise is:
   a. An asset.
   b. A liability.
   c. An increase in Accounts Payable.
   d. A revenue.

9. A sale of merchandise results in a reduction in inventory. This *reduction* should be reflected in an organization's accounting records as:
   a. An increase in the expense Cost of Goods Sold only.
   b. An increase in Sales Revenue.
   c. A decrease in the asset Merchandise Inventory only.
   d. Both a decrease in the asset Merchandise Inventory and an increase in the expense Cost of Goods Sold.

10. An employee who has just earned $350 will not be paid for another week. How should the employer report this transaction with the employee?
    a. The employer has nothing to report until payday.
    b. The employer should report only Wages Payable of $350.
    c. The employer should report only Wages Expense of $350.
    d. The employer should report both Wages Payable and Wages Expense of $350 each.

11.   An organization borrows $100,000 from a bank on November 1st Year 1 and agrees to pay $12,000 interest on November 1st Year 2. How should this interest be reflected in the accounts of the borrower at the end of Year 1?

a.   Interest Expense of $2,000.
b.   No reporting is required until the interest is paid in Year 2.
c.   Interest Payable of $2,000.
d.   Both Interest Expense and Interest Payable of $2,000 each.

12.   An organization acquires a new machine that it expects to use for five years in its operations. When would the organization report an expense for this machine?

a.   When the machine was acquired.
b.   Each year as the machine is used.
c.   No expense is reported because the machine is an asset.
d.   When the machine reaches the end of its useful life.

13.   Costs associated with specific goods might be called:

a.   Product costs.
b.   Cost of Goods Sold.
c.   Merchandise Inventory.
d.   All of the above could apply to costs associated with specific goods.

14.   The statement of cash flows reports:

a.   Only the cash results of operations.
b.   The net profits of the organization.
c.   The amount of cash spent by an organization.
d.   The effects of operating, investing, and financing activities on an organization's cash position.

15.   To measure the results of the transformation process, a decision maker should review:

a.   The income statement.
b.   The balance sheet.
c.   The statement of cash flows.
d.   All three statements should be reviewed to measure the results of the transformation process.

Exercises: These questions require the analysis of economic situations and the application of accounting concepts.

1. Matching Accounts and Account Types. Each account within an accounting information system belongs to a specific account type. Using the code identified in the first table, identify the account type of each account in the second table.

Account Type	Code
Assets	A
Liabilities	L
Owner's Equity	O
Revenues	R
Expenses	E

Account	Code
Example:	
Common Stock	O
Cash	
Accounts Payable	
Sales	
Retained Earnings	
Accounts Receivable	
Land	
Wages Expense	
Rent Expense	
Supplies	
Utilities Payable	
Automobiles	
Cost of Goods Sold	
Inventory	
Wages Payable	
Prepaid Rent	

2.   Calculating Sales Revenue and Cash Collected. The Hollyburn Company
is a merchandising firm with a particularly popular line of merchandise. In
any given month, 60% of sales are collected immediately in cash while
40% are made on credit. The credit terms provide that all credit sales
must be paid before the end of the following month.

a.   If the company sold a total of $50,000, $100,000, $150,000, and
$200,000 of merchandise in May, June, July, and August, what
were its sales revenues and cash collections in June, July and
August?   (Use the following table to organize the sales revenues
and cash flows by month.)

Activity	June	July	August
Sales Revenue:			
Cash Collected:			

b.   Why is the distinction between sales revenue and cash collected
from sales important for decision makers?

3.   <u>Analyzing Transactions</u>. Tom Robinson's kayaking and fishing business described in the Chapter 1 continues to prosper. During the most recent week, the following transactions took place:

(1)   Tom took several clients out for trips and earned $3,000. One client discovered that he had left his wallet at home and promised to send a check to Tom the following week for $150. All of the other clients paid cash.

(2)   Tom used $50 worth of gas (paid in cash) transporting boats and another $200 worth of other supplies.

(3)   The part-time bookkeeper has earned $150, and Tom has earned $1,000 wages for the week. These wages will be paid next week.

(4)   Estimated interest for the week is $20 on the loan owed to the bank and $10 on the loan made by Tom to the business.

(5)   The estimated depreciation charge for the week is $70.

Enter these new transactions for Tom's business into the table on the next page and demonstrate that Assets = Liabilities + Owner's Equity + Revenues - Expenses. Also show that once the net income is added to owners' equity, then Assets = Liabilities + Owner's Equity.

(The account balances with which Tom began the week are already entered under *Prior Activity*.)

		Balance Sheet				Income Statement	
	Account	Cash	+ Other Assets	= Liabilities	+ Equity	+ Revenues	- Expenses
	Prior Activity::						
	Cash	1,500					
	Equipment		22,500				
	Inventory		850				
	Supplies		4,320				
	Notes Payable			10,000			
	Notes Payable			5,000			
	Capital Stock				10,000		
	Retained						
	Earnings				4,170		
	Prior Activity Totals:	1,500	27,670	15,000	14,170		
	New Activity:						
1.							
2.							
3.							
4.							
5.							
	New Activity Totals:						

Short Essays: The following short essay questions not only reinforce important concepts but also give you a chance to practice writing skills. Answer these questions in complete sentences.

1.   Recognizing Events under Accrual Accounting. What general recognition guidelines govern the recognition of revenues and expenses in an accrual accounting system?

2.   Distinguishing Between Assets and Expenses. Would *asset* or *expense* recognition be appropriate when a business buys and pays for inventory for resale?

3.   <u>Comparing Expenses and Cash Flows</u>. Why should an organization recognize an expense for employees' completed work even though they have not yet been paid?

4.   <u>Identifying Assets, Expenses, and Liabilities</u>. At various times during the transformation process, *rent* activity can be recorded as an asset, an expense, or a liability. Describe the specific circumstances for these three alternatives as well as the specific accounts used.

5.   <u>Contrasting Income and Cash Flow Information</u>. Discuss the reasons why decision makers need one report that shows net income and another that shows cash flows.

Suggested Answers for Review Questions, Exercises, and Short Essays

<u>Multiple Choice Questions</u>:

1.   (b) A legal right to the good or service exists when the organization pays for the item. This right is a valuable resource and the payment should be recorded as an increase in an asset such as Prepaid Rent or Prepaid Insurance. When the good or service is consumed, an expense such as Rent Expense or Insurance Expense has been incurred.

2.   (a) At the end of an accounting period, the owners' equity account is not up to date because transactions have been recorded in two temporary sets of accounts: *revenues* and *expenses*. Asset and liability accounts are current because increases and decreases have been recorded directly in those accounts   Revenues result in increases in owners' equity and expenses result in decreases; therefore, adding revenues and subtracting expenses will adjust owners' equity to the proper level.

3.   (c) Until the customer makes payment, the contract is incomplete. The seller has performed under the terms of the contract, but the buyer has not. Presenting the bill simply reminds the customer of his or her obligations under the terms of the contract.

4.   (c) The term *going concern* refers to the assumption that an organization will continue operating long enough to complete current transformation activities. While a long-term lack of profitability or other major problems would certainly call the going concern assumption into question, the going concern concept is broader than just profitability.

5.   (b) *Periodic measurement* refers to the concept that an accounting system measures and reports performance for a particular period. Although the transformation process is continuous, the need to provide information for decisions in a timely manner requires that managers divide the organizational processes into distinct periods.

6.   (d) Cash is not an adequate measure of activities because many activities may not involve the use of cash, or cash flows may not occur at the time activities and decisions take place. For example, credit sales may occur in one period and the resulting cash inflow may take place in another period. Conversely, some current expenses may not be paid in cash until the next time period.

7.   (b) Accrual accounting is based on broader concepts than the receipt and disbursement of cash. Thus, revenue is defined not as cash inflows but as *resources created* through normal operating activities Revenue recognition usually occurs when products are *sold*. Expenses are not defined as cash outflows but as *resources consumed* as part of operating activities.

8.   (a) A promise of future payment that arises out of a sale is called an Account Receivable. This account is an asset because the holder is entitled to receive a future cash payment.

9.   (d) The reduction of inventory triggered by a sale of merchandise creates two accounting changes. First, the Merchandise Inventory asset account is decreased because inventory has been sold. In addition, an expense, Cost of Goods Sold, must be increased since a resource has been consumed in the transformation process.

10.   (d) The employer has used a resource, and, therefore, an expense, Wages Expense, has been incurred. In addition, a liability, Wages Payable, currently exists since the employer has not yet paid the employee.

11.   (d) The organization has "rented" a resource -- cash belonging to another organization. In Year1, the borrower used the resource for 2/12 of the year, so the Interest Expense for Year1 is 2/12 of the annual $12,000 interest charge. Because the amount has not been paid to the lender, it also must be recognized as an obligation -- Interest Payable.

12.   (b) A portion of the asset's value must be expensed during each year of its use. The portion of the asset's cost assigned to each year is recorded as Depreciation Expense.

13.   (d) Costs associated with specific goods are called *product costs*. Product costs initially become an asset -- Merchandise Inventory. When the goods are sold, the product costs are transferred to Cost of Goods Sold.

14.   (d) The statement of cash flows presents a comprehensive view of the cash inflows and outflows that result from an organization's operating, investing, and financing activities.

15.   (d) Taken together, all three financial statements provide decision makers with a composite view of organizational performance. An income statement displays the results of operations measured on an accrual basis. The balance sheet presents the firm's resources, obligations, and owners' investment. The statement of cash flows provides a summary record of cash inflows and outflows from operation, investing, and financing activities.

Exercises:

1.   Matching Accounts and Account Types.

The accounts listed should be categorized into the following account types:

Account Type	Code
Assets	A
Liabilities	L
Owner's equity	O
Revenues	R
Expenses	E

(The classification of specific accounts continues on the next page.)

Account	Code
Example:	
Common Stock	O
Cash	A
Accounts Payable	L
Sales	R
Retained Earnings	O
Accounts Receivable	A
Land	A
Wages Expense	E
Rent Expense	E
Supplies	A
Utilities Payable	L
Automobiles	A
Cost of Goods Sold	E
Inventory	A
Wages Payable	L
Prepaid Rent	A

2. Calculating Sales Revenue and Cash Collected.

Because of the timing of sales and subsequent cash collections, sales revenue for a given month and cash collected from sales for that same month may be two different amounts.

a. Comparison of Sales Revenue and Cash Collected from Sales:

	June	July	August
Sales Revenue:	$100,000	$150,000	$200,000
Cash Collected:			
From Previous Month	$ 20,000	$ 40,000	$ 60,000
From Current Month	60,000	90,000	120,000
Total Cash Received	$ 80,000	$130,000	$180,000

b. Sales revenue and cash collected from sales are two important but *very different* bits of managerial information for decision makers. Cash information will alert managers to an organization's ability to meet short-term obligations or acquire new resources in the near future. Sales revenue information provides information about the success of an organization's operations. Since current sales should ultimately result in future cash flows, the sales revenue information provides a basis for managers to forecast future cash inflows.

3.   Analyzing Transactions.

The events described in transactions (1) through (5) have the following impact on the accounting equation:

		Balance Sheet			Income Statement	
Account	Cash	+ Other Assets	= Liabilities	+ Equity	+ Revenues	- Expenses
Prior Activity::						
Cash	1,500					
Equipment		22,500				
Inventory		850				
Supplies		4,320				
Notes Payable			10,000			
Notes Payable			5,000			
Capital Stock				10,000		
Retained Earnings				4,170		
Prior Activity Totals:	1,500	27,670	15,000	14,170		
New Activity:						
1. Cash	2,850					
Accounts Receivable		150				
Sales					3,000	
2. Cash	-50					
Supplies		-200				
Gas Expense						-50
Supplies Expense						-200
3. Wages Payable			1,150			
Wages Expense						-1,150
4. Interest Payable			30			
Interest Expense						-30
5. Accumulated Depreciation		-70				
Depreciation Expense						-70
New Activity Totals:	2,800	-120	1,180		3,000	-1,500

Notice that Tom's accounting records up to the current week balance: $1,500 + $27,670 = $15,000 + $14,170. The retained earnings of $4,170 summarizes all prior revenues and expenses. His new transactions balance as well: $2,800 + $ -120 = $1,180 + $0 + $3,000 - $1,500. In this case, the expanded accounting equation is appropriate since the current period's revenues and expenses have not yet been added to retained earnings.

Also, notice that his net income is the amount by which his *net* assets (assets - liabilities) increased because revenues represent resources (assets) created while expenses represent resources consumed in the creation of the income. Also, note that Tom's loan to the business is treated just like the bank loan and that Tom is paid a salary. Recall that a corporation is a separate legal entity from the owners, and the contracts with Tom are treated just like any other contracts.

1.   Recognizing Events under Accrual Accounting.

Under the accrual basis of accounting, revenue is recognized (recorded) when *resources are created as part of an organization's operating activities*, and expenses are recognized when *resources are consumed as part of operating activities*. In both cases, recognition is based on underlying economic events: the creation and consumption of resources. The accrual basis of accounting differs substantially from cash basis accounting where recognition of revenue and expenses is closely linked to the movement of cash.

2.   Distinguishing Between Assets and Expenses.

When an organization purchases merchandise for resale, additional resources or *assets* have been acquired. Since the organization has already paid for the merchandise, managers merely exchanged one asset -- Cash -- for another asset of equal value -- Inventory. An *expense* would not be recognized until the merchandise is subsequently sold. At that time, an asset -- Inventory -- would decrease, and an expense -- Cost of Goods Sold -- would increase to reflect the consumption of resources.

3.   Comparing Expenses and Cash Flows.

Under even the most informal employment contracts, an obligation to pay for work completed exists once employees conclude work for a given project or period of time. An expense -- Wages Expense -- should be recognized since organizational resources have been consumed and committed to the employees even if payment takes place at a later date.

4.   Identifying Assets, Expenses, and Liabilities.

A rental contract involves the exchange of cash for the right to occupy a particular space for a specific time period. If a rental payment is made in advance, Cash is decreased in exchange for another asset -- Prepaid Rent. This transaction indicates that an organization has a right to occupy a given space for some future time period. Once a rental period has elapsed, Prepaid Rent has decreased since the right to occupy no longer exists. At this point, the organization has incurred Rent Expense. If an organization occupies space for which a rental payment has not yet been made, a liability -- Rent Payable -- must be recognized until payment is made. The treatment of any transaction, therefore, depends upon timing as well as specific activities and management decisions.

5.   <u>Contrasting Income and Cash Flow Information</u>.

Although an income statement provides vital managerial information on an organization's revenues and expenses, the statement of cash flows provides significant information that cannot be found on either an income statement or a balance sheet. A cash flow statement summarizes all operating, investing, and financing activities that resulted in either cash inflows or outflows. The statement, therefore, provides a clearer view of an organization's cash activities than the income statement or balance sheet. Since net income is not the same as net cash inflow, an organization's decision makers must be keenly aware of cash position.

CHAPTER F4: PROCESSING ACCOUNTING INFORMATION

Chapter Focus

Major Theme: Accountants use specific procedures to record, store, and summarize information in forms useful to decision makers. These procedures and policies represent important components of an organization's accounting system. This chapter examines information processing in both manual and computerized systems and concludes with a discussion of controls that increase the reliability of accounting information.

Important Elements: As you study the chapter, look for the following topics:

The accounting cycle
The effect of business processes on accounting records and reports
Components and functions of accounting systems
Controls to improve the reliability of accounting systems

Learning Objectives: After studying this chapter, you should be able to:

Identify:	Basic information processes that occur in an accounting system.
	Primary components of a computerized accounting system.
Describe and Explain:	Double-entry accounting and the purpose of debits and credits.
Explain:	The processing of transactions in a computerized accounting system.
	The purpose of internal controls and their importance for accounting systems.

Chapter Review

Introduction. Transactions occur when financial or nonfinancial resources are acquired, resources are consumed, or goods and services are sold. An organization's accounting staff uses the accounting processing system to record, summarize, and report the economic effects of the various transactions that occur throughout the transformation process.

1. **Using the Accounting Cycle to Process Transactions**. The process of converting accounting data to useful information is called the <u>accounting cycle</u>.

    A.   In general, an accounting cycle has six steps: <u>obtaining data from business activities</u>, <u>recording transactions</u>, <u>updating accounting balances</u>, <u>making end-of-period adjustments</u>, <u>preparing financial statements</u>, and <u>closing the books</u>.

    B.   Because of different business practices, the details of accounting systems vary across companies. An examination of these systems, however, reveals that each has the six general steps that make up the accounting cycle.

    C.   Information that summarizes various business transactions is recorded in specific accounts that are affected by those activities.

        1.   <u>Subsidiary accounts</u> record financial data on individual items such as a specific customer's obligation to a firm (Accounts Receivable) or the firm's specific obligation to a vendor (Accounts Payable).

        2.   <u>Control accounts</u> represent summary accounts that track the total of a group of subsidiary accounts. For example, the Accounts Receivable control account tracks all accounts receivable from customers and the Accounts Payable control account tracks all obligations to vendors.

    D.   A <u>general ledger</u> represents an accounting record of each control account and its balance.

    E.   The end-of-period adjustment phase of the accounting cycle provides an opportunity to adjust account balances for the impact of events that take place over time. The recording of interest charges, use of insurance coverage, and depreciation are examples of this type of adjustment. <u>Adjusting entries</u> represent end-of-period transactions to update account balances when necessary.

F.   When the account balances have been updated, financial statements may be prepared using the information from the general ledger.

   1.   The income statement is prepared first followed by the balance sheet. The statement of cash flows is usually prepared last.

   2.   In addition to the financial statements, firms issue notes to accompany the three primary financial statements. These notes provide supplementary, detailed information helpful in understanding the summarized financial statements

G.   The last step in the accounting cycle -- closing the books -- prepares the accounting system to receive transaction information for the next time period.

   1.   Revenue and expense accounts collect information for one time period only.

   2.   At the end of each time period, revenues and expenses must be reset to zero and their balances must be transferred to Retained Earnings. This transaction accomplishes two objectives.

      a.   The Retained Earnings account is increased by the amount of income (revenues - expenses).

      b.   The revenue and expense accounts are emptied out to prepare for the next period's transactions.

H.   Once the accounting cycle is complete, decision makers can analyze the information reported in the financial statements and notes. These statements often serve as a basis for comparison with other similar organizations and forecasts of future performance.

2.   **Double-Entry Accounting.** Double-entry accounting represents an approach to processing accounting information. The double-entry mechanism is very useful whether transactions are processed manually or through a computerized system. The language and concepts of double-entry are useful in communicating the impact of a transaction.

Essentially, double-entry accounting is the process of recording transactions in offsetting accounts.

A.   The double-entry format uses the accounting equation as a basis. The following equation must always balance:

Assets = Liabilities + Owners' Equity +
(Revenues – Expenses)

Any increase or decrease in one account must be balanced by a corresponding change in another account. For each transaction, therefore, at least two accounts must be affected.

B.   The summary notation -- or shorthand -- used to record these increases or decreases to various accounts is based on several principles.

1.   A transaction impacts any account in one of two possible ways. Account balances only increase or decrease.

2.   The system relies on a left -- or debit -- column and a right or -- credit -- column to track these increase or decreases.

3.   Elements within the accounting equation [Assets = Liabilities + Owners' Equity + (Revenues - Expenses)] have different characteristics. Therefore, the increase / decrease notation for various accounts is different.

a.   Assets and expenses track the acquisition and consumption of resources.

(1)   In addition, assets stand alone on one side of the equation while expenses represent a reduction on the other side of the equation.

(2)   For assets and expenses, debits (left side entries) represent increases and credits (right side entries) represent decreases.

b.   Liabilities, owners' equity, and revenues represent financing sources for organizational resources.

(1)   In addition, these three account categories are grouped together on the same side of the accounting equation.

(2) For <u>liabilities</u>, <u>owners' equity</u>, and <u>revenues</u>, <u>debits</u> (left side entries) <u>represent decreases</u> while <u>credits</u> (right side entries) <u>represent increases</u>.

[Important Note: Debits do not always signal increases, and credits do not always signal decreases! In double-entry accounting, *debit* only signifies *left column* and *credit* only signifies *right column*.]

4. The <u>T-account</u> is a commonly used approach for demonstrating the impact of a transaction on various accounts. The T-accounts merely organize the increases and decreases to any account in the following manner:

Assets and Expenses		Liabilities, Equities, and Revenues	
Debit	Credit	Debit	Credit
Increase	Decrease	Decrease	Increase

5. Since debits and credits track the increases and decreases to specific accounts, this approach captures the same information as the spreadsheet approach illustrated in previous chapters.

C. Sometimes, transactions are presented in a traditional <u>journal</u> format where business activities are recorded in their chronological order.

   1. The debit/credit notation system and double-entry concept based on the accounting equation can record even the most complex economic transactions in journal form.

   2. The following two journal entries serve as examples.

      a. The purchase of $1,000 of merchandise inventory for cash would appear in the journal as:

Date	Account	Debit	Credit
	Merchandise Inventory	1,000	
	Cash		1,000

One asset account balance increased while the other asset account balance decreased.

b.   Purchasing the same inventory on account would appear as:

Date	Account	Debit	Credit
	Merchandise Inventory	1,000	
	Accounts Payable		1,000

This time, an asset account balance increased, and a liability account balance also increased.

3.   In traditional accounting systems, the journal format and the ledger format represent two views of the same business activities. Once business activities are recorded in chronological order in the journal, the resulting information is then posted or transferred to the ledger where information is organized by account, and the account balances may be determined.

3.   **Computer Processing of Accounting Data.** A computerized management information system includes major components that relate to sales and distribution, purchasing, human resources (payroll), and production (in manufacturing firms).

A.   The sales and distribution component of the management information system focuses information from transactions with customers.

1.   A customer submits a purchase order either on paper or electronically. This order becomes a source document – a document containing data that describes a transaction and will be entered into the accounting system.

2.   Information from the purchase order such as the customer's name, the specific products desired, and the quantity is transferred electronically to the firm's distribution center. Here, clerks prepare a packing slip to accompany the goods and a bill of lading that specifies transportation information.

3. The sales order department and distribution center then send the purchase order, packing slip, and bill of lading to the accounts receivable department where a <u>sales invoice</u> is prepared.

4. This sales invoice triggers the recording of business activity in the accounting system. A sale has been made on account. Therefore, both Accounts Receivable and Sales must be increased. (Note: the change in accounts receivable will be recorded in both the customer's subsidiary account and the Accounts Receivable control account.)

5. In a subsequent transaction in the accounting system, the cost of the goods shipped to the customer are removed from Merchandise Inventory and recorded as Cost of Goods Sold. Thus, an asset has decreased and an expense has increased.

6. Later, when the customer pays for the merchandise, a third accounting transaction has taken place. The selling firm receives cash in exchange for the customer's account receivable. One asset – Cash -- has increased while the other – Accounts Receivable – has decreased.

B. The <u>purchases and inventory</u> component of a management information system also generates information for the accounting system.

1. Purchasing activity begins with a <u>purchase requisition</u> that represents a request to purchase supplies or inventory. This request is translated into a <u>purchase order</u> that is sent to a vendor and a <u>receiving report</u> when the goods are received.

2. The purchase requisition, purchase order, and receiving report represent source documents that provide information for an accounting transaction. An asset has been purchased and an account payable created.

3. The three source documents also serve as the basis for a <u>voucher</u> – the authorization to pay the vendor. When the payment is sent to the vendor, Cash decreases and Accounts Payable decreases as well.

C.   The <u>payroll</u> component of a management information system provides accounting information on the wages, salaries, benefits, taxes, and other costs associated with payroll activities.

D.   Non-routine transactions represent accounting activities that are not triggered by business events.

1.   In the case of <u>adjusting entries</u>, several account balances are adjusted because of the passage of time or new information available at the end of the accounting period. Recording depreciation expense and doubtful accounts expense are examples of adjustments.

2.   Other non-routine transactions are <u>closing entries</u> that update Retained Earnings and prepare the revenue and expense accounts to receive information for a new fiscal period.

a.   Retained Earnings is a <u>permanent account</u>. The balance in Retained Earnings and other permanent accounts is carried from year to year on the balance sheet.

b.   Revenue and expense accounts are <u>temporary accounts</u>. These accounts must have a zero balance at the end of the period in order to be ready to track activities for the next period.

c.   The process of closing the books moves the balance from the revenue and expense accounts to Retained Earnings. This action prepares the temporary accounts for the next period and updates Retained Earnings by adding the net income or deducting the net loss.

4.   **Computerized Accounting Systems**. In a computerized accounting system, records are maintained through the use of relational databases and computer networks.

A.   A <u>relational database</u> is a linked set of computer files that permit the easy entry and retrieval of information. Data is entered in forms and stored in electronic tables. <u>Queries</u> allow managers and staff members to retrieve information in a variety of ways.

B.   A <u>computer network</u> represents a group of linked computers that can interact with one another as well as with the internet.

     1.   Local area networks (LANs) link several computers in one particular location.

     2.   Wide area networks (WANs) link computers in different locations.

5.   **Internal Controls**. The reliability of accounting information represents an important concern for all decision makers in an organization. Management must develop and maintain a system of <u>internal controls</u> that protect organizational resources and assure the reliability of accounting information.

A.   The basis of an effective system of internal controls is management's overall philosophy about appropriate security and behavior within the organization. An important component of this overall philosophy is the development of a system of rewards and incentives for employees.

B.   In computerized systems, internal controls include controlled-access to the system; specific functional responsibility, built-in error checking, careful checks during installation of any new hardware or software; regular backup of data, and system documentation.

C.   Some internal control elements relate to the management of human resources. These general controls include items such as qualified employees; clear policies on authority, responsibility, and transaction processing; and separation of duties.

D.   Physical controls represent another component of an effective internal control system. Both documents and physical assets such as inventory must be protected.

6.   **Setting Accounting Standards**. Since 1973, the Financial Accounting Standards Board (FASB) has been the primary organization for setting accounting standards for business and not-for-profit organizations in the United States. A parallel organization, the Governmental Accounting Standards Board (GASB) sets accounting standards for state and local governmental units. The regulation of accounting standards is also an international activity, and since 1973, the International Accounting Standards Committee (IASC) has issued standards that identify preferred accounting methods.

Review Questions, Exercises, and Short Essays

<u>Multiple Choice Questions</u>: These questions reinforce vocabulary and basic concepts from the chapter. In each case, select the answer you believe to be the *best*.

1.   The accounting cycle includes:
    a.   Recording transactions.
    b.   Hiring workers.
    c.   Checking customers' credit.
    d.   All of the above are important parts of the accounting cycle.

2.   Double-entry accounting involves:
    a.   Keeping two sets of accounting records.
    b.   Requiring two people to simultaneously operate the accounting system for security purposes.
    c.   Recording every transaction in more than one account.
    d.   Using both cash and accrual basis recognition rules.

3.   In an accounting processing system, a *journal* is:
    a.   A record of travel expenses.
    b.   A record of all transactions in the sequence in which they occur.
    c.   A book or computer file that summarizes account balances.
    d.   A summary financial report for management.

4.   In an accounting processing system, a *control account* is:
    a.   A book or computer file that records financial data about individual items of importance to the organization.
    b.   A record of specific transactions in chronological order.
    c.   A summary account of all subsidiary accounts of a particular type.
    d.   A summary financial report for management.

5.   Source documents may be:
    a.   Invoices.
    b.   Purchase orders.
    c.   Cash register receipts.
    d.   All of the above may be source documents.

6.   In a double-entry accounting system, the term *credit* refers to:
    a.   A decrease in an account balance.
    b.   An increase in an account balance.
    c.   Either an increase or a decrease in an account balance.
    d.   An increase in a customer's account balance.

7. When a sale is made on credit, the SALES REVENUE account increases. To maintain the balance of the accounting equation:
   a. ACCOUNTS PAYABLE decreases.
   b. ACCOUNTS PAYABLE increases.
   c. ACCOUNTS RECEIVABLE increases.
   d. CASH increases.

8. When a sale is made either for cash or on credit, MERCHANDISE INVENTORY decreases. To maintain the balance of the accounting equation:
   a. ACCOUNTS PAYABLE increases..
   b. ACCOUNTS PAYABLE decreases..
   c. COST OF GOODS SOLD increases.
   d. COST OF GOODS SOLD decreases.

9. The expression *FOB destination* in the context of a purchase means:
   a. Title to purchased goods transfers to the purchaser when the goods are shipped.
   b. The buyer of goods pays shipping charges.
   c. Title to purchased goods transfers to the purchaser when the goods are delivered.
   d. The seller agrees to deliver to the shipper without charge to the buyer.

10. The component of a computer-based accounting system that is most likely to include a routine for recording cost of goods sold is:
    a. The general ledger system.
    b. The payroll system.
    c. The purchasing and inventory system.
    d. The sales order and distribution system.

11. The components of a computer-based accounting system most likely to provide information useful for the management of an organization's marketing are:
    a. The sales order and distribution system.
    b. The purchasing and inventory system.
    c. The payroll system.
    d. The relational database.

12. A relational database is:
    a. A computerized system for managing customer relations.
    b. A set of linked computer files, organized as tables for the efficient updating and retrieval of information.
    c. A listing relating account types and balances.
    d. None of the above.

13.   A disgruntled employee gained access to the accounts payable module in an organization's microcomputer accounting system and wrote a series of checks to fictitious vendors. What internal control steps could have prevented this?
    a.   Carefully checking computer programs before installation.
    b.   Identification of responsibility for specific functions.
    c.   Error checking routines built into the computer system
    d.   Thorough system documentation.

14.   When an organization received an upgrade for the payroll module of its automated accounting system, a computer programmer modified the new program so that it would automatically eliminate *all* payroll and payroll-related tax records if the programmer was terminated. What initial internal control step could have prevented this?
    a.   Carefully checking computer programs before installation.
    b.   Identification of responsibility for specific functions.
    c.   Segregation of duties among data-processing employees.
    d.   Thorough system documentation.

15.   A payroll clerk mistakenly enters the incorrect number of hours worked by an employee. Instead of 40 hours, the clerk enters 400 hours. What internal control steps could have prevented this?
    a.   Identify responsibility for specific functions.
    b.   Backup of data files at the end of the day and off site storage of the backup files.
    c.   Segregation of duties among data-processing employees.
    d.   An error-checking routine in the payroll program that examines number of hours worked for reasonableness.

Exercises: These questions require the analysis of economic situations and the application of accounting concepts.

1.   Analyzing Transactions. The Mt. Baker Snowboarding School -- a profit-seeking business -- is staging its first annual snowboarding competition. The following transactions relate to the week-long competition:

a.   Participant entry fees for $5,000 were received.

b.   Mt. Baker made a payment of $2,200 for liability insurance.

c.   The firm purchased 500 T-shirts that display the *MBSS* Competition logo. Management intends to pay the $2,500 bill after the competition.

d.   School managers arranged for the printing of advertising posters and flyers, and the $1,500 bill was paid immediately.

e.   Customers ordered and paid for 250 T-shirts at $15 per shirt. The orders were shipped immediately.

f.   The event manager purchased supplies for $500 cash.

g.   School staff members earned $2,000 during the week, and they were paid at week's end.

Using the journal format that appears on the next page, record the transactions in general journal form.

Date	Account	Debit	Credit
a.			
b.			
c.			
d.			
e.			
f.			
g.			

2.   <u>Recording Non-routine Transactions</u>. Using the information provided, record the effects of these year-end adjustments in general journal form:

a.   On January 1, the Islander Co. borrowed $10,000 from a bank at 12% interest per year . Financial statements are prepared at the end of the year.

b.   Islander's sales for the year were $1,500,000. All sales were on credit and the company's controller estimates that 1% of the sales are uncollectible.

c.   Islander owns equipment that had cost $500,000 and should be depreciated at $100,000 per year.

d.   Islander's employees earned $8,000 in the last week of December. They will be paid on the first Friday in January.

Date	Account	Debit	Credit
a.			
b.			
c.			
d.			

3.   <u>Recognizing Internal Control Issues</u>. The following three business
      situations highlight common internal control measures.

      a.   A local ice cream parlor is generally staffed by two young workers
            who are paid minimum wage and all the ice cream they can eat.
            The owner is frequently absent. Recently customers noticed a sign
            on the cash register offering a free serving of ice cream to any
            customer who received a cash register receipt with a red star
            printed on it. What could be the purpose of this offer?

      b.   Order tickets in restaurants are often printed with a sequential
            number at the top. Discuss the internal control purpose of these
            numbers.

      c.   Why do utilities and credit card companies often include a return
            stub with their bills? Why do some also ask customers to write the
            amount remitted on the stub and the customer's account number
            on the check?

<u>Short Essays</u>: The following short essay questions not only reinforce important concepts but also give you a chance to practice writing skills. Answer these questions in complete sentences.

1.   <u>Closing the Books</u>. Discuss two important reasons for performing the step in the accounting process known as *closing the books*.

2.   <u>Using Debits and Credits</u>. Describe the use of the terms *debit* and *credit* within an accounting system. In addition, explain why debits are not always increases to accounts and why credits are not always decreases to accounts.

3.   <u>Recognizing Source Documents</u>. Describe what is meant by *source documents* and provide several examples.

4.   <u>Tracking Receivables and Payables</u>. Explain an effective method for tracking not only the total balance in Accounts Receivable and Accounts Payable but also the balance for any single customer or vendor.

5.   <u>Describing Internal Control Elements</u>. Internal controls represent important elements of an effective accounting information system.   What are the general objectives of internal controls? What are the general control polices and procedures?

Suggested Answers to Review Questions, Exercises, and Short Essays

Multiple Choice Questions:

1.   (a) One of the initial activities within the accounting cycle is the recording of transactions. Hiring workers or checking customers credit may precede transactions such as paying new employees or selling to a customer on credit. The hiring and the checking, however, are not accounting transactions.

2.   (c) The term *double-entry* refers to the fact that each transaction is recorded in at least two accounts.

3.   (b) A *journal* can be described as a financial diary—a chronological record of events. A book or file that summarizes account balances is a *ledger*. Summary financial reports include the income statement, the balance sheet, and the statement of cash flows.

4.   (c) A *control account* is an account that maintains a control total for a set of subsidiary accounts. The balance of the control account must, at all times be equal to the sum of the balances of the subsidiary accounts in order to act as a check on the correct processing of transactions in the subsidiary accounts..

5.   (d) All of the items mentioned can be source documents because they all provide information on economic transactions.

6.   (c) *Debit* and *credit* refer only to the left and right side of an account. Historically, writing all of the increases in an account on one side of a page and all of the decreases on the other side proved quite helpful. Because decreases in asset and expense accounts appear on the credit side and increases in owners' equity, liabilities, and revenues also appear on the credit side, *credits* can represent either increases or decreases. The terms are still in use because they provide a quick way to describe changes to various accounts.

7.   (c) Accounts Receivable represent obligations that other parties have to an organization arising from credit sales. No obligation (liability) exists which attaches to the seller, and cash has not yet been received.

8.   (c) When Merchandise Inventory decreases as part of a sales transaction, an asset -- or resource -- has been consumed. The consumption of resources increases the expense Cost of Goods Sold.

9.   (c) The expression *FOB destination* is used to denote the fact that the ownership of goods purchased transfers to the buyer when they are delivered. Normally, this means that the owner of the goods during shipping, the seller, pays the shipping charges and bears the risk of loss in transit.

10.   (d) *Cost of Goods Sold* is normally recorded when goods are sold, so information about the cost of a sale is likely to be captured and recorded as part of the sales recording process in the sales order and distribution system..

11.   (a) Marketers are most likely to be interested in what products are selling to which customers, how sales respond to promotional efforts, etc. Therefore, the output of the sales order and distribution system will be of great interest. Note that a *relational database* could be the source of the information, but that expression is used for a

particular way of organizing information, not to refer to a component of the accounting system.

12.   (b) A *relational database* is a set of computer records that can be thought of as being organized as a set of linked tables. It is a very flexible and powerful organizational form that may be used to organize all manner of related data items.

13.   (b) Identification of responsibility refers to the description of employee authorization as well as the controls used to limit individuals to authorized functions. This internal control function can be accomplished by controlling physical access to files, programs, and machines or by using password access to control sensitive functions such as payroll.

14.   (a) Careful review of computer programs before implementation and control over access to programs that are operational are essential parts of internal control over computer systems. Of course, there is no guarantee that a review will find a minor change. The other possible steps would also be helpful, but the initial careful review of new software applications would be the first, very important internal control step.

15.   (d) Errors of this type can be easily prevented by a reasonableness check - a computer routine that examines input data to determine whether it seems reasonable given the constraints of the type of data being processed.

Exercises:

1.   Analyzing Transactions.

Explanation of Mt. Baker Snowboarding School transactions:

a.   The receipt of entry fees results in a cash increase. The cash represents a resource created by the operating activities of the Committee, and these receipts also represent an increase in revenues.

b.   Cash decreases to reflect the payment of $2,200 for insurance. Consumption of an asset is an expense, and, therefore, insurance expense increases.

c.   The organization has acquired new assets in the form of inventory. These assets were acquired in exchange for the promise to deliver another asset -- cash -- to the supplier in the future. This obligation for a future payment is recorded as an increase in accounts payable of $2,500.

d. $1,500 of cash was consumed on advertising. Cash decreases and advertising expense increases to represent the consumption of an organizational resource.

e.   The cash that accompanied the orders represents a resource created by the organization's activities. Cash is increased, and the increase in assets from the productive activities of the organization is represented also as a revenue increase. In addition, the consumption of assets triggers the decrease in merchandise inventory and the increase in cost of goods sold.

f.   The supplies represent a new asset. Total assets, however, have not increased since the increase in supplies is balanced by the decrease in cash. No resources have been consumed yet. When the supplies are subsequently consumed, an expense will be recorded..

g.   The employees' wages represent a decrease in cash and the recording of an expense to the firm.

In journal form, the Mt. Baker Snowboarding School's transactions appears as follows:

Date	Account	Debit	Credit
a.	Cash	5,000	
	Revenues		5,000
b.	Insurance Expense	2,200	
	Cash		2,200
c.	Merchandise Inventory	2,500	
	Accounts Payable		2,500
d.	Advertising Expense	1,500	
	Cash		1,500
e.	Cash	3,750	
	Revenue		3,750
	Cost of Goods Sold	1,250	
	Merchandise Inventory		1,250
f.	Supplies	500	
	Cash		500
g.	Wages Expense	2,000	
	Cash		2,000

2.   Recording Non-routine Transactions.

Explanation of Islander Co. non-routine transactions:

a.   The loan results in interest that Islander will have to pay when the loan is repaid. At the end of the year Islander owes $10,000 x .12 = $1,200 interest. This must be recorded as an adjustment at the end of the year as Interest Expense and Interest Payable.

b.   Islander must adjust its accounts to recognize the fact that it will not be able to collect from some, presently unidentifiable, customers. It does this by recording Doubtful Accounts Expense and reducing Accounts Receivable with a contra account called Allowance for Doubtful Accounts.

c.   Islander must record depreciation expense as a reduction in assets – using a contra account -- and an increase in an expense.

d.   Islander must record the $8,000 obligation to employees and the expense representing the cost of the labor for this period.

The adjustment information for the Islander Co. can be recorded in journal form as follows:

Date	Account	Debit	Credit
a.	Interest Expense	$ 1,200	
	Interest Payable		$ 1,200
b.	Doubtful Accounts Expense	15,000	
	Allowance for Doubtful Accounts		15,000
c.	Depreciation Expense	100,000	
	Accumulated Depreciation		100,000
d.	Wages Expense	8,000	
	wages Payable		8000

3.   Recognizing Internal Control Issues.

a.   From a marketing perspective, potential customers would probably not go to an ice cream parlor in the hopes of receiving an additional free scoop of ice cream when checking out. Patrons decide to buy ice cream before going to the shop. While this offer doesn't make sense as a promotional device, it does encourage customers to make sure that they receive a receipt. In turn, this customer interest insures that employees, who might be tempted to pocket the cash received, offer receipts to all customers. The offer is an internal control step rather than a marketing device. In fact, offering all customers a receipt is one of the few controls that can insure the complete recording of all sales transactions in the store cash register. The customer has become part of the internal control process.

b.   Like cash register tickets, the order tickets in a restaurant serve as a control device if they are prenumbered. Accounting for all prenumbered order tickets assures an accounting for all sales. An effective internal control system, however, is really a series of interlocking policies and procedures. Prenumbered documents may not be effective if other internal control elements are not also in place.

c.   By asking customers to write account numbers on checks and amounts paid on remittance forms, organizations can link specific payments and specific accounts more easily. These steps act as important internal control elements. In addition, by reducing clerical processing, they reduce the likelihood of an information processing error.

Short Essays:

1.   Closing the Books.

At the end of each accounting period, staff members must align information from the accounting system with the information reported on the financial statements and prepare the system to receive transaction information for the next accounting period. The process of closing the books accomplishes these goals by completing two specific steps. First, balances in all revenue and expense accounts are removed to prepare for the accumulation of revenue and expenses in the next period. Secondly, the net value of all these revenues and expenses -- the net income for the current period -- is added to the balance in retained earnings to determine the Retained Earnings account balance at period's end. The closing process, therefore, is a technical step that has important conceptual consequences.

2.   Using Debits and Credits.

The terms debit and credit refer to the left and right sides of specific accounts. Debits always refer to entries on the left side while credits always refer to entries on the right side of an account. Debits may represent either increases or decreases. *Increases* in asset and expense accounts and *decreases* in liability, owners' equity and revenue accounts take place on the left -- or debit -- side. Credits may also be either increases or decreases. *Increases* in liability, owner's equity and revenue accounts and *decreases* in asset and expense accounts take place on the right -- or credit -- side. The different treatment of increases and decreases to the various account types is based upon the accounting equation:

$$Assets = Liabilities + Owners' \ Equity + (Revenues - Expenses)$$

Because the assets appear on a different side of the equation from liabilities and owners' equity, increases in asset accounts occur on the left side while increases in liabilities and owners' equity occur on the credit side. Since revenues increase owners' equity, revenues are also increased with an entry on the right or credit side. Since expenses reduce owners' equity, increases in expenses are really decreases in owners' equity, and, therefore, increases in expenses appear on the debit side.

3.   Recognizing Source Documents.

A wide variety of specific documents qualify as source documents for an accounting information system. Source documents contain any original information that is entered into an accounting system. They act not only as sources, however, but also as important evidence that the information is valid. Examples include checks, invoices, purchase orders, time sheets, sales tickets, contracts and cash register tapes.

4.   Tracking Receivables and Payables.

Both receivables and payables provide a specific challenge within the accounting information system. The system must track not only the total of the Accounts Receivable and Accounts Payable accounts, but staff members must also be able to quickly determine the balance of a single customer or vendor account. Generally, only total receivables and payables are kept in the main Accounts Receivable or Accounts Payable accounts. These accounts, therefore, are considered *control accounts* that are designed to track total receivables and payables without providing specific customer or vendor details.

Accounts receivable or accounts payable *subsidiary accounts* represent sets of detailed accounts for individual customers or vendors. As supporting documents, subsidiary accounts provide the details needed to manage certain organizational functions.

5.   Describing Internal Control Elements.

As an important component of the accounting system, internal control includes the policies and procedures that an organization follows to protect its assets from theft or unauthorized use and to assure the accuracy and reliability of its records. General internal control elements include such policies as hiring qualified employees; establishing clear policies on authority, responsibility, and transaction processing; using prenumbered forms and documents; maintaining control over documents; and relying on independent audits of both account balances and physical quantities.

CHAPTER F5: REPORTING ACCOUNTING INFORMATION

Chapter Focus

Major Theme: After the accounting effects of transactions are measured and processed, information must be effectively summarized and reported to decision makers.

Important Elements: As you study the chapter, look for the following major topics:

    The purpose and content of financial statements
    Reporting rules used in preparing financial statements
    Special attributes and limitations of financial statements

Learning Objectives: After studying this chapter, you should be able to:

Identify: The primary financial statements used by businesses.
    Some of the primary limitations of financial statements.
    The purpose and basic concepts of an audit report.

Summarize: The reporting rules and the information presented on a company's income statement.
    The reporting rules and the information presented on a company's statement of stockholders' equity.
    The reporting rules and the information presented on a company's balance sheet.

Discuss: How financial statements work together to present a picture of a company for a fiscal period and the purpose of consolidated financial statements.

Chapter Review

Introduction. For most business organizations, <u>general purpose financial statements</u> include an <u>income statement</u>, a <u>balance sheet</u>, and a <u>statement of cash flows</u>. Many firms also include a <u>statement of stockholders' equity</u>. (This chapter describes the income statement, balance sheet, and statement of owners' equity, and Chapter Six analyzes the statement of cash flows.) These statements are prepared in accordance with GAAP, and, taken together, they present a picture of the financing, investing, and operating activities that make up an organization's specific transformation process.

1.   **The Purpose of Financial Statements**. Transactions during a fiscal period result in increases and decreases to various accounts. All these increases and decreases can be summarized in a presentation of account balances at the end of a fiscal period. Financial statements present various account balance summaries.

A.   An <u>income statement</u> reports an organization's revenues and expenses for a fiscal period. This report may also be called an <u>earnings statement</u> or a <u>profit and loss statement (P&L)</u>. An income statement reports the results of operating activities for a fiscal period.

1.   An income statement reports <u>net income</u> for a fiscal period and does not report cash flow activities.

2.   The income statement presents revenue and expense information in several sections:

Sales Revenue
- <u>Cost of Goods Sold</u>
= Gross Profit
- <u>Operating Expenses</u>
= Operating Income
+Other (Nonoperating) Revenues
- <u>Other (Nonoperating) Expenses</u>
= Pretax Income
- <u>Income Taxes</u>
= <u>Net Income</u>

Earnings per Share =
(Net Income ÷ Shares of Stock)

3. The difference between the selling price of goods and services and the cost of those goods and services represents the gross profit of a business.

4. Operating expenses include the cost of other resources consumed in the fiscal period that are part of operating activities.

5. Operating income represents sales revenue minus both cost of goods sold and operating expenses.

6. Other revenues and expenses include revenues and expenses that are not part of an organization's normal operating activities. For most organizations, financing costs such as interest expenses on borrowed money represents a large portion of other revenues and expenses.

7. Net income represents operating income adjusted for the impact of other revenues and expenses and income taxes. Earnings per share expresses income on a per share basis.

8. New reporting requirements also require the disclosure of comprehensive income. Comprehensive income is the change in a firm's equity resulting from all nonowner transactions. Owner transactions include the activities such as selling stock or paying dividends. Nonowner transaction impact retained earnings and include net income and other specific adjustments not included on the income statement.

B. A statement of stockholders' equity reports changes in a corporation's stockholders' equity during a fiscal period.

1. Stockholders' equity consists of two major categories: contributed capital (the amount of direct investment by owners) and retained earnings (the amount of cumulative net income that has been reinvested in the organization).

2. The balances in specific contributed capital accounts may change during a fiscal period as stock is sold or repurchased and retired.

3. Dividends decrease retained earnings since they represent the amount of net income that has been distributed directly to stockholders.

C.   A <u>balance sheet</u> reports the balances in asset, liability, and owners' equity accounts at the end of the fiscal period or other specific date. This report may also be called a <u>statement of financial position</u> or a <u>statement of financial condition</u>.

1.   <u>Comparative balance sheets</u> provide information for more than one fiscal period.

2.   <u>Classified balance sheets</u> separate assets, liabilities, and owners' equity into the following specific categories:

Assets:

Current Assets
Property, Plant, and Equipment
Long-Term Investments
<u>**Other Long-Term Assets**</u>
<u>**Total Assets**</u>

Liabilities and Owners' Equity:

Liabilities:
Current Liabilities
<u>**Long-Term Liabilities**</u>
Total Liabilities

Owners' Equity:
Contributed Capital
<u>**Retained Earnings**</u>
Total Owners' Equity

<u>**Total Liabilities and Owner's Equity**</u>

3.   Assets are classified according to their specific attributes.

a)   <u>Current assets</u> include resources that management expects to convert to cash within a year. <u>Liquid assets</u> are those resources that management expects to convert to cash in a very short time. Examples of current assets include Cash, Accounts Receivable, Inventory, and Supplies.

      b)   <u>Property, plant, and equipment</u> (often called <u>fixed assets</u> or <u>plant assets</u>) represent long-term, tangible resources that contribute to a firm's operations. This category includes depreciable items such as Buildings and Equipment along with Land, which is not depreciated.

      c)   <u>Long-term investments</u> occur when one organization buys the stock or bonds of another organization.

      d)   <u>Other long-term assets</u> include legal rights such as patents, copyrights, and trademarks along with noncurrent receivables and fixed assets held for sale. The long-term legal rights may be subject to <u>amortization</u> -- a process that reduces the value of an <u>intangible asset</u> over time.

4.   Liabilities are classified according to the time they <u>mature</u> (become due).

      a)   <u>Current liabilities</u> will be paid during the next fiscal year. This category includes any current portion of long-term debt to be paid during the next fiscal year.

      b)   <u>Long-term liabilities</u> have maturity dates beyond the next fiscal year.

5.   <u>Working capital</u> represents the excess of current assets over current liabilities.

      a)   This measure of <u>liquidity</u> describes an organization's capacity to pay its immediate obligations.

      b)   The <u>working capital ratio</u> or <u>current ratio</u> represents another measure of organizational liquidity.

Current Ratio =
Current Assets ÷ Current Liabilities

6.   The stockholders' equity section of the balance sheet reports the ending contributed capital and retained earnings balances from the statement of stockholders' equity.

2.   **Use of Financial Statements**. The income statement, statement of stockholders' equity, balance sheet, and statement of cash flows provide important information for external decision makers.

   A.   Taken together, these four statements describe the economic events that change an organization's financial position during a fiscal period.

   B.   The statements <u>articulate</u> or work together in the following way:

   Beginning Balance Sheet Account Balances

   + or -

   **Changes Reported on the
   Income Statement
   and
   Statement of Cash Flows**

   =

   Ending Balance Sheet Account Balances

   C.   <u>Consolidated financial statements</u> report the economic activities of several corporations owned by the same stockholders. A <u>parent</u> corporation may control many <u>subsidiary</u> corporations, and consolidated financial statements report the economic activities of the group of corporations as though they are a single business organization.

   D.   Specific aspects of the reporting process limit the usefulness of financial statements.

      1.   Many numbers reported on financial statements are estimates or allocations such as depreciation and amortization. Different organizations may use different methods to make these estimates and allocations.

      2.   While certain assets and liabilities are reported at market value, account balances for many other balance sheet items are based <u>historical costs</u> or the price of various assets and liabilities when they were acquired. These amounts are not adjusted for inflation.

3. Since GAAP changes over time, certain transactions may be omitted from the statements because disclosure was not required when the transaction occurred.

4. Certain important information such as the value of well-trained, dedicated employees is not reported in the financial statements.

5. Significant time lags may occur between the end of a fiscal period and the release of organizational financial reports.

3. **Financial Statements and the Transformation Process**. Accounting information displays the economic consequences of operating, investing, and financing events that represent a transformation process during a specific period of time.

   A. In addition to financial statements, firms include other information in their reports to external users. For example, external reports often include a description of the company's products and activities, a discussion of the organization's recent performance, and notes to the financial statements.

   B. External reports also contain an <u>audit report</u> where the firm's independent auditor expresses an opinion on the fair presentation of the financial statements. The process is also called <u>attestation</u>, and the audit report is divided into several specific paragraphs.

      1. The first paragraph identifies the statements and time period covered by the audit and the responsibilities of both auditors and management of the firm.

      2. The second paragraph summarizes the audit process that is based on <u>generally accepted audit standards (GAAS)</u>. The firm's records and procedures are examined on a <u>test basis</u> to determine if significant -- or <u>material</u> -- errors exist.

      3. The third paragraph includes the auditor's opinion. Most firms receive an <u>unqualified opinion</u> stating that the financial statements are fairly presented.

      4. A fourth paragraph is only included if the auditor believes that additional information should be presented to readers of the financial statements.

      5. The audit report must be signed by the audit firm.

4.   **Creating Accounting Standards**. Accounting standards protect the interest of investors, managers, and the public. The standards that form GAAP are developed through an open process sponsored by the FASB that includes specific steps.

A.   After an accounting issue has been identified, the FASB issues a discussion memorandum that describes the major issues to be examined. The public is invited to comment on the discussion memorandum, and FASB considers these comments before issuing an exposure draft -- a proposed accounting standard.

B.   Responses to the exposure draft are solicited by the FASB, and these comments are considered prior to the issuance of a new accounting standard. This new standard becomes part of GAAP, and these standards are subject to review by the FASB.

Review Questions, Exercises, and Short Essays

Multiple Choice Questions: These questions reinforce vocabulary and basic concepts from the chapter. In each case, select the answer you believe to be the *best*.

1.   Which of the following financial statements reports revenues and expenses?
   a.   Income Statement.
   b.   Earnings Statement.
   c.   Profit and Loss Statement.
   d.   All of the above.

2.   Assets and liability account balances at a particular date appear on which of the following accounting reports:
   a.   Statement of Financial Position.
   b.   Statement of Stockholders' Equity.
   c.   Statement of Cash Flows.
   d.   Statement of Earnings.

3.   Which of the following statements presents an *estimate* of the ultimate cash impact of current operating activities?
   a.   Income Statement.
   b.   Balance Sheet.
   c.   Statement of Cash Flows.
   d.   Statement of Shareholders' Equity.

4.   *Earnings per share* is:
     a.   Cash that a company can distribute to shareholders..
     b.   Equal to net income divided by the number of common stock shares outstanding.
     c.   The share of a company's earnings distributed to each shareholder.
     d.   Cash inflows a firm receives during the current time period.

5.   The first step on an income statement for a merchandising firm is the calculation:
     a.   Sales revenue - expenses = operating income.
     b.   Sales revenue - operating expenses = gross profit.
     c.   Sales revenue - operating expenses - income taxes = net income.
     d.   Sales revenue - cost of goods or services sold = gross profit.

6.   *Operating expenses* usually include all of the following *except*:
     a.   Salaries for managers and support staff.
     b.   Depreciation on office furnishings.
     c.   Insurance on office buildings and equipment.
     d.   Materials converted into products for sale.

7.   *Other revenues and expenses* most often include:
     a.   Taxes
     b.   Expenses associated with financing activities.
     c.   Revenues from service activities.
     d.   Expenses associated with investing activities.

8.   The income statement category labeled Other Revenues and Expenses would include::
     a.   Uncollectible accounts expense.
     b.   Interest expense
     c.   Salaries expense.
     d.   Cost of goods sold.

9.   *Contributed capital* represents:
     a.   The amount of cash provided by shareholders and bondholders of a company.
     b.   The amount invested by owners of a corporation.
     c.   A contra-owners' equity account.
     d.   A specific group of assets.

10.   *Retained earnings* represents:
      a.   The amount of cash available for the payment of dividends.
      b.   Net income minus taxes paid.
      c.   The total amount of income earned that has not been distributed as dividends.
      d.   A contra-owners' equity account.

11.   *Current assets* include:
      a.   Assets that are presently in use.
      b.   Assets acquired with current liabilities rather than cash.
      c.   Cash and bank deposits.
      d.   Cash and other assets that will be used up or converted to cash in the next fiscal year.

12.   A *patent* would be classified on a balance sheet with:
      a.   Property, plant and equipment.
      b.   Other long-term assets.
      c.   Current assets.
      d.   Long-term investments.

13.   The phrase *working capital* describes:
      a.   The difference between current assets and current liabilities.
      b.   Current assets divided by current liabilities.
      c.   A company's ability to pay its long-term obligations.
      d.   The capital -- or machinery -- that is actually working to produce products.

14.   Comprehensive income is:
      a.   Only the amount of net income received as cash.
      b.   All income before expenses are deducted.
      c.   Only the amount of income received from operations.
      d.   The change in equity during a period resulting from non-owner transactions.

15.   *Consolidated financial statements*:
      a.   Report the result of adding all the corresponding account balances for a parent company and one or more subsidiaries.
      b.   Report financial results of more than one company as if they were a single company.
      c.   Are rarely used in the United States.
      d.   Are only used when a parent company owns 100% of a subsidiary.

Exercises: These questions require the analysis of economic situations and the application of accounting concepts.

1. Formulating a Balance Sheet. The Mojave Company had the following account balances on December 31, 2001. Prepare a balance sheet modeled after text Exhibit 7. (Note: This balance sheet will be at the end of one year only rather than two as displayed in the text exhibit.)

Account	Account Balance
Cash	$ 10,000
Contributed Capital	420,000
Accounts Receivable	75,000
Mortgage Payable (Long-Term)	210,000
Inventory	35,000
Accounts Payable	20,000
Equipment	150,000
Buildings	350,000
Accumulated Depreciation	10,000
Trademarks	80,000
Land	120,000
Retained Earnings	160.000

2.   <u>Formulating an Income Statement</u>. The Mojave Company had the
following account balances on December 31, 2001. Prepare an income
statement modeled after text Exhibit 2.

Account	Account Balance
Sales Revenue	$350,000
Income Tax Expense	9,000
Salaries and Wages Expense	85,000
Utilities Expense	13,500
Advertising Expense	6,300
Depreciation Expense	3,200
Cost of Goods Sold	210,000
Shares of Common Stock Outstanding	10,000 shares

3. <u>Formulating a Statement of Stockholders' Equity</u>. The Mojave Company accounting staff gathered the following summary of transactions affecting stockholders' equity for the period ending December 31, 2001. Prepare a statement of stockholders' equity modeled after text Exhibit 5.

Activity	Amount
Contributed capital, December 31, 2000	$250,000
Common stock issued	50,000
Dividends declared	10,000
Net income	126,000
Retained earnings, December 31, 2000	215,000

<u>Short Essays</u>: The following short essay questions not only reinforce important concepts but also give you a chance to practice writing skills. Answer these questions in complete sentences.

1.   <u>Consolidating Financial Statements</u>. When would an organization be required to issue consolidated financial statements? What is the objective of these statements?

2.   <u>Relying on Estimates and Allocations</u>. Discuss the reasons why the reliance on estimates and allocations is regarded as a limitation of financial statements. What alternatives exist?

3.   <u>Using Historical Cost</u>. Discuss the reasons why the use of historical cost is regarded as a limitation of financial statements. What alternatives exist?

4.   <u>Analyzing the Audit Report</u>. What is the purpose of each paragraph of the audit report?

5.   <u>Outlining the Standard-Setting Process</u>. Outline the general process of accounting standard-setting in the US. Provide a brief explanation of the purpose of each step.

Suggested Answers to Review Questions, Exercises, and Short Essays

Multiple Choice:

1.   (d) Revenues and expenses are reported on the income statement. *Earnings statement* and *profit and loss statement* are equivalent -- although somewhat obsolete -- terms for the income statement.

2.   (a) The *statement of financial position* represents a formal title for a balance sheet. This statement presents asset, liability, and owners' equity balances at a specific time.

3.   (a) The income statement reports transactions that will result in cash flows when all contracts associated with current period activities are completed. This completion may occur over several accounting periods. The cash flow statement reports the cash flows received in any one period.

4.   (b) Earnings per share is defined as net income divided by the number of common stock shares outstanding and it is a measure of earnings performance per share. The term does not refer to any distributions to shareholders.

5.   (d) The first step on an income statement is to determine gross profit. Gross profit equals sales revenues minus cost of goods sold.

6.   (d) The cost of materials used to make a product become part of the cost of inventory on the balance sheet or the cost of goods sold on the income statement. The other choices are all operating expenses.

7.   (b) Expenses that are not part of a company's primary operating activities are reported as part of *other revenues and expenses*. This category often includes items such as interest expense on debt.

8.   (b) Interest expense is a common item in the Other Revenues and Expenses category. The other expenses are operating items that would be listed in a different portion of the income statement.

9.   (b) Contributed capital includes the resources contributed to a corporation by the owners. Contributions can take the form of cash or other assets. In many cases, contributed capital is a group of accounts made up of a common stock account and one or more accounts representing additional contributions by owners. In general, *contra accounts* are subtracted from another account.

10.   (c) Retained earnings represents the amount of net income that has not been distributed to shareholders. At the end of each accounting period, net income is added to the existing amount of retained earnings and any dividends paid are subtracted from retained earnings. Retained earnings is not cash. Because retained earnings belong to the owners, retained earnings are part of owners' equity and are added to not subtracted from owners' equity.

11.   (d) Current assets are assets that will be used up or converted to cash in the next fiscal year. Cash and bank deposits are examples of current assets, but other resources such as short-term investments, inventories, and supplies (that will be used up during the current or next year) also fit the definition of current assets.

12.   (b) A patent would be classified with *other long-term assets*. Because a patent is both intangible and long-lived, it is neither property, plant and equipment nor a current asset.

13.   (a) Working capital represents the difference between current assets and current liabilities and measures the extent to which sources of cash in the near future -- current assets -- exceed the need for cash in the near future (current liabilities). Current assets divided by current liabilities -- defined as the *current ratio* -- also measures the ability to meet financial obligations in the immediate future, but it is different from working capital.

14.   (d) Net income does not include certain transactions that increase stockholders' equity. To provide a picture of earnings with all transactions, except those with owners, the FASB requires that companies compute and report *comprehensive income* as well as *net income*.

15.   (b) Consolidated financial reports represent the activities of two or more companies as if they were one entity. This is appropriate when one company owns another. Because the *parent firm* controls the activities of the subsidiary, the organizations are not independent. The process of consolidation is more complex than just adding the financial statement numbers. For example, any transactions between companies must be eliminated.

Suggested answers for exercises and short essays begin on the next page.

1.   Formulating a Balance Sheet.

The balance sheet for Mojave Company appears as follows:

The Mojave Company
Balance Sheet
December 31, 2001

Assets:		
Current Assets:		
Cash	$10,000	
Accounts Receivable	75,000	
Inventory	35,000	
Total Current Assets		$120,000
Property, Plant, and Equipment:		
Equipment	$150,000	
Buildings	350,000	
	500,000	
Less: Accumulated Depreciation	10,000	
	490,000	
Land	120,000	
Total Property, Plant, and Equipment		610,000
Other Assets: Trademarks		80,000
Total Assets		$810,000
Liabilities and Shareholders' Equity:		
Liabilities:		
Current Liabilities: Accounts Payable	$ 20,000	
Long-term Liabilities: Mortgage Payable	210,000	
Total Liabilities		$230,000
Shareholders' Equity:		
Contributed Capital	420,000	
Retained Earnings	160,000	
Total Shareholders' Equity		580,000
Total Liabilities and Shareholders' Equity		$810,000

2. <u>Formulating an Income Statement</u>.

The income statement for **Mojave Company** appears as follows:

The Mojave Company
Income Statement
For the Year Ended December 31, 2001

Sales Revenue		$350,000
Cost of Goods Sold		210,000
Gross Profit		140,000
Operating Expenses:		
Salaries and Wages Expense	$85,000	
Utilities Expense	13,500	
Advertising Expense	6,300	
Depreciation Expense	3,200	
Total Operating Expenses		108,000
Income from Operations		32,000
Income Tax Expense		9,000
Net Income		$ 23,000
Earnings per share of Common Stock		$2.30

3.   <u>Formulating a Statement of Stockholders' Equity</u>.

The Statement of Stockholders' Equity for Mojave Company appears as follows:

The Mojave Company
Statement of Stockholders' Equity
December 31, 2001

Activity	*Contributed Capital*	*Retained Earnings*	*Total*
Balance as of December 31, 2000	$ 250,000	$ 215,000	$465,000
Common stock issued	50,000		50,000
Net income		126,000	126,000
Dividends declared		(10,000)	(10,000)
Balance as of December 31, 2001	$ 300,000	$ 331,000	$ 631,000

<u>Short Essays</u>:

1.   <u>Consolidating Financial Statements</u>.

If one corporation controls another because it owns more than **50%** of the other firm's stock, the controlling company is known as a *parent* and the controlled corporation is known as a *subsidiary*. The parent corporation would issue *consolidated financial statements* to report the combined economic activities of the two organizations. This reporting is required because the senior managers and directors of the parent firm control the operating, investing, and financing activities of both organizations to a large extent. The consolidation process includes the determination of the total resources and obligations of the combined entity as well as the revenues and expenses incurred in transactions with other organizations.

2.   <u>Relying on Estimates and Allocations</u>.

Reliance on estimates and allocations in the determination of income and asset values represents a limitation of financial statements because, by their very nature, estimates and allocations reduce the precision of the financial reports. Because of the need to report financial results for specific time periods in a cost-effective manner, however, the estimates are unavoidable. For example, depreciation expense allocates the cost of a long-lived asset over its useful life.

3.   Using Historical Cost.

Because the purchasing power of the dollar changes, assets or expenses measured in historical dollars may not represent the true value of a resource consumed. For example, depreciation expense is based on the historical cost of a depreciable asset. Some assets, however, have very long lives and when the asset is used up, it must be replaced at the current cost. The depreciation calculated over the life of the asset will probably understate the value consumed when measured at replacement cost.

Some alternatives to historical cost valuation do exist. Some non-US accounting systems rely on current replacement costs or general price-level adjustments. In the US, GAAP requires the valuation of some investments at current market values rather than their corresponding historical costs.

4.   Analyzing the Audit Report.

The paragraphs of a standard audit opinion each contribute important element to the scope and content of the document.

The first paragraph outlines the scope and responsibility for the accompanying statements. Typical content includes the fiscal periods covered by the audit and statements included along with a description of both auditor and management responsibility.

The second paragraph summarizes the audit process and references GAAS procedures.

The third paragraph expresses the auditor's opinion. Firms often receive an unqualified opinion.

A fourth paragraph contains additional information if necessary.

5.   Outlining the Standard-Setting Process.

In the United States, accounting standards are developed by a private standard-setting body -- the FASB. The standard-setting process consists of the following formal steps:

Identification of an accounting issue for consideration. (New economic situations constantly emerge that need specific accounting standards.)

Preparation of a discussion memorandum intended to solicit responses. (The discussion memorandum contains an analysis of the issues and alternative solution strategies.)

Public hearings. (Representatives from accounting firms, corporations, the public, investor groups, and governmental agencies express opinions on the issue and possible solutions.)

Preparation of an exposure draft of the new standard. (The exposure draft outlines a proposed solution and solicits additional opinions.)

Public hearings. (This round permits interested groups to comment on the proposed standard.)

Issuance of the new standard. (The new standard becomes part of GAAP.)

Review of existing standards. (As economic conditions change, older standards may be reinterpreted, modified, or superseded by new requirements.)

CHAPTER F6: FINANCIAL REPORTING: STATEMENT OF CASH FLOWS

Chapter Focus

Major Theme: This chapter continues the description of the reporting phase of an accounting information system by analyzing the statement of cash flows. The statement of cash flows is an integral part of a firm's annual report. This analysis focuses on the presentation of the statement of cash flows using either the direct or the indirect format.

Important Elements: As you study the chapter, look for the following major topics:

    The direct format of the statement of cash flows
    The indirect format of the statement of cash flows
    Using cash flow information in making business decisions

Learning Objectives: After studying this chapter, you should be able to:

    Summarize: Information reported on a statement of cash flows using the direct format.
    Information reported on a statement of cash flows using the indirect format.

    Interpret: Cash flow information as a basis for analyzing financial performance.

Chapter Review

Introduction. A <u>statement of cash flows</u> reports events during the fiscal period that resulted in either cash inflows or cash outflows. This report includes operating, investing, and financing activities. Organizations report cash flows using either the <u>direct format</u> or the <u>indirect format</u>.

e.   **The Direct Format**. The direct method of reporting cash flows emphasizes each major source and use of cash.

   a.   Operating cash flows include cash received from customers and cash paid to suppliers of resources.

   b.   Investing cash flows include cash received from the disposal of long-term assets and cash paid for the acquisition of these assets.

   c.   Financing cash flows include cash received from the sale of stock or debt and cash paid to reacquire stock, pay dividends, or refund debt.

   d.   Transactions that affected the cash account provide the source data for the preparation of the direct format. By organizing this information, the direct format answers two important questions for decision makers: where did cash come from and where did cash go?

f.   **The Indirect Format**. Most organizations use the indirect format to prepare and present the statement of cash flows. This indirect format reconciles net income and cash flow information.

   a.   While the financing activities and investing activities sections of the statement of cash flows look the same for both the direct and indirect approaches, the section describing cash flow from operating activities looks quite different.

   b.   The indirect approach begins with net income and through a series of adjustments determines cash flows from operations. Adjustments to net income fall into three categories.

      i.   Noncash expenses that were subtracted from revenue to calculate net income are added back to net income to move closer to cash flow from operations.

      ii.   Changes in current assets related to operations are either added to net income or subtracted from net income to more nearly reflect cash flow from operations.

         1.   Increases in these current assets are subtracted from net income. Increases in current assets mean that cash received from operations was less than the revenue recognized.

2. <u>Decreases in these current assets</u> are <u>added</u> to net income. Decreases in current assets mean that cash received from operations exceeds the revenue recognized.

iii. <u>Changes in current liabilities</u> related to operations are either added to net income or subtracted from net income to more nearly reflect cash flow from operations.

1. <u>Increases in these current liabilities</u> are <u>added</u> to net income. Increases in current liabilities mean that cash paid for operations was less than the expenses recognized.

2. <u>Decreases in these current liabilities</u> are <u>subtracted</u> from net income. Decreases in current liabilities mean that cash paid for operations was greater than the expenses recognized.

c. The reconciliation of net income to cash flow from operations may be summarized in the following way.

Net Income
+ or –
Changes in Current Assets Related to Operations
+ or –
Changes in Current Liabilities Related to Operations
+
<u>**Noncash Expenses**</u> **=**
Cash Flow from Operating Activities

g. **Interpreting of Cash Flows.** Net income and cash flow from operating activities both provide insights into organizational operations. Along with cash flow information on both financing and investing activities, income and cash flow from operations provide decision makers inside and outside the organization with perspectives on both profitability and liquidity.

a. Because of depreciation and amortization as well as changes in certain current assets and liabilities, a firm's net income and operating cash flow are often very different.

b. Cash flows from operating activities are normally equal to the net cash flows from investing activities plus the net cash flows from financing activities.

i. A firm that is performing well normally generates sufficient cash from operations to expand operations. Therefore, the combination of positive operating cash flows and negative investing cash flows can be a sign of good performance and growth.

ii. Alternatively, decision makers may decide to use the positive cash flow from operating activities to repay debt, repurchase stock, or pay dividends.

iii. A firm may also raise money through financing activities to invest in opportunities for growth. In this situation, positive cash flow from financing activities is a good sign.

iv. By contrast, a positive cash flow from financing activities is a negative sign if the cash is used to cover negative cash flow from operations.

h. **The Conceptual Framework for Accounting Standards**. To provide guidance in the development of future accounting standards, the Financial Accounting Standards Board (FASB) developed a conceptual framework or set of objectives, definitions, and principles. The conceptual framework includes four major components: objectives, qualitative characteristics, elements, and recognition and measurement issues.

a. The objective of financial reports is to provide information useful to current and potential investors, creditors, and other users in making decisions.

b. Understandability and usefulness in making decisions are the most important qualitative characteristics. Both relevance and reliability support these characteristics.

c. Elements of the financial statements include assets, liabilities, equity, investments by owners, distributions to owners, revenues, expenses, gains, and losses.

d. Recognition and measurement criteria identify the information that should be included in each statement.

Review Questions, Exercises, and Short Essays

<u>Multiple Choice Questions</u>: These questions reinforce vocabulary and basic concepts from the chapter. In each case, select the answer you believe to be the *best*.

1. The primary purpose of the statement of cash flows is:
    a. To report cash provided by operating activities.
    b. To provide information about cash inflows and outflows.
    c. To substitute for the income statement.
    d. To provide information about financing and investing activities.

2. The statement of cash flows reports:
    a. Only the amount of net income received as cash.
    b. Only the amount of cash sales minus the amount of cash paid for expenses.
    c. Only the amounts of cash paid or received from operations.
    d. The amounts of cash received or paid from operations, investing, and financing activities.

3. Cash flow statements may be prepared in two formats. The formats differ in:
    a. The computation of operating cash flows.
    b. The computation of investing cash flows.
    c. The computation of financing cash flows.
    d. In the reporting of cash collections from customers.

4. Investing activities include which of the following?
    a. The recording of depreciation on equipment.
    b. The acquisition of equipment.
    c. The acquisition of new ownership capital.
    d. The acquisition of capital from the issuance of long-term debt.

5. Operating activities include which of the following?
    a. The acquisition of stock in another company.
    b. The payment of dividends.
    c. The payment of interest.
    d. The purchase of a copyright.

6. Financing activities include which of the following?
    a. The issuance of bonds.
    b. The payment of dividends
    c. The purchase of stock in another company.
    d. The sale of goods on credit.

7.   A company has $1,500 of supplies on hand at the end of Year 1. During Year 2, $2,750 of supplies were purchased. A count of supplies on hand at the end of Year 2 found an inventory of $875. How is this inventory change reported in cash flows from operations (indirect method)?
    a.   Increase $1,875.
    b.   Decrease $3,375.
    c.   Increase $4,250.
    d.   Increase $625.

8.   At the beginning of Year 1, a company purchased a fire insurance policy covering a plant for a period of two years. The $5,600 cost of the policy was paid in cash. At the end of Year 1 How is this change reported in cash flows from operations (indirect method)?:
    a. $0.
    b.   Decrease $2,800.
    c.   Decrease $5,600.
    d.   None of the above.

9.   A company that pays employees every two weeks has paid workers wages and salaries for work completed during Year 1 of $367,500. In addition, the employees earned one week's salary of $7,200 at the end of December that will be reported as salaries and wages payable for Year 1. How is the effect reported in cash flows from operations (indirect method)?
    a.   Decrease $367,500.
    b.   Decrease $374,700.
    c.   Decrease $360,300.
    d.   Increase $ 7,200.

10.   When a service is rendered before receipt of cash, the seller, using the indirect method of preparing the statement of cash flows:
    a.   Records revenue and deducts the amount from net income to compute cash flow from operations.
    b.   Records an asset and deducts the amount from net income to compute cash flow from operations.
    c.   Records revenue and a liability without an adjustment on the cash flow statement.
    d.   Both (a) and (b) are correct.

11. On the statement of cash flows, indirect method, depreciation is an adjustment to net income because:
     a.   It is a source of cash.
     b.   It reduces net income but does not involve a payment of cash.
     c.   It reduces net income and involves a saving of cash.
     d.   It represents cash saved to replace the assets.

12. The purchase of inventory:
     a.   Is an operating activity.
     b.   Is an investing activity.
     c.   Is a financing activity.
     d.   Is an expense.

13. If a business acquires a piece of land and borrows the purchase price from its bank, what disclosure is appropriate on the Statement of Cash Flows?
     a.   Cash flows from investing activities are increased.
     b.   Cash flows from financing activities are increased.
     c.   Cash flows from operating activities are increased.
     d.   Cash flows impacting both the investing and financing categories..

14. In adjusting net income to operating cash flows in the indirect method, which of the following would be a positive adjustment:
     a.   An increase in Accounts Payable.
     b.   An increase in Supplies.
     c.   A decrease in Accounts payable.
     d.   An increase in inventory

15. An increase in Unearned Revenue would be reflected in the Statement of Cash Flows:
     a.   As a negative adjustment to net income in the operating cash flows section.
     b.   As a financing cash flow.
     c.   As an investing cash flow.
     d.   As a positive adjustment to net income in the operating cash flows section.

<u>Exercises</u>: These questions require the analysis of economic situations as well as the application of accounting concepts.

1.   <u>Associating Balance Sheet Changes and Cash Flows</u>. The following chart describes changes in balance sheet accounts reported by an organization.

  a.   In the column next to each description, enter a (+) or (-) to indicate whether the change would result in an inflow or an outflow on the statement of cash flows prepared using the indirect method.

Change in Account Balance	*Cash Flow Impact: (+) or (-)*
1. Accounts Payable has increased.	
2. Accounts Receivable has increased.	
3. Prepaid Insurance has decreased.	
4. Accrued Wages Payable has decreased.	
5. Inventory has increased.	
6. Property, Plant and Equipment has increased.	
7. Short-Term Notes Payable has increased.	
8. Intangible Assets has increased.	
9. Long-Term Notes Payable has decreased.	
10. Long-Term Investments has increased.	

  b.   Why are changes in current assets and current liabilities related to operations considered cash flows from operating activities while changes in long-term assets are considered investing activities and changes in long-term liabilities are considered financing activities?

2. <u>Recognizing Cash Flows, Revenues, and Expenses</u>. For each transaction below, enter the cash flow, related revenue or expense and the asset (other than cash) or liability changed in the respective column and row. The first transaction has been provided as an example.

Event	Month 1	Month 2	Month 3
a. A three-month insurance policy was purchased for $900, and cash was paid at the beginning of Month 1.			
Cash flow	($900)		
Revenue (expense)	($300)	($300)	($300)
Prepaid rent	600	(300)	(300)
b. A $1,500 prepayment of three months rent was received from a tenant at the beginning of Month 1.			
Cash flows			
Revenue (expense)			
c. Supplies were purchased for $2,300 cash in Month 1. At the end of each month, physical counts found $1,500, $800, and $300 of supplies remaining respectively.			
Cash flow			
Revenue (expense)			
d. A machine with an expected useful life of three years was purchased at the beginning of Month 1 for $7,200.			
Cash flow			
Revenue (expense)			
e. A contract was signed for services to be provided over a three-month period. The contract amount of $12,000 was received in advance at the beginning of Month 1. One third of the work was completed in each of the next three months.			
Cash flow			
Revenue (expense)			

3.   <u>Linking Net Income and Cash Flow from Operations</u>. The Blue Ridge Commercial Bakery reported net income of $175,000 for the most recent period. An examination of the firm's income statement and balance sheet showed the following changes:

a.   Accounts Receivable increased $5,000.

b.   Accounts Payable increased $3,000.

c.   Unearned Revenues increased $750.

d.   Accrued Wages Payable decreased $500.

e.   Property, Plant and Equipment increased by $15,000.

f.   Depreciation Expense was $20,000.

Compute the cash flow from operations using the indirect approach.

<u>Short Essays</u>: The following short essay questions not only reinforce important concepts but also give you a chance to practice writing skills. Answer these questions in complete sentences

1. <u>Linking Revenues and Cash Flows</u>. Revenues are often associated with increases in cash. Why is revenue received for services yet to be performed recorded as a positive adjustment to net income when the indirect method is used for the Statement of Cash Flows?

2. <u>Linking Receivables and Cash Flows</u>. Why is an increase in Accounts Receivable shown as a decrease in cash flows from operations when the indirect method is used for the statement of cash flows?

3.   <u>Linking Payables and Cash Flows</u>. Why is a decrease in Accounts Payable shown as a decrease in cash flows from operations when the indirect method is used for the statement of cash flows?

4.   <u>Using the Income Statement and Balance Sheet to Describe Cash Flows</u>. Describe why the current asset, current liability, and noncash adjustments to net income under the indirect method are necessary to explain the timing differences between income recognition and cash flow recognition.

5.   <u>Analyzing Cash Flow Information</u>. A member of an investment club has recommended an investment in a well-known and well-established retail firm. Another member of the club discovers that the firm has recently had large negative operating cash flows, positive financing cash flows, and insignificant investing cash flows. What conclusions can be drawn about the potential investment?

Solutions to Review Questions, Exercises, and Short Essays

1.   (b) The primary purpose of the Statement of Cash Flows is to report on cash inflows and cash outflows. It provides information about cash provided by and used for operations, investing activities and financing activities. The information supplements information provided by the income statement and balance sheet, but is not a substitute.

2.   (d) The Statement of Cash Flows provides information about all three major classes of activities: operations, investing activities and financing activities.

3.   (a) The Statement of Cash Flows may be prepared using the direct or indirect method. The indirect method differs in that it begins with net income and eliminates from net income all non-cash transactions.

4.   (b) Investing activities are concerned with the acquisition of assets other than current assets. Depreciation is a non-cash expense and does not involve cash, the acquisition of ownership and debt capital is a financing activity.

5.   (c) The payment of interest is considered to be an operating activity, while the payment of dividends is a financing activity. The acquisition of stock in another company is an investing activity, as is the purchase of a copyright.

6.   (a) Bonds are issued to obtain debt capital, so issuance of bonds is a financing activity.

7.   (d) The Statement of Cash Flows, indirect method would show the decrease in inventory as a positive adjustment to net income for $625 because a larger amount of supplies was used and reported on the income statement as an expense. The adjustment reduces the expense because the cash for the inventory used was spent in an earlier period.

8.   (c) Deferred expenses are recorded when cash is paid for a resource that will not be consumed until some later period. When the resource is consumed, the consumption is recorded as an expense. In this case, net income would have been reduced for one half of the prepayment, but cash would have been reduced for the full amount of the policy. Deducting the balance of the prepaid expense from net income would result in net income being reduced by the full amount of cash paid.

9.   (d) The fact that employees have worked requires the recognition of a current liability. An increase in current liabilities represents expenses that have not yet been paid, so net income must be increased to get to operating cash flows.

10.   (a) The rendering of a service is recorded by increasing revenues and increasing a current asset. Therefore to convert the revenue to a cash flow the increase is deducted from the revenue.

11.   (b) Depreciation is deducted from net income, but it does not involve a cash payment. There is no saving or expenditure of cash for any reason. Cash is spent when the asset is acquired.

12.   (a) The purchase of inventory is an operating activity.

13.   (d) The business neither receives nor pays cash, so there these are investing and financing activities with no effect on cash.

14.   (a) An increase in accounts payable implies that an expense has been recognized, but not paid. Therefore we add the increase back to net income to adjust net income to the cash flow.

15.   (d) An increase in Unearned Revenue represents the fact that cash was received from a customer but no revenue has been earned. So, to convert net income to cash flow, we add the increase to net income.

Exercises:

1.   Associating Balance Sheet Changes and Cash Flows.

Changes in balance sheet account balances reflect either cash increases or decreases.

a.   An increase in asset account balances represents a reduction in cash to acquire the asset. An increase in liability accounts represents an increase in cash. The rationale works like this. If an asset is acquired, it must either be paid for now -- a reduction in cash -- or paid for in the future -- represented by a liability. This related increase in a liability leaves cash available for other uses; and, therefore, it is treated as an increase in cash.

Change in Account Balance	*Cash Flow Impact: (+) or (-)*
1. Accounts Payable has increased.	+
2. Accounts Receivable has increased.	-
3. Prepaid Insurance has decreased.	+
4. Accrued Wages Payable has decreased.	-
5. Inventory has increased.	-
6. Property, Plant and Equipment has increased.	-
7. Short-Term Notes Payable has increased.	+
8. Intangible Assets has increased.	-
9. Long-Term Notes Payable has decreased.	-
10. Long-Term Investments has increased.	-

b.   Changes in the account balances of current assets and current liabilities result from timing differences between revenues or expense recognition and cash flows related to operating activities. These assets and liabilities facilitate the operations of an organization and do not represent permanent investing or financing decisions by management. Conversely, long-term asset or liability decisions do represent significant investing or financing activities. Increases or decreases in noncurrent asset balances reflect investing decisions while changes in noncurrent liability account balances reflect financing decisions.

2. <u>Recognizing Cash Flows, Revenues, and Expenses</u>.

The cash flow and related revenue or expense information appear below.

Event	Month 1	Month 2	Month 3
a. A three-month insurance policy was purchased for $900, and cash was paid at the beginning of Month 1.			
Cash flow	($900)		
Revenue (expense)	($300)	($300)	($300)
Prepaid insurance	600	(300)	(300)
b. A $1,500 prepayment of three months rent was received from a tenant at the beginning of Month 1.			
Cash flows	$1,500		
Revenue (expense)	$500	$500	$500
Unearned rent revenue	1,000	(500)	(500)
c. Supplies were purchased for $2,300 cash in Month 1. At the end of each month, physical counts found $1,500, $800, and $300 of supplies remaining respectively.			
Cash flow	($2,300)		
Revenue (expense)	($800)	($700)	($500)
Supplies	1,500	(700)	(500)
d. A machine with an expected useful life of three years was purchased at the beginning of Month 1 for $7,200 cash.			
Cash flow	($7,200)		
Revenue (expense)	($200)	($200)	($200)
Equipment	7,000	(200)	(200)
e. A contract was signed for services to be provided over a three-month period. The contract amount of $12,000 was received in advance at the beginning of Month 1. One third of the work was completed in each of the next three months.			
Cash flow	$12,000		
Revenue (expense)	$4,000	$4,000	$4,000
Unearned revenue	8,000	(4,000)	(4,000)

Explanations of these recognition differences appear on the next page.

Explanations of recognition differences:

a.   The cash outflow occurs immediately while the related expense is charged uniformly over three months as the insurance coverage is used and expenses are incurred. The cash outflow results in the acquisition of an asset, prepaid insurance, which is reduced as the benefit derived from it is used up.

b.   The cash inflow occurs immediately while the related revenue is recognized uniformly over three months as the tenant occupies the building and the revenue is earned. The prepayment is recorded as a liability and, as revenue is earned the liability is reduced.

c.   The payment for supplies -- a cash outflow -- takes place immediately. The use of supplies, however, must be measured on a month-by-month basis. In the first month, $800 of supplies are used ($2,300 - $1,500 = $800). In the second month, $700 of supplies are used ($1,500 - $800 = $700), and $500 of supplies are used in the third month ($800 - $300 = $500). Initially, the payment results in an asset and as the asset is used up, the consumption is recorded as an expense.

d.   The machinery will last for three years or 36 months. The monthly depreciation expense, therefore, should be $200 ($7,200 / 36 months = $200 per month). The $7,200, however, is an immediate cash outflow and results in the recognition of an asset; the expense is recorded as the asset is used up..

e.   The $12,000 cash inflow is recognized immediately and a liability is recorded; the associated revenue will be recognized equally over the three months in which it is earned and the liability is reduced.

3.   <u>Linking Net Income and Cash Flow from Operations</u>.

The following schedule represents the adjustments to net income to calculate cash flow from operations. The change in property, plant, and equipment is not included in this calculation because it represents an *investing activity* rather than an *operating activity*.

		$175,000
Net income		
Noncash adjustments to income:		
Depreciation expense	$20,000	
Increase in accounts receivable	(5,000)	
Increase in accounts payable	3,000	
Increase in deferred revenues	750	
Decrease in accrued wages	(500)	
Net adjustments to income		18,250
Net cash flow from operations		$193,250

Short Essays:

1. ### Linking Revenues and Liabilities.

    Revenues usually increase assets since resources are created as part of the transformation process. Deferred revenue, however, arises through a slightly different economic situation. The term deferred means *postponed*. In the case of deferred revenue, the recognition (recording) of the revenue must be postponed until it has been earned – even though cash has been received. Revenue recognition will take place when the activities required to render the goods or services to the customer are completed. Therefore, the advanced receipt of cash must be treated as a liability or obligation until the earning activities are complete.

2. ### Linking Receivables and Cash Flows.

    An increase in accounts receivable is an increase in an asset account. A sale has been completed and included in net income, but no cash has yet been received. The increase in accounts receivable represents a portion of net income not collected in cash, and, therefore, this increase in accounts receivable represents a decrease in cash flow from operations.

3. ### Linking Payables and Cash Flows.

    Accounts payable increase as operating items are purchased from vendors on short-term credit. A decrease in accounts payable implies that an organization is paying off short-term obligations in cash. When accounts payable are paid, both a liability and an asset -- cash -- decrease. Since no revenue or expenses are recognized at this point, however, net income is not affected by the payment of the payable. Subtracting the decrease in accounts payable from net income adjusts for this increased cash outflow from operating activities.

4. ### Using the Income Statement and Balance Sheet to Determine Cash Flows.

    If all revenues were immediately collected in cash and all expenses immediately paid in cash, net income and cash flow from operations would always be identical. Timing differences, however, can accelerate or delay cash flows while revenues and expenses are always recognized when the underlying operating activities take place. The timing differences are reflected in the changes in current assets, current liabilities, and noncash expenses such as depreciation. Adjusting net income for these changes in current accounts and noncash items transforms an accrual basis measure -- net income -- into a cash basis measure -- cash flow from operations.

5.   <u>Analyzing Cash Flow Information</u>. While the retailer may be well-known and well-respected, the investment club members should think very carefully about this investment opportunity. The firm has large negative operating cash flows suggesting that operating activities have not been very successful. Management is covering these negative operating cash flows with positive financing cash flows. Normally, a firm uses cash inflows from financing activities to make investments in assets to expand the firms operations. However, since investing cash flows are insignificant, the financing cash flows are supporting the firm's operations. While this scenario may be acceptable for a start-up firm or a firm in a major transition, it is not a positive sign for an established firm.

SECTION F2: ANALYSIS AND INTERPRETATION OF FINANCIAL ACCOUNTING INFORMATION

CHAPTER F7: THE TIME VALUE OF MONEY

Chapter Focus

Major Theme: The second section of the text presents an analysis of accounting for operating, investing, and financing activities. This chapter describes an important concept of accounting measurement -- the time value of money. The time value of money is applicable to a variety of transformation activities. This concept is quite helpful in understanding information reported in financial statements.

Important Elements: As you study this chapter, look for the following important concepts:

      Determining the future value of single amounts and annuities
      Determining the present value of single amounts and annuities
      Determining investment values and interest earned

Learning Objectives: After studying this chapter, you should be able to:

Define: Future and present value.

Determine: The future value of a single amount invested at the present time.
                 The future value of an annuity.
                 The present value of a single amount to be received in the future.
                 The present value of an annuity.
                 Investment values and interest expense or revenue for various periods.

Chapter Review

Introduction. Prior chapters focused on <u>recognition issues</u>. Both cash and accrual basis concepts were used to identify when an activity and related cash flow would be recognized in an organization's accounting system. This chapter focuses on <u>valuation -- or measurement -- issues</u>. <u>The time value of money</u> concept can be used to determine the financial value of many assets, liabilities, and equity items.

1.   **Future Value**. Because money has earning power of its own through the ability to accumulate interest, the value of an initial sum of money changes over time. The <u>future value</u> of an amount is the value of that amount at a particular time in the future. The <u>present value</u> of an amount is the current value of that amount to be paid or received at some future date.

   A.   For example, an investment with a present value of $100 that earns 10% interest will have a future value of $110 one year from now. This association between present value and future value can be expressed by the following general relationship:

$$FV = PV(1 + R)$$

   where:
   FV = Future Value
   PV = Present Value
   R = Interest Rate

   B.   In many circumstances, interest earnings are compounded. <u>Compound interest</u> occurs when interest is earned on interest earned in earlier periods.

   1.   For example, the investment previously described that earned $10 interest in the first year would earn compound interest of $11 the second year ($110 at the end of Year 1 earns an additional 10% or $11 in Year 2).

2. The general equation for a future value with compound interest is:

$$FV = PV(1 + R)^t$$

where:
   FV = Future Value
   PV = Present Value
   R = Interest Rate
   t = the number of periods of investment

3. The interest factor $(1 + R)^t$ may be determine with a calculator, electronic spreadsheet, or predetermined table.

**[Tables of predetermined interest factors
appear on the inside front and back covers
of the text.]**

For example, text Table 3 displays predetermined interest factors (IF) to help determine future values of single sums.

4. The future value formula can, therefore, be rewritten as:

$$FV = PV \text{ x } IF(\text{Table 3})$$

where:
   FV = Future Value
   PV = Present Value
   IF(Table 3) = the appropriate interest factor in Table 3.

5. For example, if a $500 investment today will earn 7% for 2 periods, the relevant interest factor from text Table 3 is 1.14490 -- the number in the cell at the intersection of the 7% column and the two period row. The future value of this investment at the end of two periods is $572.45 (FV = PV x IF; FV = $500 x 1.14490 = $572.45).

C. In addition to finding the future value of a single sum, the general future value-present value relationship may be used to find the future value of an annuity. An <u>annuity</u> is a series of equal amounts paid or received over a specified number of equal time periods.

1. Since an annuity is a series of equal amounts, the future value may be computed by treating each amount as a single sum.

2.   For example, if an investor plans to deposit $100 at the end of each year for three years into an investment earning 6%, the future value of this investment at the end of the third year could be determined by summing the future values of each of the three deposits of $100.

3.   This approach uses the future value formula:

FV = PV x IF(Table 3)

a)   The deposit made at the end of Year 1 earns interest for two years. Therefore,

FV = $100 x 1.12360 = $112.36

b)   The deposit made at the end of Year 2 earns interest for one year. Therefore,

FV = $100 x 1.06 = $106

c)   The deposit made at the end of Year 3 has no opportunity to earn interest, and its FV at the end of the third year is $100.

d)   The FV of this annuity, therefore, is $318.36 ($112.36 + $106 + $100 = $318.36).

4.   A quicker way to determine the future value of an annuity is to use the special features of calculators, electronic spreadsheets, or future value of annuity tables such as text Table 4.

a)   The future value equation can be modified to find the future value of an annuity. The future value of an annuity equation is:

FVA = A x IF(Table 4)

where:
FVA = The Future Value of the Annuity
A = The Amount Paid Each Period.
IF = the appropriate interest factor from Table 4

b) Applying this equation to the previous example of the three-year, $100 annuity that earns 6%, the future value is $318.36:

$$FVA = A \times IF(Table\ 4)$$
$$FVA = \$100 \times 3.1836 = \$318.36$$

(The IF of 3.1836 is the cell at the intersection of the 6% column and the three period row.)

2. **Present Value.** In some business situations, decisions makers know the <u>future value</u> of an investment and want to determine its <u>present value</u>.

A. The process of determining present value -- called <u>discounting</u> -- relies on the relationship of present and future values previously described:

$$FV = PV(1 + R)^t$$

where:
FV = Future Value
PV = Present Value
R = Interest Rate
t = the number of periods of investment

1. This future value equation may become a present value equation by solving for PV. Once the equation has been rewritten, it appears as:

$$PV = FV \times [1 \div (1 + R)^t]$$

2. For example, the equation may be used to determine the present value of an investment that will pay $5,000 in two years if an investor wishes to earn 9% interest:

$$PV = \$5,000 \times [1 \div (1 + .09)^2]$$
$$PV = \$5,000 \times (1 \div 1.1881)$$
$$PV = \$5,000 \times (0.84168)$$
$$PV = \$4,208.40$$

3.   Just as with future value calculations, tables, calculators, and electronic spreadsheets provide present value factors. Text Table 1 presents present value factors for single sums, and the present value equation can be expressed as:

PV = FV x IF(Table 1)

where:
  FV = Future Value
  PV = Present Value
  IF = the appropriate interest factor from Table 1

4.   For example, the IF(Table 1) for 2 years and 9% is 0.84168 -- the same factor as $[1 \div (1 + .09)^2]$.

B.   In addition to determining the present value of single sums, decision makers also must calculate the present value of an annuity -- a series of equal future payments.

1.   Using a process similar to that used with future values, the present value of an annuity is really the sum of the present values of each annuity payment.

2.   For example, an investor may determine the present value of an annuity of three annual payments of $5,000 each and earning 9%.

a)   The calculation may be approached as the calculation of present value for three single sums corresponding to the three annuity payments.

(1)   Using the present value equation PV = FV x IF(Table 1), the value of the first payment is $5,000 x 0.91743 = $4,587.15

(2)   The value of the second payment is $5,000 x 0.84168 = $4,208.40.

(3)   The value of the third payment is $5,000 x 0.77218 = $3,860,90.

(4)   Therefore, the total value of this annuity is $4,587.15 + $4,208.40 + $3,860.90 = $12,656.45.

b) A faster method of determining present values for annuities is to rely on the present value factors for annuities from tables, calculators, or electronic spreadsheets. Text Table 2 presents present value factors for annuities, and the present value equation may be expressed as

PVA = A x IF(Table 2)

where:
PVA = The Present Value of an Annuity
A = The Amount Paid Each Period
IF = the appropriate interest factor from Table 2

(1) Using the IF(Table 2) the present value of the three-year, $5,000 annuity earning 9% is determined as follows:

PVA = A x IF(Table 2)
PVA = $5,000 x 2.53129
PVA = $12,656.45

(2) The results of the two methods are the same because the annuity factor in Table 2 (2.53129) is the sum of the three relevant interest factors from Table 1 (0.91743 + 0.84168 + 0.77218 = 2.53129).

3. **Loan Payments and Amortization**. As previously stated, decision makers frequently use present and future value concepts. One common application of present value concepts is a loan and the associated amortization -- or repayment schedule.

A. In a loan transaction, understanding the relationship between the amount borrowed and the total amount repaid requires the use of present value concepts.

1. A loan transaction involves the initial amount borrowed (a present value), a series of payments (an annuity), and an interest rate (the discount rate).

2. A loan transaction is really an application of the equation for the present value of an annuity:

PVA = A x IF(Table 2)

3.   In this case, the PVA is the amount borrowed, the IF(Table 2) is related to the interest rate and length of the loan, and A -- the periodic payment -- is the unknown value.

4.   For example, a decision maker can determine the periodic repayments associated with a $10,000, 9%, 3 year loan in the following manner:

$$PVA = A \times IF(Table\ 2)$$
$$\$10,000 = A \times 2.53129$$
$$A = \$10,000 \div 2.53129$$
$$A = \$3,950.55\ (Rounded)$$

(The interest factor 2.53129 from Table 2 is found at the intersection of the 9% column and the three-year row.)

B.   From the preceding calculation, a decision maker now knows that three annual payments of $3,950.55 will be required to repay the $10,000 borrowed along with 9% interest.

1.   Each payment, therefore, includes some principal repayment and some payment of interest. This is an important distinction.

a)   The repayment of the loan represents a reduction in the decision maker's liability.

b)   The payment of interest represents the decision maker's interest expense for the period involved.

c)   The portion of the periodic payment that represents repayment of the loan impacts the decision maker's balance sheet and statement of cash flows.

d)   The portion of the periodic payment that represents the payment of interest impacts the decision maker's income statement and statement of cash flows.

2.   The three payments of $3,950.55 will, however, have different proportions of loan repayment and interest payments.

a)   For the first annual payment, the interest charge is $900 ($10,000 x 9% = $900). The remaining

$3050.55 is a repayment of the principal portion of the loan ($3,950.55 - $900 = $3,050.55).

b)   In the second year, the loan balance is now only $6,949.45, and the associated interest is $625.45 ($6949.45 x 9% = $625.45). Therefore, the loan repayment in the second year is $3,325.10 ($3,950.55 - $625.45 = $3,325.10).

c)   The final payment includes interest on the remaining loan balance of $3,624.35. This interest charge is $326.19 ($3,624.35 x 9% = $326.19). The remainder of the payment repays the last portion of the loan $3,624.36 ($3,950.55 - $326.19 = $3,624.36. The extra $.01 is due to rounding.)

3.   For the entire loan transaction, the loan repayments equal the $10,000 amount borrowed ($3,050.55 + $3,325.10 + $3,624.36 = $10,000.01), and interest has been paid at 9% on the loan balance.

4.   **Unequal Payments**. When future payments such as loan repayments are made in unequal amounts, an annuity no longer exists. Therefore, the analysis of these situations must consider the payments as single sums and employ appropriate present or future value single sum factors.

5.   **Combining Single Amounts and Annuities**. Decision makers may determine the present or future values inherent in transactions that include both single sums and annuities. In analyzing a transaction with both single sums and annuities, a decision maker should determine single sum value and annuity value separately and then combine the results.

6.   **Summary of Future and Present Value Concepts**. These future and present value concepts are all based on the ability of money to earn interest and increase over time. In addition to the technical aspects of determining future and present values for both single sums and annuities, two important concepts emerge from the illustrations presented.

A.   The difference between a present value and the associated future value increases as the interest rate inherent in the transaction increases.

B.   The difference between a present value and the associated future value increases as the amount of time in the transaction increases.

Review Questions, Exercises, and Short Essays

<u>Multiple Choice Questions</u>: These questions reinforce vocabulary and basic concepts from the chapter. In each case, select the answer you believe to be the *best*.

1.   The term *present value* means:
   a.   The current value of an investment or obligation.
   b.   The amount an investment or obligation is worth at some future date.
   c.   The amount of cash that will be received or paid on the due date.
   d.   The current amount of revenue or expense to be recognized.

2.   The term *future value* may refer to:
   a.   The amount an investment or obligation is worth at some future date.
   b.   The amount that a sum of money placed in a savings account will equal at some future date.
   c.   The value of a share of stock in the future.
   d.   Each of the above alternatives describes a future value.

3.   The relationship between present value (PV) and future value (FV) for one time period given an interest rate (R) can be expressed as:
   a. $PV = FV \times R$.
   b. $PV = FV \times (1+R)$.
   c. $PV = FV \div R$.
   d. $PV = FV \div (1+R)$.

4.   The process of earning interest on an earlier amount of interest is called:
   a.   Complicating
   b.   Compounding.
   c.   Discounting.
   d.   Amortizing.

5.   The future value of $100 earning interest for 3 periods at 9% is equal to:
   a. $100 x.09 x 3.
   b.   ($100 x .09)^{3.}
   c. $100 x 1.09 x1.09 x 1.09.
   d. $100 x 1.09 x 3.

6. A series of equal payments made over a specific number of equal time periods is called a(n):
   a. Bond.
   b. Maturity value.
   c. Annuity.
   d. Yield to maturity.

7. When annuity payments are made at the end of a period, the annuity is called:
   a. An ordinary annuity.
   b. An annuity due.
   c. An annuity in arrears.
   d. A prepaid annuity.

8. The *present value* of a *future amount* is:
   a. Always more than the amount.
   b. Always less that the amount.
   c. Equal to the amount.
   d. More or less than the amount depending on the interest rate.

9. The *present value* of $100 three periods in the future at 9% interest is equal to:
   a. $100 \div (09 \times 3)$.
   b. $100 \div (.09)^{3.}$
   c. $100 \times 1.09 \times 3$.
   d. $100 \div (1.09 \times 1.09 \times 1.09)$.

10. If the interest rate is 5%, how much would a decision maker have in a savings account if a payment of $100 were made into the account at the end of each year for three years?
    a. 100×3.15250.
    b. 100×2.72325.
    c. 100×1.15763.
    d. $100 \div 1.15763$.

11 If the interest rate is 5%, the present value of three end-of-year payments of $100 each is:
    a. 100×3.15250.
    b. 100×2.72325.
    c. 100×1.15763.
    d. $100 \div 1.15763$.

12.   A decision maker must pay $5,000 to a creditor in three years. In order
       to have the total payment ready, the decision maker wishes to make three
       equal end-of-year payments into a savings account that earns 7%. What
       is the size of each of the three payments?
       a. $1,360.50
       b. $1,905.26
       c. $1,555.26
       d. $1,666.67

Questions 13-15 are based on the following loan transaction:

       A decision maker has agreed to pay $15,000 for a new car. The
       individual is anxious to pay off the necessary financing as soon as
       possible. The dealer arranges a loan with an annual rate of 12% for two
       years to pay off the entire $15,000. The payments would be $706.10 per
       month.

13.   What is the present value of this stream of loan payments?
       a. $18,371.65.
       b. $16,346.40.
       c. $15,000.00.
       d.   Cannot be determined from this information.

14.   How much interest will the lender earn in the month leading up to the first
       payment?
       a. $0.
       b. $150.00.
       c. $143.19.
       d. $56.10.

15.   What is the principal amount outstanding at the end of the first month?
       a. $556.10.
       b. $14,293.90
       c. $14,443.90
       d. $14,462.09

Exercises: These questions require the analysis of economic situations and the application of accounting concepts.

1.   Calculating Compound Interest. The concept of compound interest applies to both single sums and annuities as demonstrated by the following exercises.

        a.   If a saver deposits $1,000 in an account earning 5% at the beginning of a year, how much money would he or she have at the end of the year? In two years? In three years?

        b.   If a saver deposits $1,000 *per year* in an account earning 5% at the end of each year for three years, how much money would he or she have at the end of each year?

2.   Applying Present Value Concepts. In order to attend college, a student forgoes an opportunity to earn $18,000 per year. In addition, the student has $12,000 of college costs per year for four years. If attending college is viewed strictly as an investment decision, calculate how much more income this student will have to earn each year over a 25 year career to equal the present value of the costs incurred over 4 years of college. How do the results change if the student takes 5 years to graduate? (Use 7% as the relevant interest rate.)

3. <u>Calculating a Loan Amortization</u>. A loan officer at The Columbia Bank agrees to lend one of the bank's customers $10,000 for four years at 12%. The customer will make four equal payments of principal and interest at the end of each of the four years. Prepare a loan amortization schedule for this loan similar to text Exhibit 5.

<u>Short Essays</u>: The following short essay questions not only reinforce important concepts but also give you a chance to practice writing skills. Answer these questions in complete sentences.

1.   <u>Linking Interest Rates and Future Values</u>. How do *future values* change when interest rates go up or down?

2.   <u>Linking Interest Rates and Present Values</u>. How do *present* values change when interest rates go up or down?

3. <u>Relating the General Level of Interest Rates and Investment Values</u>. Individuals and organizations invest in order to receive future payments from the investment. How would a change in the prevailing interest rate affect the current value of investments?

4. <u>Describing the Impact of Time on the Relationship Between Present Values and Future Values</u>. Present values and future values are linked together through both time and interest rates. As the length of time between present values and future values changes, what happens to the difference between these two measures?

5. <u>Using Present Values to Analyze Business Decisions</u>. A common business decision involves the choice between buying or leasing an asset. In either case, a business has the use of the asset, but the financing decision can be significant. A lease requires a series of payments of a specific time. How could a manager use present value concepts to analyze this decision?

Solutions to Review Questions, Exercises, and Short Essays

<u>Multiple Choice</u>:

1.   (a) *Present value* refers the current value of a sum of money to be paid or received in the future.

2.   (d) *Future value* refers the value in the future of a current sum of money. It may be thought of as the amount to which a current amount will grow if interest or earnings are allowed to accumulate to the future date. All three options describe future value situations.

3.   (d) The future value is computed by adding interest to a present value. The formula is [FV = PV x (1+R)]. Rearranging terms, an equivalent form of this equation is [PV = FV ÷ (1+R)].

4.   (b) Compounding refers to the familiar process where interest is calculated on previously earned interest.

5.   (c) The future value is calculated as $100 x 1.09 x 1.09 x 1.09, or 100 x 1.09^3. This is consistent with the interest factor from Table 3. These interest factors equal to $(1+R)^t$ where R is the interest rate -- the columns -- and t is the number of periods -- the rows.

6   (c) A series of equal payments spaced over a set of equal time periods is an *annuity*.

7.   (a) An ordinary annuity is paid or received at the end of a period. An annuity due is paid or received at the beginning of a period.

8.   (b) A present value grows into a future value by earning compound interest. The present value, therefore, must be smaller than the related future value.

9.   (d) The present value is $100 ÷ $(1.09)^3$ or $100 ÷ (1.09 x 1.09 x 1.09)

10.   (a) The annuity payments will accumulate interest. Therefore, the future value must be more than 3 x $100. From Table 4, the interest factor is 3.15250, and the future value of the annuity will be $315.25 ($100 x 3.15250 = $315.25).

11.   (b) The future payments must all have a present value of less than $100 each. Therefore, the present value of the three payments must total less than 3 x $100. From Table 2, the interest factor is 2.72325, and the present value of the annuity is $272.33 ($100 x 2.72325 = $272.33 rounded).

12.   (c) The future value of $5,000 is known, and the value of the annuity is determined by the equation [FVA = A x IF(Table 4)]. With an interest factor of 3.21490 (7%, 3 years), the payment must be $1,555.26 ($5,000 ÷ 3.21490 = $1,555.26).

13.   (c) The present value of the payments must be equal to the total amount borrowed or $15,000.

14.   (b) The lender will earn $150 interest during the first month. The initial amount outstanding on the loan is $15,000. At 1% interest per month (12% per year ÷ 12 months = 1% per month), the interest would be $150 ($15,000 x 1% = $150).

15. (c). The first payment of $706.10 is made up of $150.00 interest and $556.10 principal ($706.10 - $150.00 = $556.10). Therefore, the balance of the principal after the first month's payment is $14,443.90 ($15,000 - $556.10 = $14,443.90).

Exercises:

1. Calculating Compound Interest. The concept of compound interest applies to both single sums and annuity calculations.

   a. Compound Interest for a Single Sum. The ending value of an investment is the beginning value plus the interest earned during the fiscal period:

   General Formula for Future Value: $FV = PV \times (1 + R)^t$

   Year 1: FV at End of Year 1 = $1,000 x (1 + .05) = $1,050
   Year 2: FV at End of Year 2 = $1,050 x (1 + .05) = $1,102.50
   Year 3: FV at End of Year 3 = $1,102.50 x (1 + ,05) = $1,157.625

   b. Compound Interest for an Annuity. The ending value of an annuity investment is the beginning value plus the interest earned during the period plus any additional annuity payments invested.

   [Note: This exercise describes a *series of payments* made at the *end of each year*. The prior exercise described a *single payment* made at the *beginning of a year.*]

Year 1	Year 2	Year 3
$1,000	$1,000 x (1 + .05) = $1,050	$1,050 x (1 + .05) = $1,102.50
	$1,000	$1,000 x (1 + .05) = $1,050
		$1,000
Total: $1,000	Total: $2,050	Total: $3,152.50

2. Applying Present Value Concepts.

   [Note: Specific opportunity costs and out-of-pocket costs for college differ widely from one student to the next. This exercise is presented to both practice the concepts and techniques of future and present value as well as examine a familiar investment decision.]

   The central issues in this question are:

   Considering both outlay costs and opportunity costs.
   Ignoring expenses that would be incurred anyway.
   Applying present value concepts appropriately.

   Outlay Costs: While education costs vary widely, school-related expenses such as tuition, books, and supplies require $12,000 per year in this case.

   Opportunity Costs: In addition to the out-of-pocket costs, students also give up some amount of income to attend college. In this case, the amount is $18,000 per year.

Living Expenses: Living expenses would not be considered in this analysis because they would have to be paid whether or not an individual attended college.

The total cost, therefore, is $30,000 per year ($12,000 + $18,000 = $30,000).

In addition, present value calculations require an interest rate. This analysis uses 7% interest since a high-quality corporate bond might yield about 7%.

Present Value Calculations:

[In order to use Table 2 on the inside back cover of the text, payments must be made at the end of each year. This may not be completely accurate, but that's how the table is organized.]

The present value (PV) of $30,000 for four years at 7% using Table 2 is:

PV = FV x IF(Table 2)
PV = $30,000 x (3.38721) = $101,616

The PV of $30,000 for five years at 7% is:

PV = FV x IF(Table 2)
PV = $30,000 x (4.10020) = $123,006

What increase in earnings is necessary to justify this investment strictly on financial terms? Another way of asking this question is: What stream of payments over a 25-year career is equivalent to the present value $101,616? (Careers may easily span more than 25 years, but this is the highest year presented in Table 2.) From Table 2, the appropriate annuity factor for 25 years at 7% is 11.65358. The calculation is:

Four years of study:

PVA = A x IF(Table 2)
$101,616 = A (11.65358)
A = $8,720 (rounded)

Five years of study:

PVA = A x IF(Table 2)
$123,006 = A x (11.65358)
A = $10,555 (rounded)

Using these data and assumptions, a yearly increase in income of over $8,700 is necessary to justify the investment in education on purely financial terms. Statistics suggest that education is a good investment and that this increase in income may be likely, but notice how quickly the incremental income required goes up with an additional year of education! Of course, the decision to pursue a college education should involve more than just thoughts of increased income and present value calculation. Noneconomic factors also represent critical considerations.

3. <u>Calculating a Loan Amortization</u>. For the $10,000 loan to be repaid over 4 years at 12%, the amortization schedule would be:

Explanation of column titles:
Value at Beginning of Year = Unpaid portion of the loan at the beginning of the year.
Interest Incurred = Unpaid portion of loan x 12%
Amount Paid = $10,000 original loan value ÷ 3.03735 interest factor = $3,292.34
Principal Paid = Amount Paid - Interest Incurred
Value at End of Year = Value at Beginning of Year - Principal Paid

Year	Value at Beginning of Year	Interest Incurred	Amount Paid	Principal Paid	Value at End of Year
1	10,000.00	1,200.00	3.292.34	2,092.34	7,907.66
2	7,907.66	948.92	3,292.34	2,343.42	5,564.24
3	5,564.24	667.71	3,292.34	2,624.63	2,939.61
4	2,939.61	352.73*	3,292.34	2,939.61	0

*Rounded

This payment schedule will repay the loan principal over four years and pay 12% interest per year on the unpaid loan balance.

Short Essays:

1. <u>Linking Interest Rates and Future Values</u>.

Interest rates and future values move in the same direction. As interest rates increase, any present value will grow to a higher future value. With higher interest rates, the interest added each year is greater than in periods of lower interest rates. When interest rates decrease, a given principal earns less each year and the related future value decreases.

2. <u>Linking Interest Rates and Present Values</u>.

Interest rates and present values move in opposite direction. A future value is composed of a related present value and interest earnings. As interest rates and, therefore, interest earnings increase, the present value component of any future value decreases. Conversely, when interest rates are relatively low and interest earnings small, present values and related future values must be closer together since the interest component of any future value will be smaller.

3.   <u>Relating the General Level of Interest Rates and Investment Values</u>.

If the general level of interest rates rises, other things equal, the rate applied to a particular investment also increases. As discussed in the previous question, higher interest rates mean lower present values. As interest rates increase, present values -- in this case, the value of investments -- decrease. From another perspective, investments with a fixed return -- a specific number of dollars earned per year -- will fall in value if similar investments pay a higher percentage return. Conversely, as the general level of interest rates fall, investments with fixed returns increase in value.

4.   <u>Describing the Impact of Time on the Relationship Between Present Values and Future Values</u>.

Future values are composed of present values and interest earned -- and compounded -- over time. Increasing the time between a present value and an associated measure of future value increases both the number of periods interest is paid and the impact of interest compounding. Increasing the time, therefore, increases the difference between a present value and the associated future value. Decreasing the time interval brings the present value and future value closer together.

5.   <u>Using Present Values to Analyze Business Decisions</u>.

The management decision to buy or lease an asset is based on several important factors including the cash flow impact and total cost of each option. Leasing an asset requires a firm to make a series of payments for a defined period of time. Alternatively, buying an asset requires current payment in full or some type of financing from a lender. Analyzing the financial impact of these alternatives can challenge an inexperienced manager since payments from several different time periods must be compared. Both a lease and a loan can be analyzed as annuities. Using present value methods, managers can compare the present values of future lease payments, the present value of loan payments, and current outlay to buy the asset. All the cash flows have been measured at the same time -- their present values today. These present values allow managers to evaluate these alternatives more appropriately.

CHAPTER F8: FINANCING ACTIVITIES

Chapter Focus

Major Theme: Managers and other decision makers engage in a variety of financing activities on behalf of their respective organizations. These financing activities focus on a number of debt and equity transactions. This chapter describes the accounting rules that organizations use to measure and report debt and equity activities.

Important Elements: As you study the chapter, look for the following topics:

> Debt transactions
> Measurement and reporting of debt obligations
> Stockholders' equity transactions
> Measurement and reporting of stockholders' equity

Learning Objectives: After studying this chapter, you should be able to:

Identify and Explain:	Information that companies report about obligations to lenders and the transaction affecting long-term debt.
Describe:	Appropriate accounting procedures for contingencies and commitments, including capital leases.
Identify and Distinguish:	Information reported in the stockholders' equity section of a corporate balance sheet and contributed capital from retained earnings.
Explain and Describe:	Transactions affecting stockholders' equity and how these transactions are reported in a company's financial statements.
Distinguish and Discuss:	Between preferred stock and common stock and why corporations may issue more than one type of stock.

Chapter Review

Introduction. Debt and equity transactions serve as major sources of financing for most organizations. Organizations receive cash as part of these financing transactions in exchange for obligations to creditors or expectations of returns by owners. These debt and equity transactions are reported on the income statement, balance sheet, statement of cash flows, and statement of stockholders' equity.

1.   **Types of Obligations**. An organization may engage in numerous types of debt transactions that are reported as liabilities on the organization's balance sheet.

      A.   Contracts that involve liabilities may occur between an organization and its lenders, suppliers, customers, employees, and governmental units.

      B.   A liability has three specific elements:

            1.   Responsibility must exist for a future transfer of resources.

            2.   The responsibility may not be avoided.

            3.   The event causing the responsibility must have already taken place.

2.   **Debt Obligations**. Organizations often have a variety of short-term and long-term debt contracts.

      A.   Short-term debt includes all liabilities that mature in the coming fiscal year -- including any maturing portion of long-term liabilities.

      B.   Long-term debt includes a variety of bonds and notes payable. Bonds and bond contracts may include specific features that give the debt distinguishing characteristics.

            1.   Some debt is <u>secured</u> by specific assets of the firm. Alternatively, an organization may issue <u>debentures</u> or unsecured debt.

            2.   <u>Serial</u> debt issues include bonds that mature at different times so that management may repay the debt as the different bonds mature.

3. <u>Callable</u> bonds may be repaid -- or retired -- by an organization after a specified period of time.

C. Debt transactions involving bonds include some important valuation issues.

   1. Bonds are issued by a corporation -- the borrower -- with both a <u>maturity value</u> and a <u>stated interest rate</u>.

      a) The <u>maturity value</u> -- or <u>face value</u> -- is the amount a bondholder -- the investor -- will receive when the bonds mature.

      b) The <u>stated interest rate</u> -- or <u>nominal rate</u> -- is the interest rate the borrower will pay on the maturity value of the debt.

      c) For example, a $1,000, 10%, 20-year bond will pay the investor interest of $100 per year for 20 years ($1,000 x 10% = $100) and also pay $1,000 at maturity -- the end of Year 20.

   2. Despite the interest rate stated by the corporation issuing the bonds, investors might desire a different interest rate.

      a) Investors' expectations of interest rates are influenced by interest rates and returns available on other bonds or investments of similar risk.

      b) If a bond's stated interest rate is lower than the interest rates paid on similar investments, that bond will be less attractive to potential investors. These investors will adjust their offer price for the bond downward, and the bond will sell at a <u>discount</u>.

      c) If a bond's stated interest rate is higher than the interest rates paid on similar investments, that bond will be more attractive to potential investors. These investors will be willing to pay more for the bond, and the bond will sell at a <u>premium</u>.

   3. The process of determining the initial price of a bond requires the use of both the present value of a single sum and the present value of an annuity.

a)   For example, if similar investments return 12% while a $1,000, 20 year bond has a stated interest rate of 10%, an investor can determine an initial bond price that will return 12% as follows:

PV of Single Sum:
  $1,000 x IF(Table 1: 20 years, 12%)
  $1,000 x 0.10367 = $103.67

PVA of Annuity:
  $100 x IF(Table 2: 20 years, 12%)
  $100 x 7.46944 = $746.94 (Rounded)

The initial price of the bond in order to earn 12% is $850.61 ($103.67 + $746.94 = $850.61).

b)   Since the bond carried a lower stated interest rate than the return on similar investments, the corporation issuing the bond would only receive $850.61 at the time the bond was sold.

4.   As just illustrated, a firm may receive less than face value for its bonds at the point of sale. The firm must, however, pay the investor face value at maturity.

a)   The difference between the initial cash received and the face value of the bonds must be amortized over the life of the bonds so that the financial statements reflect the maturity value of the bonds on the maturity date.

b)   When an investor pays less than face value for a bond, the bonds are sold at a discount. If the bonds are sold at a discount, the firm reports yearly interest expense in excess of the yearly interest paid in cash, and the value of the bonds is amortized upward to the maturity level.

c)   When an investor pays more than face value for a bond, the bonds are sold at a premium. If the bonds are sold at a premium, the firm reports interest expense less than the yearly interest paid in cash, and the value of the bonds is amortized downward to the maturity level.

3. **Financial Reporting of Debt**. Debt and the associated interest and amortization are reported on an organization's financial statements.

   A. The present value of a firm's long-term debt is reported on the balance sheet.

   B. Interest expense based on the real rate of interest is reported each year on the income statement.

   C. Interest paid in cash is reported on the statement of cash flows. In addition, when debt is issued, firms report a cash inflow from financing activities. When a debt is repaid, firms report a cash outflow from financing activities.

4. **Other Obligations**. Organizations may report other obligations besides those associated with lenders, suppliers, customers, employees, or governmental units. These other obligations include contingencies and commitments.

   A. A <u>contingency</u> represents an existing condition that may have a future economic effect on a firm. For example, contingencies may result from litigation of environmental regulations. A contingency should be recognized as a liability if the loss is probable and can be reasonably estimated.

   B. While a <u>commitment</u> -- a promise to engage in future activity -- does not represent an existing liability, future liabilities may result from existing commitments once these activities take place. Leases serve as an example of commitments.

      1. An <u>operating lease</u> allows an organization access to specific assets that are not owned by the organization. These lease payments are expenses of the fiscal period during which the lease is valid. Although not yet liabilities, future lease commitments are reported in the notes to the financial statements.

      2. A <u>capital lease</u> represents a financing arrangement in which actual liabilities are created and recorded at their present value. In addition, the leased property is recorded as an asset.

        a)   The present value of a capital lease -- and the leased asset -- is the present value of the annuity of lease payments.

        b)   The lease payments include two components: interest and the payment of principal. (This is much like the loan payments discussed in the last chapter.)

        c)   As lease payments are made, the value of the lease obligation decreases, and at the end of the lease, the firm has no lease obligation left on the balance sheet.

5.   **Stockholders' Equity**. Shareholders contribute resources to the corporation in return for a share of ownership. These same shareholders share in the earnings of the organization. The contributions of capital and retained earnings transactions, therefore, make up two central activities in accounting for shareholders' equity. A third activity involves <u>treasury stock</u> -- shares of a corporation's own stock that are repurchased.

    A.   Contributed capital increases as potential shareholders exchange resources for <u>common stock</u>. This stock represents the ownership rights of investors in a corporation.

        1.   Each corporation has a <u>charter</u> granted by a state that allows the organization to exist. The charter usually assigns a <u>par value</u> to each share of stock. Since the par value is often quite small, potential shareholders routinely pay much more than par value for a share. The amount paid above the par value represents <u>paid in capital in excess of par value</u>.

        2.   Occasionally, a corporation issues either <u>stated value</u>, <u>nominal</u>, or <u>no par stock</u> instead of par value stock.

        3.   A corporation may have different amounts of stock authorized, issued, and outstanding.

            a)   <u>Authorized shares</u> establish a maximum number of shares that may be sold without amending the corporate charter.

            b)   <u>Issued shares</u> include all shares that have ever been sold to investors.

        c)   <u>Outstanding shares</u> represent the number of shares currently held by investors.

B.   As discussed in prior chapters, <u>retained earnings</u> is the sum of all prior corporate earnings not distributed as dividends.

C.   The primary transactions in the transformation process that affect shareholder equity are the issuance of stock (contributed capital) and the reinvestment of income (retained earnings).

D.   Issued shares that have been repurchased by a corporation are classified as <u>treasury stock</u>. The cost of treasury stock is deducted from shareholders' equity because it represents the amount that has been repaid to shareholders.

6.   **Changes in Shareholders' Equity**. The statement of shareholders equity reports the impact of transactions that change equity balances from the beginning to the end of a fiscal period. Generally, these events include earning net income, paying cash dividends, selling stock, and issuing stock dividends.

A.   These changes are summarized on a statement of shareholders' equity.

B.   A firm cannot recognize income from its own equity transactions. These transactions are financing activities rather than operating activities.

C.   As previously discussed, <u>net income</u> increases the retained earnings of a corporation.

D.   <u>Cash dividends</u> decrease shareholders' equity by decreasing retained earnings. Several specific dates define the process of declaring and paying dividends.

        1.   The board of directors declares the payment of a dividend on the <u>date of declaration</u>.

        2.   The shareholders eligible to receive the dividend are determined on the <u>date of record</u>.

        3.   The dividend checks are mailed to recipients on the <u>date of payment</u>.

E.   Additional shares of stock may be issued for a variety of reasons.

1.   When a corporation issues more stock, an investor-shareholder always has a <u>preemptive right</u> to maintain the existing percentage of ownership in the organization.

2.   <u>Stock rights</u> authorize a shareholder to purchase more shares of stock. If the original recipient does not use the rights, they may be sold to another individual.

F.   If a corporation lacks the cash to pay a cash dividend, managers may declare a <u>stock dividend</u> for shareholders. A stock dividend -- or the closely associated <u>stock split</u> -- does not reduce shareholders' equity. In the case of a stock dividend, managers decide to shift value from retained earnings to contributed capital. Total financing in shareholders' equity remains unchanged.

7.   **Preferred Stock.** <u>Preferred stock</u> has a higher claim on dividends and assets than common stock. Preferred stock attracts investors who desire less risk than common stock. Several features contribute to this lower risk.

A.   Preferred stock is often <u>cumulative</u>. Any dividends not paid in a prior year must be paid before any new dividends can be paid.

B.   Preferred stock often carries a stated percentage dividend.

C.   Preferred stock could participate in additional dividends after receiving its stated percentage dividend.

D.   Hybrid securities such as <u>redeemable preferred stock</u> blur the traditional line between debt and equity financial instruments.

8.   **International Reporting**. Although many similarities exist in debt and equity reporting among the GAAP of various nations, some significant differences in measurement do occur. Decision makers must act with caution when evaluating debt and equity disclosures made under the accounting standards of different nations.

9.   **Additional Financing Activities.** Some corporations have special financing activities and disclosures such as stock options, convertible securities, minority interest, appropriations of retained earnings, and foreign currency adjustments.

A.   A company may issue <u>stock options</u> as part of compensation to
       employees. The stock options -- or rights to purchase shares of
       company stock at a specified price -- may be compensation to key
       executives or part of an employee stock ownership plan (ESOP).
       Accounting for these stock options varies according to the specific
       stock option plan provided by a firm.

B.   <u>Convertible securities</u> represent one type of financing that can be
       converted to another type. For example bonds may be converted
       to common stock or preferred stock may be converted to common
       stock. Convertible securities appeal to potential investors who
       initially want less risk but later may prefer the earning potential of
       common stock.

C.   When one corporation buys another organization, the parent may
       not acquire all the shares of the subsidiary firm. Any outstanding
       equity of a subsidiary firm is reported by the parent firm as a
       <u>minority interest</u> in the equity portion of the balance sheet.

D.   Within the general retained earnings category, some retained
       earnings may be segregated for a specific purpose. These items
       are reported as <u>appropriations of retained earnings</u>.

E.   As international currencies fluctuate in value, corporate assets,
       liabilities, and earnings denominated in other currencies can
       change in value between the beginning and end of a fiscal period.
       Since equity value is linked to the value of assets, liabilities, and
       earnings, currency changes affect the value of shareholders'
       equity. A <u>translation adjustment</u> represents the impact of currency
       fluctuations on the shareholders' equity.

Review Questions, Exercises, and Short Essays

Multiple Choice Questions: These questions reinforce vocabulary and basic concepts from the chapter. In each case, select the answer you believe to be the *best*.

1.   Long-term debt reported on a company's balance sheet might include:
      a.   Accounts payable.
      b.   Capital leases.
      c.   Operating leases.
      d.   Contributed capital.

2.   *Serial bonds* are liabilities that:
      a.   Represent a set of related obligations that are due for payment after specific time intervals.
      b.   Can be paid by the borrower at any time.
      c.   Come due at one fixed date.
      d.   Are unsecured bonds.

3.   *Debentures* are:
      a.   Short-term notes payable.
      b.   Bonds that can be redeemed at any time by the issuer.
      c.   Bonds that are due for payment after a series of specific time intervals.
      d.   Bonds that are not secured by a pledge of specific assets.

4.   The Maple Company issued $500,000 of debentures paying 6% interest and maturing in 10 years. If the purchasers of the bonds require an 8% return their investment, how much will Maple receive for the debentures?
      a. $500,000.
      b. $432,897
      c. $499,998.
      d. $768,401.

5.   When the real rate of interest is *higher* than the stated rate:
      a.   Investors buy the bonds at a discount.
      b.   Investors buy the bonds at a premium.
      c.   Investors will earn the stated rate.
      d.   The amount of interest earned by the investor will be less than the amount of cash interest paid by the issuer.

6. *Capital leases:*
    a. Are disclosed as liabilities and the assets leased are disclosed as assets on the balance sheet.
    b. Are reported as if the asset had been purchased.
    c. Are recorded when a lease covers most of the useful life of an asset.
    d. Have all of these characteristics.

7. A *commitment*:
    a. Is a promise to engage in some future activity that will have an economic effect.
    b. Is reported only in the notes to a company's financial statements.
    c. May be in the form of an operating lease.
    d. Has all of these attributes.

8. The Aspen Corporation occasionally needs a small tractor. Various jobs require this machine for several months at a time. During a particular job, a tractor may be leased for part of a year and then returned to the lessor. This lease would be reported as a(n):
    a. Operating lease.
    b. Capital lease.
    c. Prepaid asset.
    d. Special financing arrangement.

9. If Aspen Corporation decided that it had enough jobs requiring a tractor to commit itself to a lease that would cover the expected life of a new tractor, this commitment would be reported as a(n):
    a. Operating lease.
    b. Capital lease.
    c. Rent expense.
    d. Special financing arrangement.

10. An existing condition that may result in an economic effect if a future event happens is:
    a. A contingency.
    b. A commitment.
    c. An expense on the income statement.
    d. A prepaid expense on the balance sheet.

11. *Contributed capital* includes:
    a. The direct investment of cash by shareholders in a corporation.
    b. The sum of the capital stock and capital in excess of par value.
    c. The value of common stock given by a corporation in exchange for fixed assets.
    d. All of these are included in contributed capital.

12.   The *par value* of stock represents all of the following *except*:
    a.   The average market value of stock.
    b.   The value assigned to a corporation's stock in its charter.
    c.   An amount of cash that cannot be transferred back to stockholders unless the corporation is liquidated.
    d.   The minimum legal value of a corporation's stock.

13.   The number of shares of stock of a corporation currently held by shareholders is called:
    a.   Shares issued.
    b.   Shares outstanding.
    c.   Shares authorized.
    d.   Shares circulating.

14.   Differences between the number of issued and outstanding shares of stock are due to:
    a.   Treasury shares.
    b.   Shares that have been authorized but not sold.
    c.   Shares that have been sold to investors but not yet issued.
    d.   Share that are outstanding but not circulating.

15.   The right to purchase a certain number of shares of stock *at a predetermined price* is called:
    a.   A preemptive right.
    b.   A stock dividend.
    c.   A stock option.
    d.   A stock split.

Exercises: These questions require the analysis of economic situations and the application of accounting concepts.

1. Calculating Components of Contributed Capital. Apple Computer reported net income of $601 million for fiscal 1999. The company's balance sheet reported the following shareholders' equity information:

Shareholders' Equity:	1999 (Millions)	1998 (Millions)
Series A nonvoting convertible preferred stock, no par value; 150,000 shares authorized, issued and outstanding	150	150
Common stock, no par value; 320,000,000 shares authorized; 160,799,061 and 135,192,769 shares issued and outstanding, respectively.	$1,349	$633
Retained Earnings	$1,499	$898

Source: *SEC Form 10-K*

a. What is Apple's contributed capital balance at the end of 1998?

b. What was the average price per share of the shares of common stock purchased *from the corporation* during 1999?

2.   <u>Calculating Components of Retained Earnings</u>. The Saco Corporation reported net income of $53 million and dividends of $1.50 per common share for Year 2. Furthermore, the balance sheet reported common stock; $5 par value; 20,000,000 shares authorized; 12,900,000 shares issued and outstanding in Year 2. Retained earnings at the end of Year 1 had been $38 million. What is Saco's retained earnings balance at the end of Year 2?

3. <u>Preparing Amortization Tables for Bonds and Leases</u>. The amortization of long-term debt such as bonds and capital leases requires the determination of the interest expense to be reported each year.

   a. The Platte Company issued $500,000 of debentures with a stated interest rate of 5% at a real interest rate of 7%. The bonds were issued on January 2, 1997 and will mature in five years. Prepare an amortization table for the bonds similar to text Exhibit 3.

   b. The Astoria Company is a small, luxury yacht manufacturer. For various tax and cash flow reasons, Astoria leases some of its manufacturing equipment from a leasing firm. The lease requires Astoria to make annual lease payments of $20,000 at the end of each of five years. Assuming a 10% interest rate, prepare a lease amortization schedule for Astoria similar to text Exhibit 6.

Short Essays: The following short essay questions not only reinforce important concepts but also give you a chance to practice writing skills. Answer these questions in complete sentences.

1.   Describing the Attributes of Liabilities. What are the characteristics that define a financial statement item as a liability?

2.   Describing the Attributes of Contingencies. What are the characteristics of contingencies. Provide an example that illustrates the characteristics.

3. <u>Distinguishing Among Dividend Dates</u>. Define the three important dates associated with the payment of dividends and explain the specific actions that take place on each date.

4. <u>Comparing Stock Dividends and Cash Dividends</u>. How are cash dividends and stock dividends different?

5. <u>Contrasting Preferred Stock and Common Stock</u>. How is preferred stock different from common stock?

Solutions to Review Questions, Exercises, and Short Essays

<u>Multiple Choice:</u>

1.   (b) Capital leases are long-term rental agreements that provide that the lessee rent an asset for most of its useful life. They are recorded as long-term debt. Accounts payable are a form of short term debt, operating leases are short term rentals that do not result in long term liabilities, and contributed capital is a category of owners' equity.

2.   (a) Serial bonds mature at specific intervals; they represent a set of related obligations with different due dates.

3.   (d) The term *debenture* refers to bonds that are not secured by pledges of specific property. They are backed solely by the credit of the issuer. They may be callable and may mature serially, but the term debenture refers specifically to the lack of a pledged asset.

4.   (b) The value of a bond is the present value of the interest payments made at the stated rate plus the present value of the principal repayment. Both of these cash flows are discounted at the real rate of interest for the appropriate number of periods. In this case, the cash flows are discounted at 8% for 10 years. The value of the bonds is $432,897 [($30,000 x 6.71008) + ($500,000 x 0.46319) = $432,897].

5.   (a) When the real interest is higher than the stated rate, bond buyers will reduce the amount they will pay for a bond to less than the maturity amount. Investors will buy the bonds at a discount and earn the real rate of interest.

6.   (d) The economic essence of a capital lease is that the lessor sells the productive capacity of an asset but not the legal title. By allowing the lessee, the renter, to pay over time for this benefit, the lessor is providing financing to the lessee. Therefore, to faithfully represent the transaction, the lessee records a liability and an asset as if the asset had been acquired and financed by the seller.

7.   (d) A commitment is a promise to engage in some future activity that has an economic effect. Commitments are recorded in the notes to financial statements, and operating leases are examples of commitments.

8.   (a) An operating lease is a rental agreement that uses only a relatively small fraction of the useful life of an asset. The rental of the tractor seems to fit that definition and is classified as an operating lease. Lease payments would be recorded as rent expense.

9.   (b) A capital lease is a rental agreement that uses most of the useful life of an asset. The lessee would record both an asset and a liability. Periodic payments would include interest expense and an amount to repay principal.

10.   (a) An existing condition that may result in an economic effect if a future event happens is called a *contingency*.

11.   (d) Contributed capital represents the direct investment of cash or other resources by shareholders in a corporation and is measured as the sum of capital stock and capital in excess of par value.

12. (a) The par value of stock represent the value assigned to a corporation's stock in its charter. This is the minimum legal value of a corporations stock, and this amount cannot be transferred back to owners unless the corporation is liquidating. It is a legal, not an economic, concept and does not represent the market value of the stock.

13. (b) The number of shares of stock of a corporation currently held by shareholders is called the number of *outstanding* shares.

14. (a) Differences between the number of *issued* and *outstanding* shares of stock are due to treasury shares -- shares that had been issued to shareholders but that the corporation repurchased from the owners.

15. (c) A right to purchase a certain number of shares of stock *at a predetermined price* is called a stock option.

Exercises:

1. Calculating Components of Contributed Capital.

   a. Apple's common and preferred stock has no par value; therefore, the full amount of the shareholders' investment on the original issue of the stock is added to the capital stock accounts. In 1998, the total contributed capital, therefore, is $783 million ($150 million + $633 million = $783 million).

   b. During fiscal 1999, the contributed capital increased by $716 million ($1349 million - $633 million = $716 million). During that same time the number of issued and outstanding shares increased by 25,606,292 million shares (160,799,061 shares - 135,192,769 share = 25,606,29 additional shares). Investors must have, therefore, paid an average of about $27.96 per share ($716,000,000 ÷ 25,606,292 = $27.962 per share).

2. Calculating the Components of Retained Earnings.

   Retained earnings represents the total net income of a corporation less any amounts distributed as dividends. Saco's beginning retained earnings of $38 million must be adjusted for both net income and dividends. Net income is $53 million. Dividends are paid on the outstanding shares; therefore, dividends are 12,900,000 x $1.50 per share or $19,350,000. Retained earnings at the end of the year are, therefore, $71.65 million ($38 million + $53 million - $19.35 million = $71.65 million).

3. Preparing Amortization Tables. The amortization of both the Platte Company bonds and the Astoria Company capital lease requires the determination of the present value of the liability and, subsequently, the determination of the interest expenses.

   a. Platte Company Bond Amortization:

   Step 1: Calculate the present value of the bonds using the real interest rate.

Total PV of Bonds = PV of Lump Sum Principal Repayment + PVA of the Annuity of Interest Payments.

PV of Single Sum Repayment of Principal:
PV = FV x IF (Table 1; 7%, 5 periods)
PV = $500,000 x 0.71299
PV = $356,495

PVA of Annuity of Interest Payments:
PVA = A x IF (Table 2; 7%, 5 periods)
PVA = $25,000 x 4.1002
PVA = $102,505

Total PV of Bonds = $356,495 + $102,505 = $459,000

Step 2: For each year calculate the real interest incurred and the cash payments for the stated interest. Increase the principal to give the new present value. At maturity, the present value is the maturity value.

Value at Beginning of Year	Interest Incurred	Amount Paid	Amortization of Principal	Value at the End of Year
459,000.00	32,130.00	25,000.00	7,130.00	466,130.00
466,130.00	32,629.10	25,000.00	7,629.10	473,759.10
473,759.10	33,163.14	25,000.00	8,163.14	481,922.24
481,922.24	33,734.56	25,000.00	8,734.56	490,656.80
490,656.80	34,343.20*	25,000.00	9,343.20	500,000.00

*Rounded

b.   Astoria Company Lease Amortization:

Step 1: Calculate the present value of the payments:

PVA = A x IF (Table 2; 10% for 5 periods)
PVA = $20,000 x 3.79079
PVA = $75,815,80

Step 2. Just as in the bond amortization, calculate the difference in the interest amounts. In this case, the interest paid is greater than the interest incurred. The difference reduces the principal amount each year.

Value at Beginning of Year	Interest Incurred	Interest Paid	Amortization of Principal	Value at the End of Year
75,815.80	7,581.58	20,000.00	(12,418.42)	63,397.38
63,397.38	6,339.74	20,000.00	(13,660.26)	49,737.12
49,737.12	4,973.71	20,000.00	(15,026.29)	34,710.83
34,710.83	3,471.08	20,000.00	(16,528.92)	18,181.91
18,181.91	1,818.09*	20,000.00	(18,181.91)	0.00

*Rounded

Short Essays:

1.   Describing the Attributes of Liabilities.

Strictly defined, liabilities have three specific attributes. First, a present obligation to transfer resources in the future to another party must exist. Secondly, the organization cannot choose to avoid the obligation. Finally, the obligation must relate to an event that has already occurred.

2.   Describing the Attributes of Contingencies.

Contingencies are future economic sacrifices resulting from a past event that will occur if another future event occurs. For example, when a customer is injured using a product and files a law suit against the maker. The manufacturer has a contingent liability resulting from a past event -- the injury -- that may result in material future economic sacrifices if the manufacturer is found liable in court.

3.   Distinguishing Among Dividend Dates.

Three important dates form a timeline for the payment of a corporate dividend. First, the corporate board of directors declares a dividend on the *declaration date*. Following this date, the *date of record* is established to determine who will receive the dividend. Finally, dividend checks are mailed to recipients on the *date of payment*.

4.   Comparing Stock Dividends and Cash Dividends.

Cash dividends and stock dividends differ in several important ways. Cash dividends result in the distribution of an asset -- cash -- to the investors. This leaves the corporation smaller in terms of assets. In addition, the corporation is also smaller in terms of retained earnings since a portion of net income has been distributed to shareholders. Therefore, both assets and owners' equity decrease. Alternatively, stock dividends do not result in the distribution of assets. In a stock dividend only new stock certificates are distributed. Since shareholders receives stock dividends proportionate to the percentage of shares owned, a stock dividend leaves each shareholder in the same position as before the dividend. In addition, the corporation's assets and owners' equity remain the same size as before the stock dividend.

5.   <u>Contrasting Preferred Stock and Common Stock</u>.

Preferred stock is a form of ownership that has some specific attributes very different from common stock. Generally, preferred stock is paid a fixed dividend like the interest on a bond. Although a corporation has no obligation to actually declare and pay a dividend, preferred stock has a higher claim on dividends and assets, and, therefore, preferred dividends must be paid before any dividends are paid to common shareholders. In case of a corporate liquidation, preferred shareholders have a higher claim on remaining assets than do common shareholders. As owners, however, both preferred and common shareholders are secondary to creditors -- such as bondholders -- at liquidation.

CHAPTER F9: ANALYSIS OF FINANCING ACTIVITIES

Chapter Focus

Major Theme: Managers have two principal responsibilities regarding financial activities. They must make decisions that reflect the best interests of the firm and comply with the terms of contracts with creditors and other resource providers. This chapter emphasizes management's use of accounting information about financing activities to fulfill these two responsibilities.

Important Elements: As you study this chapter, look for the following topics:

> Issues that affect financing decisions by company managers
> The effects of financing decisions on a company's risk and return
> Using accounting information to evaluate financing activities

Learning Objectives: After studying this chapter, you should be able to:

Define and Explain: Capital structure and why it is important to a company.

Explain: When it is beneficial for a company to use financial leverage.
Why cash flows are important for a company's financing decisions.
Why financing activities are important for determining company value.

Use: Companies' financial statements to evaluate their financing activities.
Cash flow and liquidity measures to evaluate financing decisions.

Determine and Explain: The effects of financial leverage on a company's risk and return.

Chapter Review

Introduction. Managers use accounting information to make decisions about the financing activities of a firm. In addition, investors use the same accounting information to analyze investment options. Both groups find accounting information helpful in assessing potential risks and returns of specific actions and decisions.

1. **Financing Decisions.** Financing for an organization involves management's use of short-term and long-term debt, common and preferred stock, retained earnings, and other financing instruments to provide the cash necessary to acquire other resources and carry on operations.

    A. The specific mix of debt and equity items on an organization's balance sheet is the firm's capital structure. The blend of debt and equity within a capital structure varies among firms due to differences in both lines of business and management philosophy.

    B. The mix of debt and equity in a capital structure affects the return to shareholders of a firm.

    C. Return on equity (ROE) represents a common measure of corporate performance. ROE may be expressed as:

    Return on Equity (ROE) =
    Net Income ÷ Stockholders' Equity

    D. The use of debt to increase a firm's ROE is called financial leverage.

    1. Two common measures of leverage are the debt to equity ratio and the debt to total assets ratio.

    Debt to Equity Ratio =
    Debt ÷ Stockholders' Equity

    Debt to Assets Ratio =
    Debt ÷ Assets

    2. Higher ratios indicate a higher degree of financial leverage.

    3. The financial leverage concept focuses on the appropriate use of debt to extend or magnify the earning power of a given amount of equity. By borrowing to acquire assets and

earning income with those assets that exceeds required interest payments, management intends to have more income to divide among the shareholders than would have been possible with no borrowing.

    4.   The impact of financial leverage on ROE can be described by the following formula:

**Return on Equity =
Return on Assets (ROA) x Financial Leverage
or
Net Income ÷ Stockholders' Equity =
(Net Income ÷ Assets) x
(Assets ÷ Stockholders' Equity)**

2.   **Effects of Financing Decisions on Cash Flow and Liquidity**.
Financing decisions can have a significant impact on a firm's cash flows and liquidity position.

    A.   When a firm acquires debt through loans, bonds, or other forms of borrowing, the firm incurs periodic interest payments

        1.   These payments require cash on a regular basis. Alternatively, many firms that incur high interest payments could use this cash to finance operations or acquire more assets.

        2.   Creditors often evaluate a borrower's <u>liquidity</u> -- the ability to meet upcoming cash obligations. A convenient measure of liquidity is the <u>current ratio</u>.

**Current Ratio =
Current Assets ÷ Current Liabilities**

    B.   Stockholders also expect returns on their investment in a company. Returns on equity investments, however, differ from returns to creditors in several important ways.

        1.   Cash payments to stockholders to distribute earnings -- dividends -- are not required. Therefore, dividends do not equal a mandatory cash outflow. Often, management of a firm will decide not to pay dividends and, therefore, maintain a higher level of retained earnings within the firm to finance investing or operating activities.

2.   Stockholders can still benefit even if a firm does not pay dividends.

    a.   As retained earnings are used to finance operations or investing activities, a firm can grow in both sales and profits.

    b.   Increased profitability of a firm increases the value of its stock, and the value of every stockholder's investment in the firm increases.

3.   Stockholders can earn returns through the receipt of dividends and/or the increase in the value of their investment through an increase in the price of the stock.

C.   Other financing activities such as leases and preferred stock also have impacts on the cash flow and liquidity of a firm.

1.   As previously described, leases represent an important financing activity for many firms. Leases should not require a large cash outflow when assets are acquired, but they do require periodic payments similar to the periodic cash outflow required to repay a loan.

2.   As another form of equity financing, preferred stock does not require periodic payments in the form of dividends. However, preferred stock holders often have a higher expectation of regular dividends. In addition, when preferred stock is issued, the common stock of the issuing firm becomes riskier since preferred stockholders have a higher claim to the firm's income and assets at liquidation.

3.   **Interpretation of Financing Activities**. Decision makers use financial information disclosed by firms to make judgments about a company's risk, return, and value.

A.   The analysis of one or more firms' financing activities includes five general steps.

1.   Identify the financing activities of the firm(s).

2.   Measure the capital structure for each firm.

3.   Evaluate the impact of financing activities on a company's risk and return.

4. Analyze the effect of financing decisions on cash flows and liquidity.

5. Examine the relationship between a firm's financing decisions and its value to its stockholders.

B. A comparison of the financing activities of several firms often requires the analysis of different size firms. With different size firms, dollar measures are not enough.

1. To improve comparability, decision makers often use financial ratios.

2. <u>Return on assets (ROA)</u> represents a common ratio measure of income or operating performance.

Return on Assets = Net Income ÷ Assets

C. The capital structure of firms -- the mix of debt and equity financing -- is often evaluated with the <u>debt to assets ratio</u> or the <u>assets to equity ratio</u>.

Debt to Assets Ratio = Debt ÷ Assets
Assets to Equity Ratio = Assets ÷ Stockholders' Equity

D. The effect of financial leverage on risk and return is often evaluated by analyzing return on equity. As previously presented:

Return on Equity (ROE) =
Return on Assets (ROA) x Financial Leverage
or
Net Income ÷ Stockholders' Equity =
(Net Income ÷ Assets) x
(Assets ÷ Stockholders' Equity)

E. Return on equity, therefore, is the product of a measure of operating performance -- ROA -- and a measure of financial leverage -- the assets to equity ratio.

1. Financial leverage carries both potential returns and potential risks.

2. Debt can be beneficial to shareholders since the debt will allow earning assets to generate income and potentially

increase returns without increasing equity. Increased earnings from a stable amount of equity leads to increased ROE.

3.   Financial leverage can increase a firm's risk since increased debt can increase volatility and uncertainty. In a difficult fiscal period, debt can depress earnings when assets fail to generate income necessary to cover interest payments.

4.   Since risk increases for a leveraged firm, investors expect higher returns. In leveraged firms, stock prices will not necessarily rise as returns increase.

4.   **Other Risk Considerations**. To further analyze a firm's risk, decision makers evaluate the ability of a firm to make both interest payments and debt repayments.

A.   Default risk is the likelihood that a firm will not be able to meet debt or interest payments when they are due.

B.   Even though a firm may use financial leverage to increase the return on equity, a firm's use of leverage is limited by its ability to make the periodic cash payments necessary to service the debt.

C.   Decision makers can analyze a firm's cash flow statement to determine the sources of cash used to make interest and debt payments.

1.   A profitable firm will likely have cash inflows from operations to use in paying interest and debt.

2.   A firm presents a much riskier picture when interest and debt payments are financed by selling assets and generating cash inflows from investing activities.

5.   **Financing Activities and Company Value**. A final step in evaluating financing activities is to assess the relationship between financing decisions and company value.

A.   A helpful measure of company value is the market to book value ratio.

Market to Book Value Ratio =
Market Value ÷ Book Value

1. <u>Market value</u> equals the price of a company's stock times the number of outstanding shares.

2. <u>Book value</u> equals the amount of stockholders' equity reported on the balance sheet.

3. Higher market to book value ratios indicate investors perception of higher company value. Lower market to book value ratios indicate a lower estimate of company value.

B. Financing activities have an impact on company value in several important ways.

1. Financial leverage should add to company value for a firm that is performing well. A positive return on equity is magnified by financial leverage. For a poorly performing firm, however, financial leverage should decrease a company's value by reducing ROE and increasing risk.

2. Financing decisions impact future cash outflows for interest and debt payments. Concerns about liquidity should decrease a firm's value.

3. The purposes underlying financing activities also impact company value. Issuing debt or stock to finance asset acquisition and expanded operations will likely enhance company value. Issuing debt or stock to provide cash for declining operations or to meet immediate cash flow needs will likely decrease company value.

Review Questions, Exercises, and Short Essays

<u>Multiple Choice Questions</u>: These questions reinforce vocabulary and basic concepts from the chapter. In each case, select the answer you believe to be the *best*.

1.   The way in which a company finances its operations and acquisition of assets is called its:
    a.   Financial leverage.
    b.   Investing activities.
    c.   Capital structure.
    d.   Asset portfolio.

2.   The use of debt to increase a company's return on equity is called:
    a.   Financial leverage.
    b.   Financing activities.
    c.   Capital structure.
    d.   Borrowing.

3.   Two summary measures of a company's overall performance from a shareholder perspective are:
    a.   Financial leverage and net income.
    b.   Net income and return on equity.
    c.   Return on equity and return on assets.
    d.   Gross margin and net income.

4.   Two successful companies are identical in both assets and operations, but one uses a moderate amount of debt in its capital structure while the other relies exclusively on equity. If profitability is evaluated using return on equity (ROE), the company that has debt will likely be:
    a.   Less profitable but more stable.
    b.   Riskier but more profitable.
    c.   Riskier and less profitable.
    d.   More stable and more profitable.

5.   The risk that a borrower will not be able to meet interest and principal payments on debt is called:
    a.   Default risk.
    b.   Bankruptcy risk.
    c.   Business failure risk.
    d.   Leverage risk.

6.   In calculating the *debt to equity ratio*, capital leases are:
    a.   Included as debt because they require regular interest and principal payments.
    b.   Included because they are a form of equity.
    c.   Excluded because they are rentals.
    d.   Ignored.

7.   As a company's debt to equity ratio *increases,* it has:
    a.   Used more debt to finance operations or asset acquisitions.
    b.   Earned more profit than a similar firm with no debt.
    c.   Likely experienced cash shortages.
    d.   Used more equity in its capital structure.

8.   The *market value* of a company is:
    a.   The amount of stockholders' equity reported on the balance sheet.
    b.   The number of shares of stock outstanding times the market price per share.
    c.   The difference between total assets and total equity.
    d.   The amount of stockholders' equity minus the total retained earnings.

9.   The *book value* of a company is:
    a.   The amount of stockholders equity reported on the balance sheet.
    b.   The number of shares outstanding times the market price per share.
    c.   The difference between total assets and total equity.
    d.   The amount of stockholders' equity minus the total retained earnings.

10.   The value that investors place on a company's equity is measured by:
    a.   Book value.
    b.   Market value.
    c.   Par value.
    d.   Stated value.

11.   A ratio used to assess a company's liquidity is the:
    a.   Financial leverage ratio.
    b.   Current ratio.
    c.   Debt to equity ratio.
    d.   Assets to equity ratio.

12.   To compare the operating performance of two firms of different size, a
        decision maker should compare the firms':
        a.   Return on equity.
        b.   Financial leverage.
        c.   Return on assets.
        d.   Current ratio.

13.   Which of the following reasons might explain why a firm is not currently
        paying dividends?
        a.   The firm has poor operations.
        b.   The firm has a cash shortage.
        c.   The firm has good opportunities to invest income internally.
        d.   All of these reasons could explain the lack of dividends.

14.   A company that has very little debt is likely to:
        a.   Be valuable to shareholders.
        b.   Pay high dividends.
        c.   Be a less risky investment compared to a similar company with
                moderate debt.
        d.   Have a high assets to equity ratio.

15.   Restrictions placed on a company's economic activities by creditors
        are called:
        a.   Financial ratios.
        b.   Credit controls.
        c.   Debt covenants.
        d.   Liability restrictions.

Exercises: These questions require the analysis of economic situations and the application of accounting concepts.

1. Calculating the Effect of Financial Leverage on Return on Assets and Return on Equity. The following two companies have selected different capital structures, but each is the same size as measured by total assets and has the same amount of revenue and operating expenses. For each firm, calculate the assets to equity ratio, the return on assets (ROA), and return on equity (ROE). Explain why the ROE results differ.

	Company A	Company B
Balance Sheet:		
Assets	$100,000	$100,000
Debt (7% interest)	--	60,000
Common Equity	100,000	40,000
(Number of shares)	(10,000)	(4,000)
Income Statement:		
Sales revenue	$30,000	$30,000
Operating expenses	18,000	18,000
Operating income		
Interest expense		
Income before income tax		
Income taxes (30%)		
Net income		
Assets to equity ratio		
Return on assets		
Return on equity		

2.   <u>Calculating the Effect of Financial Leverage on Earnings Variability (I).</u>
     Recalculate the assets to equity ratio, ROA, and ROE for the same two
     companies from the prior exercise assuming that they each experience a
     50% decrease in sales and operating expenses. Which firm's ROE is
     most affected? Explain the reason for this impact.

	Company A	*Company B*
Balance Sheet:		
Assets	$100,000	$100,000
Debt (7% interest)	--	60,000
Common Equity	100,000	40,000
(Number of shares)	(10,000)	(4,000)
Income Statement:		
Sales revenue	$15,000	$15,000
Operating expenses	9,000	9,000
Operating income		
Interest expense		
Income before income tax		
Income taxes (30%)		
Net income		
Assets to equity ratio		
Return on assets		
Return on equity		

3. Calculating the Effect of Financial Leverage on Earnings Variability (II).
Recalculate the asset to equity ratio, ROA, and ROE for the companies
from the two prior exercises assuming that they experience a 50%
increase in sales revenues and operating expenses from the original
case. Which firm's ROE is most affected? Explain the reason for this
difference.

	Company A	Company B
Balance Sheet:		
Assets	$100,000	$100,000
Debt (7% interest)	--	60,000
Common Equity	100,000	40,000
(Number of shares)	(10,000)	(4,000)
Income Statement:		
Sales revenue	$45,000	$45,000
Operating expenses	27,000	27,000
Operating income		
Interest expense		
Income before income tax		
Income taxes (30%)		
Net income		
Assets to equity ratio		
Return on assets		
Return on equity		

<u>Short Essays</u>: The following short essay questions not only reinforce important concepts but also give you a chance to practice writing skills. Answer these questions in complete sentences.

1.   <u>Explaining Capital Structure</u>. Briefly explain the concept of *capital structure*.

2.   <u>Explaining the Effects of Financial Leverage</u>. Explain the impact of debt on both ROA and ROE in a firm's capital structure.

3.   <u>Linking Capital Structure and Cash Flows</u>. Why does a firm's capital structure affect cash flows?

4.   <u>Discussing Company Attributes that Affect Capital Structure</u>.   What company attributes influence management's decisions about capital structure?

5.   <u>Linking Accounting Information and Financing Decisions</u>. How is accounting information used in financing decisions?

Solutions to Review Questions, Exercises, and Short Essays

<u>Multiple Choice</u>:

1.   (c) The term *capital structure* refers to the mix of debt and equity that a company uses to finance assets. Capital structure can be viewed as the proportions of debt and equity represented on the right side of the accounting equation: Assets = Liabilities + Owners' Equity.

2.   (a) Because the use of debt can magnify return on equity similar to the way in which a lever effects movement, the term leverage is used to describe the use of debt in the capital structure. With financial leverage, the lever of debt magnifies a small change in income. The lever, however, works in both directions. The movement of income is magnified when it moves down as well as when it moves up.

3.   (c) Return on equity and return on assets are both important performance measures from a stockholder perspective.

4.   (b) Risk and return are linked in the financial world. Since their earnings can vary more, leveraged firms are riskier. Investors, therefore, will demand a higher return. Leverage can result in a higher return on equity but only with greater risk.

5.   (a) The failure of a borrower to pay principal and interest is called default; the risk that this may happen is called default risk.

6.   (a) Capital leases -- like many other forms of financing -- require regular principal and interest payments. They are treated as a form of debt financing because the firm using the property derives most of the benefits and bears most of the risks of ownership even though legal title remains with the lessor.

7.   (a) As the debt to equity ratio *increases*, a firm has used more debt in its capital structure. The firm has *decreased* the proportion of equity in its capital structure. The firm is not *necessarily* more profitable or experiencing cash shortages.

8.   (b) The *market value* of a firm is the total value of the firm from an investor's perspective. This is the number of share outstanding times the market price per share.

9.   (a) *Book value* is the amount of stockholders' equity reported on the balance sheet. This is also equal to *total assets* less *total liabilities*.

10.   (b) The true value of a company's equity is the value assigned by the equity markets -- the price of the stock. Thus, the total value of a company's equity is the *market value* -- the number of shares outstanding times the price per share. Book value results from the rules used to record equity transactions. Many balance sheet values, however, are measures of historical costs.

11.   (b) A commonly used measure of liquidity is the current ratio -- current assets divided by current liabilities. This measures a firm's ability to meet its immediate obligations.

12.   (c) Operating performance for firms of different sizes is best compared by analyzing the firms' ROAs -- net income divided by assets. The other three measures relate more to financing activities than they do operations.

13.   (d) Nonpayment of dividends can result from a lack of cash, poor operating results, or good investment opportunities inside the firm. These investment opportunities may earn more for the stockholders than they could earn by themselves if dividends are distributed.

14.   (c) A company with very little debt has low financial leverage and, therefore, is likely to be a less risky investment compared to a similar company with more debt. This firm would have a low assets to equity ratio, and it may or may not be more valuable or pay higher dividends than another firm.

15.   (c) *Debt covenants* are agreements between a company and a group of creditors. Such agreements protect the creditors and usually include provisions about additional debt that a company may accept, the liquidity position that it must maintain, or assets that must be set aside for debt repayment.

Exercises:

1.   Calculating the Effect of Financial Leverage on Return on Assets and Return on Equity.

An analysis focus on the impact of financial leverage on a firm's profitability. Both the return and risk potential of financial leverage are evident through the comparison of the profitability results at three levels of operations.

Three formulas are necessary in these exercises:

Assets to Equity Ratio = Assets ÷ Stockholders' Equity

Return on Assets = Net Income ÷ Assets

Return on Equity = Net Income ÷ Equity

(Alternatively, Return on Equity = ROA x Assets to Equity Ratio)

An analysis of Exercise 1 continues on the next page.

Exercise 1 (Continued)

The following table shows the calculation of net income, assets to equity ratio, return on assets and return on equity for the two companies. The firms have the same amount of assets, revenues, and operating expenses. They do, however, have different capital structures.

Notice that Companies A has no debt and, therefore, no interest expense. Company B has debt and the calculation of net income includes interest expense. The differences in return on assets (ROA) and return on equity (ROE) highlight the impact of financial leverage on profitability.

	Company A	Company B
Balance Sheet:		
Assets	$100,000	$100,000
Debt (7% interest)	--	60,000
Common Equity	100,000	40,000
(Number of shares)	(10,000)	(4,000)
Income Statement:		
Sales revenue	$30,000	$30,000
Operating expenses	18,000	18,000
Operating income	12,000	12,000
Interest expense	--	4,200
Income before income tax	12,000	7,800
Income taxes (30%)	(3,600)	(2,340)
Net income	8,400	5,460
Assets to equity ratio	1.00	2.50
Return on assets	8.4%	5.46%
Return on equity	8.4%	13.65%

Interest expense for Company B = $60,000 x 0.07 = $4,200

Assets to Equity Ratios:
  Company A: $100,000 ÷ $100,000 = 1.00
  Company B: $100,000 ÷ $40,000 = 2.50
Return on Assets:
  Company A, ROA: $8,400 ÷ $100,000 = 0.084.
  Company B, ROA: $5,460 ÷ $100,000 = 0.0546
Return on Equity:
  Company A, ROE: $8,400 ÷ $100,000 = 0.084.
  Company B, ROE: $5,460 ÷ $40,000 = 0.1365

While Company A has a higher ROA because it has no interest expense, Company B has a higher ROE due to its financial leverage.

2. Calculating the Effect of Financial Leverage on Earnings Variability (I).

This exercise examines the same two companies as Exercise 1, but in this scenario, sales revenue and operating expenses have declined by 50% from $30,000 and $18,000 to $15,000 and $9,000 respectively. The following table illustrates the results of declining income on both a leveraged firm and a nonleveraged firm. The calculations that follow show that Company A's ROA and ROE decline less sharply than Company B's ROA and ROE. As discussed earlier, financial leverage magnifies the changes in earnings in both directions.

	Company A	Company B
Balance Sheet:		
Assets	$100,000	$100,000
Debt (7% interest)	--	60,000
Common Equity	100,000	40,000
(Number of shares)	(10,000)	(4,000)
Income Statement:		
Sales revenue	$15,000	$15,000
Operating expenses	9,000	9,000
Operating income	6.000	6,000
Interest expense	--	4,200
Income before income tax	6,000	1,800
Income taxes (30%)	1,800	540
Net income	4,200	1,260
Assets to equity ratio	1.00	2.50
Return on assets	4.2%	1.26%
Return on equity	4.2%	3.15%

Interest expense for Company B = $60,000 x 0.07 = $4,200

Assets to equity ratios:
 Company A: $100,000 ÷ $100,000 = 1.00
 Company B: $100,000 ÷ $40,000 = 2.50
Return on Assets:
 Company A, ROA: $4,200 ÷ $100,000 = 0.042
 Company B, ROA: $1,260 ÷ $100,000 = 0.0126
Return on Equity:
 Company A, ROE: $4,200 ÷ $100,000 = 0.042
 Company B, ROE: $1,260 ÷ $40,000 = 0.0315

Notice the magnifying effect of the leverage. Sales decreased by 50%, but ROE for Company B decreased by nearly 77% [(0.1365 - 0.0315) ÷ 0.1365 = 0.769]!

3.   <u>Calculating the Effect of Financial Leverage on Earnings Variability (II)</u>.

This exercise examines the same two companies as Exercises 1 and 2, but this scenario assumes a 50% increase in sales revenue and operating expenses from the original case. Sales revenue and operating expenses have jumped from $30,000 and $18,000 to $45,000 and $27,000 respectively. Once again, financial leverage magnified the effects of the change in income for Company B.

	Company A	*Company B*
Balance Sheet:		
Assets	$100,000	$100,000
Debt (7% interest)	--	60,000
Common Equity	100,000	40,000
(Number of shares)	(10,000)	(4,000)
Income Statement:		
Sales revenue	$45,000	$45,000
Operating expenses	27,000	27,000
Operating income	18,000	18,000
Interest expense	--	4,200
Income before income tax	18,000	13,800
Income taxes (30%)	5,400	4,140
Net income	12,600	9,660
Assets to equity ratio	1.00	2.50
Return on assets	12.6%	9.66%
Return on equity	12.6%	24.15%

Interest expense for Company B = $60,000 x 0.07 = $4,200

Assets to Equity Ratios:
  Company A: $100,000 ÷ $100,000 = 1.00
  Company B: $100,000 ÷ $40,000 = 2.50
Return on Assets:
  Company A, ROA: $12,600 ÷ $100,000 = 0.1260
  Company B, ROA: $9,660 ÷ $100,000 = 0.0966
Return on Equity:
  Company A, ROE: $12,600 ÷ $100,000 = 0.1260
  Company B, ROE: $9,660 ÷ $40,000 = 0.2415

This time sales and income have increased for both firms. The change in Company B's ROE, however, has been magnified by the financial leverage in its capital structure. Even though both firms had identical increases in sales levels, Company B's ROE is now almost double the ROE of Company A. Notice that the results for Company B are greatly affected by the firm's assets to equity ratio of 2.50. (Assets to equity ratio of 2.50 x ROA of 0.0966 = ROE of 0.2415 or 24.15%.)

1.   Explaining Capital Structure.

Capital structure refers to the manner in which a company finances its assets. Company management must decide on the mix of debt and equity it will use to provide the resources to invest in the firm's assets. Capital structure, therefore, refers to the amounts reported on the right side of the balance sheet equation: Assets = Liabilities + Owners' Equity.

2.   Explaining the Effects of Financial Leverage.

The use of debt in a company's capital structure -- financial leverage -- impacts both ROA and ROE. ROA is lower for a leveraged firm since interest expense decreases income and, therefore, lowers ROA. Financial leverage can increase ROE because a smaller owner investment can be used to acquire a larger amount of productive assets. If the company is successful, the owners will earn larger returns measured on ROE. However, leverage also multiplies the effects of variability in revenues and operating expenses on the returns earned by shareholders, and this variability increases their risk.

3.   Linking Capital Structure and Cash Flows.

When a company carries debt in its capital structure, the firm must make periodic cash payments for interest and principal. This process is called *servicing the* debt. These cash payments take the highest priority and leave less cash for other purposes such as financing operations or acquiring additional assets. Thus, a leveraged firm will have higher cash flow requirements than a similar nonleveraged firm.

4.   Discussing Company Attributes that Affect Capital Structure.

Decisions about capital structure are greatly affected by the type of specific company activities and by the variability of its revenues and expenses. A company in an industry that is very capital intensive and requires large investments in plant and equipment is more likely to use large amounts of debt. For example, a manufacturing firm may be highly leveraged because it requires large investments in assets to make its product. Conversely, a service organization that has relatively little need of plant and equipment may have no long-term debt. In addition, firms that have very stable revenues and expenses are more likely to use leverage because there is little variability to be amplified by the impact of debt in their capital structure. Firms that operate in volatile markets will be less inclined to rely on large amounts of financial leverage.

5.   <u>Linking Accounting Information and Financing Decisions</u>.

Accounting information reports the amounts of an organization's debt and equity, cash flows, due dates of debt payments, dividend payments, and many other facets of financing activities. Since many of these activities are essentially invisible to outsiders, accounting reports are the primary source of such information. Current and potential investors and creditors rely on this accounting information to assist in the formulation of a composite view of an organization's financial position and its future financial prospects.

CHAPTER F10: INVESTING ACTIVITIES

Chapter Focus

Major Theme: Investing activities include the acquisition, use, and disposal of assets. As managers engage in these investing activities, accounting issues include the recognition of asset acquisition and disposal as well as related expenses and valuation questions that arise while assets are held by an organization. This chapter focuses on investments in assets such as plant assets, short and long-term investments, intangibles, and other long-term assets.

Important Elements: As you study this chapter, look for the following topics:

Accounting for plant assets
Accounting for long-term and short-term investments
Accounting for intangible and other assets.

Learning Objectives: After studying this chapter, you should be able to:

Identify: Types of long-term assets, their purposes, and the measurement basis companies use to record their assets.

Apply: Appropriate measurement rules to the purchase, depreciation, and disposal of plant assets.
Appropriate measurement rules to the purchase and use of natural resources.
Appropriate measurement rules to the purchase, valuation, and sale of long-term and short-term investments.

Explain: Accounting issues associated with intangible and other long-term assets.

Summarize: The effects of investing activities on a company's financial statements.

Chapter Review

Introduction. Management choices about the acquisition, use, and disposal of assets are classified as investing activities. As a result, this chapter analyzes accounting for certain assets such as plant assets, long-term and short-term investments, intangibles, and other long-term assets. The general accounting issues include the acquisition and disposal of the investments, the recognition of related expenses, and valuation issues while the assets are held by a company.

1.   **Types of Assets**. Investing activities provide productive resources to an organization. These resources -- or assets -- may be classified as current or long-term.

> A.   Current assets include resources that management expects to convert to cash or consume during the coming fiscal year. Current assets include cash, receivables, inventories, prepaid expenses, and short-term investments in securities of other firms.

> B.   Long-term assets include resources that management expects to retain through several fiscal periods. These long-term items typically include long-term investments in securities, plant assets (buildings, equipment, and land), intangible assets, and other long-term assets.

2.   **Plant, Property, and Equipment**. Plant assets provide productive capacity to carry out operations and achieve organizational objectives. This category of assets includes buildings, equipment, and land. Accounting for this category of investing activities includes recording the acquisition of these assets and their subsequent disposal. While the assets are owned, they must also be valued for balance sheet purposes at the end of each fiscal period.

> A.   At acquisition, plant assets are valued at their cost (including purchase price, transportation, and preparation costs).

> > 1.   If several assets are purchased as a group for a single price, the value of each asset is determined by distributing the total cost based on the fair market value of the various assets.

> > 2.   Expenditures involving assets may be classified as either capital expenditures or operating expenditures.

a)   Expenditures made to acquire an asset, extend its life, or enhance its capabilities are known as <u>capital expenditures</u>. These expenditures become part of the value of the asset.

b)   Expenditures for routine repairs or maintenance on plant assets are considered <u>operating expenditures</u>. These expenditures immediately become expenses on the income statement. They are associated with the time period in which the repair or maintenance was completed. They do not change the value of the asset.

3.   For assets that are constructed by a firm, interest charges incurred during the construction period become part of the cost of the asset.

B.   With the exception of land, plant assets must be <u>depreciated</u> to systematically allocate their cost over the fiscal periods in which they are used. A variety of depreciation techniques are commonly used including the <u>straight-line</u>, <u>accelerated</u>, and <u>units-of-production</u> methods.

1.   <u>Straight-line depreciation</u> allocates an equal portion of a depreciable plant asset's cost to each period of expected useful life.

a)   The following equation may be used to determine the straight-line depreciation associated with a specific asset:

**Straight-Line Depreciation Expense =
(Cost - Residual Value) ÷
Expected Life of Asset**

This approach provides for equal amounts of depreciation each year.

b)   The yearly depreciation charge appears as Depreciation Expense on a firm's income statement and is added to Accumulated Depreciation on the firm's balance sheet.

c)   The <u>net value</u> or <u>book value</u> of an asset is the asset's cost minus the total accumulated depreciation to date.

d)   A depreciation charge may be modified because of several potential changes in circumstances. Capital expenditures may increase an asset's value, the estimated life may be shortened or lengthened, or the residual value estimate may change. In these situations, managers must determine a revised annual depreciation expenses as follows:

Revised Depreciation Expense =
(Book Value - Residual Value) ÷
Estimated Remaining Life

2.   <u>Accelerated depreciation</u> techniques allocate larger portions of a plant asset's cost to earlier periods. A popular accelerated depreciation technique is the <u>double-declining balance</u> method.

a)   The yearly double-declining balance depreciation expense may be determined by the following equation:

Double-Declining Balance
Depreciation Expense =
Book Value x (2 ÷ Expected Useful Life)

This method relies on the book value of the asset rather than its cost.

b)   The double-declining balance approach only considers an asset's residual value in the later years of depreciation. At this time, the depreciation charge is adjusted so that the book value of the asset will equal its residual value.

c)   Two underlying reasons support the use of accelerated depreciation.

(1)   First, an asset may be more useful in its early years if this particular type of equipment becomes obsolete quickly. A firm may accelerate the depreciation on these items to

expense most of the asset's cost during the early part of its life.

(2)   Secondly, accelerated depreciation is often used for tax purposes.

d)   Using accelerated depreciation for tax purposes often creates a <u>deferred tax liability</u>.

(1)   Compared to straight-line depreciation, accelerated depreciation reports higher depreciation expense -- and therefore, lower income -- in the early years of an asset's life.

(2)   For tax purposes, therefore, a firm may use accelerated depreciation and report lower income and pay lower income taxes.

(3)   For financial reporting purposes, however, a company prefers to report higher income. Thus, a company may use straight-line depreciation for financial reporting purposes and accelerated depreciation for tax purposes.

(4)   Using accelerated depreciation for tax purposes and straight-line depreciation for financial reporting creates a difference between Income Tax Expense --based on reported income -- and Income Taxes Payable -- based on income for tax purposes.

(5)   This difference between Income Tax Expense and Income Tax Payable is referred to as <u>deferred taxes</u> -- taxes a company would owe if the same depreciation method were used for both tax purposes and financial reporting.

(6)   Since the total depreciation expense over the life of an asset will be the same under both straight-line and accelerated depreciation, the additional tax has only been deferred -- or postponed -- to a later year.

(7)   Deferred taxes, therefore, are attributed to the differences in the timing of depreciation

expense between the accelerated and straight-line methods.

3.   The units-of-production method allocates an equal portion of the plant asset's cost to each unit of output or activity rather than equal amounts per fiscal period. The equation for determining the units-of-production depreciation rate is:

**Units-of-Production Depreciation Rate =
(Cost - Residual Value) ÷
Estimated Units**

4.   Over a plant asset's life, each depreciation technique will allocate the same total cost although the timing of the expenses will be different.

5.   The book value of an asset -- original cost minus accumulated depreciation -- is not necessarily a good indication of the market value of an asset. Often, through general inflation or specific market conditions, an asset's market value is much higher than its book value.

C.   At disposal, gains or losses are recognized when the cash received for a plant asset is greater or less than its current book value.

3.   **Natural Resources**. When natural resources are acquired and used, depletion systematically allocates the cost of the natural resources over the time periods that benefit from their use. This process resembles units-of-production depreciation. A portion of the resource's total cost is assigned to each unit of production. The value of these processed units is then added to Cost of Goods Sold and removed from the natural resource value itself.

4.   **Long-Term and Short-Term Investments**. Long-term and short-term investments represent a company's investment in the stocks and bonds of other firms. (Remember that a firm's own stocks and bonds are accounted for as financing activities in the liability and equity portions of the balance sheet.)

A.   These investments in the stock or bonds of other firms are called marketable securities if they may be readily exchangeable for cash. GAAP recognizes two broad categories of investments: those that yield significant influence or control and those that do not.

1.   <u>Investments that yield significant influence or control</u> are always considered long-term investments and occur when one firm owns between 20% and 50% of another firms stock. These investments are accounted for using the <u>equity method</u>.

2.   <u>Investments that do not yield significant influence or control</u> may be classified in one of three possible categories.

   a)   <u>Held-to-maturity securities</u> represent investments in the debt securities of other firms and are considered long-term assets

   b)   <u>Trading securities</u> represent either debt or equity investments held for resale on a regular basis. These are reported as current assets on the balance sheet.

   c)   <u>Available-for-sale securities</u> represent all other security investments that do not yield significant influence or control. They may be classified as either current or noncurrent assets.

3.   Securities in any of these three categories that do not yield significant influence or control are initially recorded at cost. The subsequent valuation and reporting, however, depends on the type and category of security.

   a)   Held-to-maturity securities -- the debt securities of other firms – are reported at amortized cost after the initial investment date. <u>Amortized cost</u> represents the initial cost adjusted for amortized premium or discount.

   b)   Both <u>trading</u> and <u>available-for-sale securities</u> are reported at their current market value. This process or revaluation is called <u>mark to market accounting</u>.

      (1)   Revaluing these investments from cost (or amortized cost) to current market value creates <u>Unrealized Holding Gains</u> or <u>Unrealized Holding Losses</u>.

         (a)   These gains and losses have not actually taken place. They are only indications of the gains or losses that would result if the stocks or bonds were sold at this time.

       (b)   For trading securities, the unrealized holding gains and losses are reported on the income statement.

       (c)   For available-for-sale securities, the unrealized holding gains and losses are reported at part of stockholders' equity rather than the income statement.

B.   If a firm owns more than 50% of the stock of another company, this investment would be accounted for as a consolidation.

C.   Text Exhibit 7 presents a comparison of the initial and subsequent treatment of these various types of investments.

5.   **Intangible Assets**. Managers and investors also have interest in the initial recognition and valuation questions associated with intangible assets.

A.   Intangible assets include legal rights such as copyrights, patents, brand names, and trademarks. These assets are initially recorded at their cost and then amortized over 40 years or less using the straight-line method.

B.   Although U.S. GAAP does not permit firms to report intangible assets at their market value, accounting regulations in other leading nations do allow fair market value reporting.

C.   A common intangible asset category is goodwill. Goodwill often arises when one firm purchases some or all of another firm.

       1.   Specifically, goodwill represents the amount of the purchase price that exceeds the fair market value of the net assets purchased. (Net assets equal assets minus liabilities.)

       2.   A firm is often willing to pay more than the fair value of the net assets acquired because the other firm has brand recognition, a distribution network, or a loyal customer base. These items make a firm valuable but do not necessarily show up on the balance sheet.

3.   Goodwill is recorded at the time of purchase and then amortized over a period representing its useful life up to a maximum of 40 years.

6.   **Other Long-Term Assets**. Other long-term assets include <u>deferred charges</u> that are long-term prepayments, assets that have been retired from service, or other specialized assets of some industries.

7.   **Financial Reporting of Investing Activities**. The impact of investing activities may be found in the balance sheet, income statement, and statement of cash flows.

A.   The long-term assets themselves appear on the balance sheet. In addition, unrealized holding gains and losses associated with investments in debt or equity securities are presented in the stockholders' equity section of the balance sheet.

B.   Depreciation, depletion, and amortization expense appear as operating expenses on the income statement. In addition, gains and losses associated with the sale of plant assets or investments appear on the income statement.

C.   The cash flows associated with the acquisition or disposal of long-term assets are listed in the investing section of the statement of cash flows.

8.   **Other Investment Issues**. Companies often own a significant interest in other companies. When one firm owns a large portion of another company's stock, special accounting rules apply.

A.   If a firm own between 20% and 50% of another firm's stock, it has a <u>significant influence</u> over the other firm and must use the <u>equity method</u> to account for this investment.

1.   Under the equity method, the initial investment is recorded at cost on the balance sheet of the investing firm.

2.   The investing firm increases the value of this investment as the other firm earns income. (As the other firm increases retained earnings through additional income, the investing firm now has a more valuable asset.)

3.   When the other firm pays dividends -- decreases its retained earnings -- the investing firm receives cash and decreases the value of its asset (the investment in the other firm).

4.   This process is called the equity method since the value of the investment for the investing firm is tied to changes in the value of stockholders' equity of the other firm.

B.   If one firm owns more than 50% of another firm, it has a <u>controlling interest</u> and must account for this investment as a <u>consolidation</u>.

1.   A consolidated set of financial statements includes financial information of the parent firm and all its subsidiaries. The statements represent the economic activities of a single consolidated entity.

2.   If a parent does not own 100% of a subsidiary firm, the portion not owned is reported as a <u>minority interest</u> on the consolidated balance sheet.

Review Questions, Exercises, and Short Essays

<u>Multiple Choice Questions</u>: These questions reinforce vocabulary and basic concepts from the chapter. In each case, select the answer you believe to be the *best*.

1. Investing activities include all of the following *except*:
   a. Purchase of a machine.
   b. Purchase of stock in another firm.
   c. Purchase of a firm's own stock.
   d. Purchase of bonds that a company plans to resell at the first favorable opportunity.

2. If a taxi company sends several of its cabs to a garage for oil changes and routine replacement of drive belts, the costs would be classified as:
   a. Capital expenditures.
   b. Operating expenditures.
   c. Depreciation expense.
   d. Depletion expense.

3. A company purchases 5% of the stock of another company and intends to hold the stock indefinitely. At year-end, the investing firm must report the investment at:
   a. Cost.
   b. Amortized cost.
   c. Market value.
   d. A value determined by the equity method.

4. A company purchases 25% of another company's bonds at face value and intends to hold the bonds to maturity. This investment must be reported at:
   a. Cost.
   b. Amortized cost.
   c. Market value.
   d. A value determined by the equity method.

5. Investor Corporation acquires 10,000 shares of the stock of another corporation, representing a 5% interest, for $200,000. Investor does not intend to sell in the near future. At the end of the year, the stock is quoted at $15 per share. Investor should report the change:
   a. As a $50,000 loss on its income statement.
   b. Investor should not report a loss until it sells the stock.
   c. As an unrealized loss in stockholders' equity.
   d. At cost on the balance sheet.

6.   Midway through an asset's useful life, managers realize that the asset will last 5 years longer than anticipated. For depreciation purposes, the firm should:
     a.   Restate income from prior periods and future years based on a new depreciation schedule.
     b.   Keep the original depreciation schedule.
     c.   Revise the future yearly depreciation expense based on current book value and remaining life of the asset.
     d.   Any of these methods is acceptable as long as the firm is consistent.

7.   A *deferred tax liability* arises because:
     a.   Tax laws change over time.
     b.   Special arrangement can be made when a firm lacks cash.
     c.   The actual tax owed is less than the tax expense on the books.
     d.   Tax obligations may be prepaid.

8.   A corporation acquires some production equipment for $150,000. The firm also incurs $60,000 for installation costs and pays $10,000 in wages to employees preparing and calibrating the machine before use. How should the firm report the investment and related costs?
     a.   Equipment $150,000; installation expense, $70,000
     b.   Equipment $220,000; installation expense, $0.
     c.   Equipment $210,000; installation expense, $10,000
     d.   Equipment $160,000; installation expense, $60,000.

9.   A company sold used equipment for $3,000. The company bought the equipment 4 years ago for $10,000 and had depreciated it for 4 full years using the straight-line method assuming a 5-year life and no salvage value. The asset had a fair market value of $4,000 at the time of sale. As a result of this disposal transaction, the company would recognize:
     a.   A loss of $1,000.
     b.   A gain of $1,000.
     c.   A loss of $7,000.
     d.   A loss of $6,000.

10. The systematic allocation of the cost of natural resources is called:
     a.   Depletion.
     b.   Depreciation.
     c.   Amortization.
     d.   Deferred charges.

11. A corporation incurred legal and accounting costs in conjunction with the organization of the firm. These costs are examples of:
    a. Ordinary operating expenditures.
    b. Intangible assets.
    c. Deferred charges.
    d. Paid-in-capital.

12. In an acquisition, if a company pays more than the fair market value of the net assets acquired, this *excess* represents:
    a. Other long-term assets.
    b. Goodwill.
    c. An operating expense of the acquisition period.
    d. Paid-in-capital for the acquired firm.

13. If a company has invested in a portfolio of corporate bonds and intends to sell them before they mature, the investment should be measured and reported at:
    a. Cost.
    b. Market value.
    c. Amortized market value.
    d. Amortized cost.

14. *Depreciation expense* represents:
    a. The allocation of the cost of plant assets to the periods that benefit from the use of the assets.
    b. The decrease in the value of plant assets as a result of use.
    c. The decrease in the value of plant assets as a result of aging.
    d. The cost of maintaining plant assets in usable condition.

15. The depreciation method that results in a constant amount of depreciation expense *for each fiscal period* over the life of an asset is the:
    a. Units-of-production method.
    b. Double-declining balance method.
    c. Straight-line method.
    d. All three methods depreciate a constant amount.

<u>Exercises</u>: These questions require the analysis of economic situations and the application of accounting concepts.

1.   <u>Comparing Alternative Depreciation Calculations</u>. The Ozark Toy Company purchased a metal stamping machine for $35,000 at the beginning of Year 1. The machine was expected to be used for 5 years and have a residual value of $5,000. Ozark Toys management, however, decided to outsource the parts produced by the machine and sold it at the end of Year 4 for $7,500.

   a.   Initially, Ozark Toy's management planned to keep this machine for 5 years. Calculate the depreciation that would be expensed for Years 1 through 5 for this machine using the straight-line method and the double-declining balance method.

Year	Straight-Line Depreciation	Double-Declining Balance Depreciation
1		
2		
3		
4		
5		

   b.   If Ozark's income *excluding depreciation* was $50,000 in Year 1, what was the firm's income after depreciation under the two depreciation methods?

   c.   What is the book value of the machine at the end of Year 4 under both depreciation alternatives?

   d.   At the time the machine was sold, what gain or loss would be recognized under the two depreciation alternatives?

2.   <u>Reporting Asset Values</u>. Allegheny Company acquires a parcel of land with a building for $240,000. The firm spends an additional $100,000 renovating the building for its own use. At the time of the acquisition, appraisers value the land at $120,000 and the building at $180,000.

   a.   What values should Allegheny assign to the land and building at acquisition?

   b.   If Allegheny depreciates this property over 20 years on a straight-line basis with no salvage value, what is the yearly depreciation expense on this property?

   c.   Allegheny also hires a consulting firm to develop a new trademark or logo. The consulting firm charged Allegheny $25,000 and delivers a logo that will enhance the firm's image for the foreseeable future. As soon as the logo is developed, an advertising agency executive states that the new Allegheny logo will be so successful that it is probably worth $1,000,000.

      (1)   How should Allegheny value the logo initially?

      (2)   What yearly amortization expense should Allegheny report for the logo?

3.   <u>Reporting the Impact of Investments in Equity</u>. The Platte Corporation paid $100,000 for 10,000 shares of Canyon Corporation on January 1st. Platte views itself as a long-term shareholder. During the year, Canyon Corporation earned net income of $350,000. The firm declared and paid a dividend of $0.50 per share. The market value of Canyon stock was $11.00 per share at the end of the year.

    a.   If Platte's holding in Canyon represents 15% of Canyon's outstanding stock, how should Platte report the acquisition, receipt of dividends, and the year-end value of its investment in Canyon stock?

    b.   If Platte's holdings in Canyon represent 25% of Canyon's outstanding stock, how should Platte report the acquisition, receipt of dividends, and year-end value of its investment in Canyon stock?

Short Essays: The following short essay questions not only reinforce important concepts but also give you a chance to practice writing skills. Answer these questions in complete sentences.

1.   Defining Intangible Assets. Define and give examples of intangible assets. Briefly explain how intangibles are valued at both acquisition and years subsequent to acquisition.

2.   Considering Straight-Line and Accelerated Depreciation. What are the issues that a company's management might consider when deciding between straight-line and accelerated depreciation methods?

3.   <u>Describing Deferred Tax Liabilities</u>. Describe deferred tax liabilities and explain their relation to the selection of depreciation method.

4.   <u>Describing Goodwill</u>. When one firm acquires another, what is *goodwill*? What circumstances may lead to the creation of goodwill?

5.   <u>Distinguishing Between Operating and Capital Expenditures</u>. How do *operating expenditures* differ from *capital expenditures*? How is the accounting for these two types of expenditures different?

Solutions to Review Questions, Exercises, and Short Essays

Multiple Choice:

1. (c) Buying machinery, stock in other firms, and corporate bonds all represent investing activities. The purchase of a company's own stock is not an investing activity. This management decision reduces both assets and total owners' equity. (Remember from Chapter 8 that these *treasury stock* transactions are financing activities.)

2. (b) These activities are routine maintenance procedures. They do not extend the normal life or increase the capacity of the cabs. Therefore, these costs would be classified as operating expenditures rather than capital expenditures. The term depreciation expenditure is not meaningful because depreciation does not involve the expenditure of cash. Depletion is a term reserved for the allocation of the cost of natural resources.

3. (c) A 5% investment would not usually give the investor significant influence over the other firm. The investor must report the investment at its market value at the balance sheet date.

4. (a) If management intends to hold the bonds to maturity and the bonds were purchased at face value, they would be valued at cost. The initial cost -- equal to maturity value -- is the amount of cash that will result from the ultimate sale of the investment.

5. (c) Investor would classify the investment as available for sale, and record unrealized gains and losses as a separate component of stockholders' equity. Also, Investor would decrease the investment account by the amount of the loss.

6. (c) If the estimates of either an asset's useful life or residual value change during the process of depreciating an asset, management should recalculate the future yearly depreciation expense based on the asset's current book value and remaining useful life.

7. (c) A *deferred tax liability* arises when the tax owed is less than the tax expense on the books. This will happen in the early years of an asset's life when accelerated depreciation is used for tax purposes while the depreciation for financial reporting is calculated on a straight-line basis.

8. (b) This corporation has spent $220,000 placing the machine in service. Assuming that all of these are normal costs associated with an asset of this type, the firm would record a $220,000 cost for the asset and no installation expenses.

9. (b) The book value for this asset is the initial cost minus the accumulated depreciation. At the end of the fourth year, the book value is $2,000 [$10,000 - (4 x $2,000) = $2,000]. The company gave up a book value of $2,000 in exchange for $3,000 in cash. Therefore, the firm has a gain of $1,000.

10. (a) The systematic allocation of the cost of natural resources is called *depletion*. The concept is the same as *depreciation* of a plant asset or the *amortization* of an intangible asset.

11. (c) Organization costs have a long-term benefit for an organization. Therefore, these costs are classified as deferred charges on the balance sheet.

12.   (b) Goodwill is the amount paid for a company in excess of the fair value of the net assets acquired. The buyer often pays more than the asset value because of the value of the company as a going concern. The acquired firm may have resources, markets, or technology that the acquiring firm considers very valuable. Goodwill is considered an intangible asset.

13.   (b) The investment would be reported at market value if management intends to sell the bonds prior to maturity. Changes in market value would normally be reported as holding gains or losses within the stockholders' equity section of the balance sheet.

14.   (a) Depreciation is a process of allocating the cost of a plant asset over time, activity, or output. It is not necessarily related to changes in values and does not represent a current cost.

15.   (c) The straight-line method results in an allocation of a constant amount of expense *per period*. The double-declining balance method results in a constant rate (percentage) of expense relative to the book value of the asset. The units-of-production method produces a constant amount of depreciation *per unit of output*.

Exercises:

1.   Comparing Alternative Depreciation Calculations. This exercise emphasizes both the determination of depreciation expense and the impact of depreciation on income and asset values.

   a.   Calculation of Depreciation Expense:

   Straight-Line Depreciation = (Cost - Residual Value) ÷ Expected Life
   Straight-Line Depreciation = ($35,000 - $5,000) ÷ 5 years = $6,000 per year

   Double-Declining Balance Depreciation = Book Value x (2 ÷ Expected Life)
   (This depreciation expense will be different for each year because the book value of the asset changes each year.)

   Year 1: $35,000 x 40% = $14,000
   Year 2: $35,000 - $14,000 = $21,000; $21,000 x 40% = $8,400
   Year 3: $35,000 - ($14,000 + $8,400) = $12,600; $12,600 x 40% = $5,040
   Year 4: $35,000 - ($14,000 + $8,400 + $5,040) = $7,560; since the residual value of the asset is $5,000, the depreciation expense is $2,560 ($7,560 - $5,000 = $2,560)
   Year 5: $0 (The book value of the asset already equals the residual value.)

Year	Straight-Line Depreciation	Double-Declining Balance Depreciation
1	$6,000	$14,000
2	$6,000	$8,400
3	$6,000	$5,040
4	$6,000	$2,560
5	$6,000	$0

b.   Year 1 Income After Depreciation:

Year 1 income excluding depreciation = $50,000

Straight-Line: $50,000 - $6,000 = $44,000 income after depreciation

Double-Declining Balance: $50,000 - $14,000 = $36,000 income after depreciation

c.   Book Value at the End of Year 4:

The book value of an asset is its initial cost minus total accumulated depreciation to date.

Straight-Line: $35,000 - (4 x $6,000) = $11,000

Double-Declining Balance: $35,000 - ($14,000 + $8,400 + $5,040 + $2,560) = $5,000

d.   Gain or loss on Disposal:

The asset was sold for $7,500 at the end of Year 4. Since the book value of the asset differs between depreciation methods, the gain or loss recognized will be different under the two methods as well.

Straight-Line: $7,500 Cash Received - $11,000 Book Value = $3,500 Loss on Disposal

Double-Declining Balance: $7,500 Cash Received - $5,000 Book Value = $2,500 Gain on Disposal.

2.   Reporting Asset Values. This exercise examines several aspects of valuation and reporting both plant assets and intangible assets.

a.   Value of Assets at Acquisition:

The $240,000 purchase price must be divided between the building -- that will depreciate -- and the land -- that will not depreciate.

The appraised value of the assets totals $300,000 ($120,000 + $180,000 = $300,000). The land represents 40% ($120,000 ÷ $300,000) while the building represents 60% ($180,000 ÷ $300,000 = 0.60).

The $240,000 cost would be distributed as follows:

Land = $240,000 x 40% = $96,000
Building = $240,000 x 60% = $144,000

The cost of the building would also include the renovations. Therefore, the total cost of the building would be $244,000 ($144,000 + $100,000 = $244,000).

b.   Yearly Straight-Line Depreciation:

The land has no yearly depreciation.

The building has $244,000 ÷ 20 years = $12,200 per year

c.   The Initial Value and Amortization of Intangible Assets:

(1)   The initial value of the trademark equals the cost of $25,000. The advertising executives estimate of $1,000,000 might be permitted in other countries, but U.S. GAAP focuses on the cost of the intangible item.

(2)   Even though the trademark is expected to last for the foreseeable future, it must be amortized over a period not to exceed 40 years. If the firm elects the maximum time limit, the yearly amortization expense will be $625 ($25,000 ÷ 40 years = $625).

3.   Reporting the Impact of Investments in Equity. The two parts of this exercise differ only in Platte's percentage of ownership in Canyon. This percentage of ownership, however, has a big impact on accounting for the investment.

a.   This level of investment -- 15% ownership -- would not be one of significant influence. Since Platte apparently intends to hold these securities as a long-term shareholder, the investment would be reported at market value at the end of the accounting period. Because the investment is deemed not to produce a significant, it is classified as available-for-sale.

At acquisition, the investment is listed at $100,000 on Platte's balance sheet

When dividends are received, Platte would recognize increases to both Cash and Dividend Revenue of $5,000 (10,000 shares x $0.50 = $5,000).

At year-end, the investment would be listed at $110,000 -- market value -- and the stockholders' equity section would include a $10,000 Holding Gain ($110,000 - $100,000 = $10,000).

b.   In this case of 25% ownership, Platte is presumed to have significant influence but not complete control over Canyon. Therefore, the equity method is appropriate. Platte's investment would be recorded at cost and then adjusted for the proportionate share of Canyon's income and dividends.

At acquisition, the investment is valued at $100,000 on Platte's balance sheet.

When Canyon reports income of $350,000, Platte increases the value of the Canyon investment by $87,500 ($350,000 x 0.25 = $87,500).

When Canyon pays dividends, Platte receives $5,000 in cash and reduces its investment in Canyon by $5,000.

The year-end value of Platte's investment in Canyon is $182,500 ($100,000 + $87,500 - $5,000 = $182,500).

Short Essays:

1. <u>Defining Intangible Assets</u>.

   Intangible assets are assets that do not have a physical existence. They often are represented by legal rights, such as copyrights and patents. U.S. GAAP does not allow the recognition of estimated values. Therefore, intangible assets are valued at their initial cost. Some other countries allow the reporting of the estimated fair values of intangibles. Recognition and reporting of fair value would result, in many cases, in significant increases in total assets and shareholders' equity. U.S. GAAP requires that the cost of intangibles be amortized over the useful life of the intangible item not to exceed 40 years.

2. <u>Comparing Straight-Line and Accelerated Depreciation</u>.

   Depreciation is the systematic allocation of an asset's cost to the time periods in which an organization will benefit from the asset's use. The straight-line approach is based on the view that the a firm will benefit equally in each time period of the asset's life. This depreciation method, therefore, expenses an equal portion of the asset's cost each year. An accelerated depreciation approach is based on the view that an asset is most beneficial early in its life. This approach, therefore, expenses more depreciation in early years. Over the life of an asset, both straight-line and accelerated depreciation methods will expense the same total depreciation -- the difference between an asset's cost and its estimated residual value.

3. <u>Describing Deferred Tax Liabilities</u>.

   Deferred tax liabilities arise when expenses for tax purposes are timed differently from expenses for financial reporting purposes. If accelerated depreciation is used for tax purposes while straight-line depreciation is used for financial reporting, the same total depreciation will be expensed over the life of the asset. The timing of the depreciation expense, however, will be very different. Accelerated depreciation will report higher depreciation expenses and lower income in the early years. A lower income for tax purposes will result in a lower tax obligation than would be expected for the income reported in the financial statements. When the tax obligation is lower than the tax expense reported in the financial statements, a deferred tax liability is created. This tax liability will be paid in the later years of the asset's life when the depreciation expensed under an accelerated approach is lower than under straight-line. Income for tax purposes is now higher than income on the financial statements, and the deferred tax liability must be paid.

4.   <u>Describing Goodwill</u>.

Goodwill often arises when one firm acquires all or part of another firm. When one firm acquires net assets (assets minus liabilities) of another firm, the purchase price may exceed the fair market value of the net assets. Goodwill is the excess of this purchase price over the value of the identifiable assets. This intangible asset reflects the value of a company's unique characteristics such as its customer and employee relations, special skills and experience, or good standing in the community. These intangibles may have existed for a long time, but they are not recorded on the balance sheet until another firm purchases them during an acquisition.

5.   <u>Distinguishing Between Operating and Capital Expenditures</u>.

Essentially, operating expenditures represent financial resources that are employed to maintain the normal operating condition of assets. Alternatively, capital expenditures represent expenditures that extend the asset's life or enhance its usefulness. Capital expenditures increase the value of an asset and are depreciated over the remaining useful life of the asset. Operating expenditures are recorded as expenses of the period in which they occur.

CHAPTER F11: ANALYSIS OF INVESTING ACTIVITIES

Chapter Focus

Major Theme: Managers and investors use accounting information in making investment decisions and evaluating the results of these decisions. A firm's performance is significantly affected by the success of these investments, and this chapter examines the use of accounting information in making and evaluating investing decisions.

Important Elements: As you study this chapter, look for the following topics:

Issues that affect investment decisions by company managers
The effects of investing activities on company risk and return
Using accounting information to evaluate investing activities

Learning Objectives: After studying this chapter, you should be able to:

Explain: Why investing decisions are important to a company and how they can affect its profits.
How operating leverage affects a company's risk and profits.
How investing activities affect company value and how accounting information is used to measure value-investing activities.
Why accounting information about long-term assets is useful for creditors.

Use: Companies' financial statements to evaluate their investing activities.

Identify: Ways in which a company can use its assets to improve effectiveness and efficiency.

Chapter Review

Introduction. Managers make investing decisions that impact a company's performance. These decisions include the acquisition, deployment, and disposal of various assets. This chapter describes the role of accounting information in making investing decisions and evaluating the results of those decisions.

1.   **Investing Decisions**. For managers, investing decisions often involve choices about the size, scope, and characteristics of operating assets such as equipment and facilities.

   A.   An important choice for many firms is the decision regarding the makeup of their specific operating process.

   1.   Some firms rely on a manual process while other firms may opt for an automated process to produce or distribute the same product or service.

   2.   A choice such as this impacts the level of investment in assets since a manual system will typically require a smaller investment in operating assets than an automated system.

   B.   The choice about the size of the investment in operating assets also has an impact on company profits.

   1.   From one perspective, a larger investment in assets means higher yearly depreciation. This higher depreciation level translates to lower income if sales revenue and all other expense categories are equal.

   2.   Alternatively, a manual system with a smaller investment in assets means higher labor costs, which can mean a lower level of income.

   3.   Depending on the sales level, one approach or the other -- automation versus manual system -- will yield a higher income because of the different expense levels involved.

   C.   This selection of operating approach also impacts the risk of the firm.

   1.   A manual system includes more variable cost in the form of workers wages.

        a)   These variable costs fluctuate up or down as sales increase or decrease.

        b)   With relatively more variable costs, a firm is less risky since the variable costs will adjust to the level of sales.

   2.   With a higher investment in assets, an automated system includes more fixed cost in the form of asset depreciation.

        a)   If sales go up, profits will increase faster than sales since the relatively large fixed costs stay the same regardless of sales level.

        b)   Alternatively, if sales go down, profits decrease faster than sales since the relatively large fixed costs, once again, stay the same regardless of sales level.

   3.   Because profits will vary more dramatically than sales, the relatively high fixed cost strategy is a more risky one.

D.   The use of fixed costs to increase net income as sales increase is <u>operating leverage</u>.

   1.   Higher operating leverage -- higher fixed costs -- increase risk as well as potential returns.

   2.   A firm's managers should consider using operating leverage if they are relatively certain of future market conditions or if other benefits -- such as lower unit product costs -- outweigh the risk involved in this strategy.

2.   **Interpretation of Investing Activities**. Interpreting the investing activities for one or more companies involves several specific steps: identifying investing activities for several fiscal periods, considering asset growth for profit and value, measuring the effects of asset growth, examining the effects of asset growth on risk, and examining the use of accounting information by creditors.

A.   Identify investing activities for one or more firms involves gathering data from the three primary financial statements.

   1.   The balance sheet provides information on the size and composition of long-term assets.

2. The statement of cash flows provides information on cash inflows and outflows resulting from investing activities.

3. The income statement provides information on sales and depreciation levels.

B. Growth in assets is important for both the value of the firm and the wealth of the stockholders. The level of investment in fixed assets often establishes the size of a firm's operations and therefore its range of sales and profitability.

C. Calculating and comparing the changes in selected performance ratios over time can evaluate the effect of asset growth.

1. A common way of measuring the outcome of a firm's investment decisions is the calculation of <u>return on assets (ROA)</u>. The ROA equation is:

$$\text{ROA} = \text{Net income} \div \text{Total Assets}$$

This ratio describes the level of income produced by a specific level of assets.

a) Managers and investors would typically use ROA to compare the performance of two or more firms of different sizes within the same or similar industries.

b) This measure can also be used to evaluate the performance of divisions or business units within the same consolidated firm.

c) By comparing net income and total assets, this measure links the income statement with the balance sheet.

2. ROA may be separated into two important components: asset turnover and profit margin.

a) <u>Asset turnover</u> is the ratio of sales to total assets. The equation for asset turnover is:

$$\text{Asset Turnover} = \text{Sales} \div \text{Total Assets}$$

This measure indicates how well the managers of a firm use assets to sell products or services.

b) <u>Profit margin</u> is the ratio of net income to sales. The formula for profit margin is:

Profit Margin = Net Income ÷ Sales

This measure describes managers' ability to generate profits from sales.

3. Return on assets, therefore, is the product of asset turnover and profit margin. In equation form, this relationship is:

ROA = Asset Turnover x Profit Margin
ROA = (Sales ÷ Total Assets) x (Net Income ÷ Sales)
ROA = (Net Income ÷ Total Assets)

4. ROA, therefore, summarizes both managers' ability to generate sales with assets and their ability to generate profits with sales.

3. **The Effect of Investment on Effectiveness and Efficiency.** By making investments in assets, managers intend to improve their firms' effectiveness and/or efficiency.

A. <u>Effectiveness</u> increases when a firm's sales increase faster than the firm's assets.

1. Increases in effectiveness are measured by increases in asset turnover.

2. If sales are increasing faster than assets, the asset turnover ratio must be increasing.

B. <u>Efficiency</u> increases when a firm's profits increase faster than the firm's sales. Increases in efficiency are measured by increases in profit margin.

1. If profits are increasing faster than sales, the profit margin must be increasing.

2. If increases in the profit margin are a result of reductions in costs, then a firm is more efficient.

C. Firm performance improves significantly when managers can increase both effectiveness and efficiency. In other words, ROA increases as either asset turnover, profit margin, or both ratios increase.

4.   **Investing Activities and Creditor Decisions**. Companies often borrow the money to invest in assets. The lenders of the money -- or creditors -- can, therefore, have an interest in the use and performance of the assets.

A.   Assets capable of generating significant sales are productive. Productive assets are valuable and generate sufficient income and cash to pay interest expenses and repay the debt.

B.   If assets do not generate sufficient sales, they lose value. These assets might not be able to generate the necessary income or cash to cover interests payments and debt repayments.

C.   Assets that are used effectively may have a higher market value than assets that are unproductive.

D.   The accounting systems of some nations permit managers to revalue operating assets to fair market values.

1.   U.S. GAAP does not allow the restatement of most long-term operating asset values from historical cost to market value.

2.   The only general exception to this policy in the U.S. is when the fair market value of an operating asset drops below its book value.

Review Questions, Exercises, and Short Essays

<u>Multiple Choice Questions</u>: These questions reinforce vocabulary and basic concepts from the chapter. In each case, select the answer you believe to be the *best*.

1.   One form of the *Return on Assets (ROA)* equation is:
  a.   ROA = Sales ÷ Total Assets.
  b.   ROA = (Sales ÷ Total Assets) x (Net income ÷ Sales)
  c.   ROA = Net Income ÷ Sales.
  d.   ROA = Net Income ÷ Stockholders' Equity.

2.   Return on assets is:
  a.   A measure of a company's ability to generate sales from its assets.
  b.   A measure of the effect of a company's investment decisions on profitability.
  c.   The product of a company's profit margin and its return on equity.
  d.   A measure of a company's ability to generate profits though its sales.

3.   When a company chooses a production process that requires large investments in equipment rather than large amounts of labor:
  a.   It commits to large variable costs.
  b.   Its return on assets will be more stable over time.
  c.   It commits to high operating leverage.
  d.   It will likely operate more efficiently

4.   Asset growth is important to a company because:
  a.   Asset growth can result in a higher ROA..
  b.   The ability to increase sales is related to asset growth.
  c.   Asset growth permits management to expand into new markets or adopt new technologies.
  d.   All of these reasons are important reasons for asset growth.

5.   When a company selects an operating strategy that requires high levels of fixed costs rather than variable costs, this decision:
  a.   Decreases risk because the company knows in advance the level of costs to expect.
  b.   Increases risk because the company cannot adjust to adverse business conditions.
  c.   Has no effect on risk because the company must find ways to sell its output regardless of the nature of the investment.
  d.   Has no effect on risk because investment risk is determined in the investment markets.

6.   When a company selects an operating strategy that requires lower levels of fixed costs, the firm's performance:
   a.   Has less associated risk.
   b.   Has greater variability.
   c.   Will consistently exceed that of a firm with higher fixed costs.
   d.   Will consistently be less than a firm with higher fixed costs.

7.   One way to assess a company's *effectiveness* is the:
   a.   Asset turnover ratio.
   b.   Profit margin.
   c.   Return on assets.
   d.   Operating leverage.

8.   One way to assess a company's *efficiency* is:
   a.   Asset turnover ratio.
   b.   Profit margin.
   c.   Return on assets.
   d.   Operating leverage.

9.   When the values of plant and equipment assets change, U.S. GAAP requires a company to:
   a.   Increase the value of the assets in the accounting records as soon as the market values of assets increase.
   b.   Increase the value of the assets in the accounting records only when the asset values have changed dramatically.
   c.   Adjust the asset value in the accounting records to correspond to increases or decreases in the fair market value.
   d.   Adjust the asset value in the accounting records to correspond to fair market value only when the asset's value has declined below its current book value.

10.   A company sells fine art through galleries and has consistently earned a 15% ROA. Another company sells inexpensive products in outlet stores and also has earned a 15% ROA. What is a logical explanation for the similarity of results?
   a.   The fine art firm has a low expense format while the other firm sells inexpensive merchandise and can earn a higher profit margin.
   b.   The fine art firm operates with a high profit margin and low asset turnover while the other firm operates with a low profit margin and a high asset turnover.
   c.   Both companies operate with similar profit margins and turnover rates.
   d.   The fine art firm operates with a low profit margin and low asset turnover while the other firm operates with a high profit margin and a high asset turnover.

11. Two firms operate in the same industry and region. The first firm has an asset turnover of 2.9 and a profit margin of 10%. The second firm has a turnover of 2.1 and a profit margin of 13%. Which company is more *efficient*?
    a. The second firm because it has a smaller turnover.
    b. The first firm because it has a higher turnover.
    c. The second firm because it has a larger profit margin.
    d. The first firm because it has a higher return on assets.

12. A company that has high *operating leverage* has:
    a. Low fixed costs.
    b. Low variable costs.
    c. A high proportion of fixed costs to total expenses.
    d. A high proportion of variable costs to total expenses.

13. As sales revenue increases, a company with higher operating leverage will have a larger increase in net income than a company with lower operating leverage because the company with higher leverage:
    a. Has higher variable costs.
    b. Always has lower expenses.
    c. Has a smaller change in total expenses.
    d. Operates in an emerging industry.

14. Firms with high operating leverage would likely be:
    a. Operating in lines of business characterized by rapid fluctuations in sales.
    b. Operating in lines of business characterized by very stable sales.
    c. Operating in the service sector.
    d. All of the above are likely locations for firms with high operating leverage.

15. *Effectiveness* will increase when:
    a. The profit margin increases.
    b. Asset turnover increases.
    c. The dollar amount of assets increases faster than the amount of new sales.
    d. The dollar amount of income increases faster than the amount of sales.

Exercises: These questions require the analysis of economic situations and the application of accounting concepts.

1.   Calculating Return on Assets and Return on Equity. Magnolia Manufacturing is a relatively new company that specializes in recycling plastic and paper products into building materials. During a recent operating period, the firm had assets of $1,030,000 and stockholder's equity of $510,000. During the period, the company earned income of $75,000.

[Note: This exercise compares return on assets (ROA) and return on equity (ROE) calculations. ROE along with the concepts of capital structure and financial leverage were discussed in Chapter 9.]

a.   Calculate Magnolia's return on assets and return on equity for this recent period.

b.   Explain why the returns are different. Do the results make sense given Magnolia's capital structure?

c.   Does Magnolia's capital structure make sense given the market in which the firm operates?

2.   <u>Calculating Return on Assets, Asset Turnover and Profit Margin.</u>
     Selected balance sheet and income statement data for Apple Computers,
     Inc. and Intel Corporation are presented in the table below. Apple is the
     firm that launched the microcomputer industry; Intel is the largest
     manufacturer of the microprocessors that operate MS-DOS computers.
     All numbers are in millions.

Category	Apple 1998	Intel 1998
Sales	5,941	26,273
Net Income	309	6,068
Total Assets	4,289	31,471
Total Equity	1,642	23,377

Source: SEC Form 10-K

a.   Calculate the return on assets (ROA) for the two corporations
     for 1998.

b.   Calculate the 1998 asset turnover and profit margin for the two
     corporations. What do these ratios suggest?

3.   Analyzing Cash Flows. The table below contains information from the cash flow statements of Apple Computers Inc. and Intel Corporation for 1997 and 1998. All numbers are in millions, and negative numbers indicate net cash outflows.

Category	Apple 1997	Apple 1998	Intel 1997	Intel 1998
Cash Flow Provided by Operating Activity:				
Net Income (Loss)	$ (1,045)	$ 309	$ 6,945	$ 6,068
Depreciation and Amortization	118	111	2,192	2,807
Net Increase (Decrease) Assets and Liabilities	1,081	395	871	151
Other Adjustments, Net	0	(40)		165
Net Cash Provided (Used) by Operations	154	775	10,008	9,191
Cash Flow Provided by Investing Activity:				
(Increase) Decrease in Property, Plant and Equip	(6)	43	(4,501)	(3,557)
(Increase) Decrease in Securities Investments	(36)	(566)	(2,358)	(2,043)
Other Cash Inflow (Outflow)	(457)	(20)	0	(906)
Net Cash Provided (Used) by Investing Activities	(499)	(543)	(6,859)	(6,506)
Cash Flow Provided by Financing Activity:				
Issue (Purchase) of Equity	184	41	(2,727)	(4,618)
Increase (Decrease) In Borrowing	(161)	(22)	(305)	86
Dividends, Other Distribution			(180)	(217)
Other Cash Inflow (Outflow)				
Net Cash Provided (Used) by Financing Activities	23	19	(3,212)	(4,749)
Net Change in Cash or Equivalents	(322)	251	(63)	(2,064)
Cash or Equivalents at Year Start	$1,552	$1,230	$4,165	$4,102
Cash or Equivalents at Year End	$1,230	$1,481	$4,102	$2,038

Source: SEC Form 10-K

Analyze the 1992 and 1993 cash flows reported by these firms. What do the results suggest about the investing activities of the two corporations?

Short Essays: The following short essay questions not only reinforce important concepts but also give you a chance to practice writing skills. Answer these questions in complete sentences.

1. Analyzing Investing Activities and Risk. Commonwealth Edison is a large public utility in the Northeast. Microsoft is the largest producer of software for personal computers. Which of these companies would you expect to have the larger investment in operating assets and higher operating leverage?

2. Distinguishing Between Operating Leverage and Financial Leverage. Clearly distinguish between the concepts of operating leverage and financial leverage. (Note: The concept of financial leverage was discussed in Chapter 9.)

3.   <u>Explaining the Asset Valuation</u>. In the U.S., the market values of long-term assets may be very different from the values reported on the balance sheet. Please explain this valuation difference.

4.   <u>Explaining the Effect of Investment Decisions</u>. Explain briefly how a company's investment decisions affect its profitability.

5.   <u>Explaining the Value of Information About Long-Term Assets for Creditors</u>. Briefly explain why information about investment decisions is important for creditors.

Solutions to Review Questions, Exercises, and Short Essays

<u>Multiple Choice</u>:

1.   (b) An expanded form of the ROA equation is based on the asset turnover and profit margin components: ROA = (Sales ÷ Total Assets) x (Net Income ÷ Sales).

2.   (b) ROA measures the effect of a company's investment decisions on profitability. The ROA equation that describes ROA as the product of asset turnover (sales ÷ total assets) and profit margin (net income ÷ sales) reinforces this link between investment decisions and profitability.

3.   (c) When a company chooses a production process that requires large investments in equipment rather than large amounts of labor, it will be faced with high fixed costs. The equipment, once acquired, will generate depreciation expenses that will continue even if production is cut back. Unlike labor, equipment costs cannot easily be reduced by small increments. This is another way of saying that a firm commits to high operating leverage. One result of this decision is that a firm's ROA will be less stable over time.

4.   (d) Asset growth can lead to sales growth, an expansion of markets, new technologies, and a higher ROA. Investments in operating assets permit managers to exercise more options to expand the firm's earning power and performance.

5.   (b) When a company commits to high levels of fixed costs, it also gives up a certain amount of flexibility. The firm's ability to respond to a less favorable environment decreases, and, as a result, the company's performance is subject to greater variability or more risk.

6.   (a) A firm with lower levels of fixed costs and higher levels of variable cost has greater flexibility and less associated risk. A higher fixed cost firm has greater variability in earnings. Neither type of firm consistently performs better than the other under all circumstances.

7.   (a) The asset turnover measures the amount of sales that a company has generated for every dollar invested. This ratio measures the company's effectiveness.

8.   (b) The profit margin is a measure of efficiency -- the amount of net income that a company is able to earn on every dollar of sales.

9.   (d) U.S. GAAP includes provisions reducing the value of assets when those values decline below book value. U.S. companies are not allowed to increase asset values to higher fair market values.

10.   (b) The nature of a business often determines the basic operating strategy. An art gallery is likely to have a relatively low asset turnover -- relatively low sales for each dollar invested. A business like this is, however, likely to have a large profit margin. A discount operation in a much more competitive line of business will attempt to keep asset turnover high but will be forced by competition to accept low profit margin.

11.   (c) The profit margin is a measure of efficiency. Thus, the second firm -- with the larger margin -- is more efficient.

12.   (c) A firm using operating leverage has a high proportion of fixed cost to total expenses. With sizable fixed costs, a firm can increase sales without a corresponding increase in expenses. The result is more rapidly increasing income and greater profitability at high sales levels.

13.   (c) A firm with higher operating leverage has a higher proportion of fixed costs. Since fixed costs do not change as sales activity increases, this firm will experience a smaller increase in expenses as sales activity increases.

14.   (b) Firms in very stable markets can take advantage of operating leverage. Firms in rapidly fluctuating markets accept a very risky strategy when they use operating leverage. Service firms often do not have a large quantity of plant and equipment when compared with a manufacturing or merchandising firm.

15.   (b) Effectiveness is measured by the asset turnover -- the ratio that represents the amount of sales generated for each dollar invested in assets. Effective firms are able to generate more sales from given investment in assets.

Exercises:

1.   Calculating Return on Assets and Return on Equity (I). This exercise compares two performance measures -- return on assets (ROA) and return on equity (ROE). (Return on equity was described in Chapter 9.)

General Equations:

ROA = Net Income ÷ Total Assets

ROE = Net Income ÷ Stockholders' Equity

a.   ROA and ROE Calculations for Magnolia Manufacturing.

ROA = $75,000 ÷ 1,030,000
ROA = 0.0728 or 7.28%

ROE = $75,000 ÷ $510,000
ROE = 0.1471 or 14.71%

b.   ROE exceeds ROA for Magnolia Manufacturing, and this result is consistent with Magnolia's capital structure. The firm is using *financial leverage*. Since about $1,000,000 in assets are financed with only about $500,000 in equity, the remaining financing must be debt. For a leveraged firm, ROE will exceed ROA since the financial leverage magnifies the operating results.

c.   Magnolia management appears to have adopted a highly leveraged capital structure in an industry that could be rather volatile. The financial leverage does enhance ROE, but the presence of debt does increase the risk of the firm.

2. <u>Calculating Return on Assets, Asset Turnover and Profit Margin</u>. This exercise expands the calculation of performance measures to include return on assets, asset turnovers and profit margins.

General Equations:

ROA = Net Income ÷ Total Assets

Asset Turnover = Sales ÷ Total Assets

Profit Margin = Net income ÷ Sales

a. Return on Assets for 1998.

Apple's ROA = $309 ÷ $4289 = 7.2%

Intel's ROA = $6,068 ÷ $31,471 = 19.3%.

b. Asset Turnover for 1998.

Apple's Asset Turnover = $5,941 ÷ $4,289 = 1.39

Intel's Asset Turnover = $26,273 ÷ $31,471 = 0.83

Profit Margin for 1998:

Apple's Profit Margin = $309 ÷ $5,941 = 5.2%

Intel's Profit Margin = $6,068 ÷ $26,273 = 23.1%

These ratios suggest that Apple is able to generate more sales per dollar invested than Intel ($1.39 of sales for every dollar invested vs. $0.83 per dollar invested). Intel, however, is able to turn those sales into profits much more efficiently (Apple has just over $0.05 of profit on every dollar of sales while Intel has $0.23 per dollar of sales). The result is that Apple generates a return of only 7.2% on the resources invested in assets, while Intel generates 19.3%.

3. <u>Analyzing Cash Flows</u>. The cash flow activities for Apple and Intel are very different from one another. The analysis of cash flows begins with the identification of cash flows from operating, investing, and financing activities. This analysis will focus specifically on the information the statement of cash flow provides about investing activities.

Analysis of cash flows from operating, investing, and financing activities:

	Operating Activities	Investing Activities	Financing Activities
Apple 1997	$ 154	$ (499)	$ 23
Apple 1998	775	(543)	19
Intel 1997	10,008	(6,859)	(3,212)
Intel 1998	$ 9,191	$ (6,506)	$ (4,749)

In both years, Apple and Intel generated cash inflows from operations. Apple generated cash from operations in 1997 despite reporting a loss for the year. Both firms used cash to invest. However, while Intel invested heavily in property, plant and equipment that represents new productive capacity, Apple in 1998 actually reduced its investment in property, plant and equipment. Apple's new investments were in securities rather than productive capacity. Apple generated some additional cash through financing activities while Intel used cash in financing activities -- primarily to repurchase its own stock.

Short Essays:

1. Analyzing Investing Activities and Risk.

   A power utility like Con Edison must invest heavily in transmitting and generating equipment. This creates a high investment in operating assets and operating leverage. The operating leverage can work to the utility's advantage since the market for power is relatively stable.

   Alternatively, Microsoft operates in an environment that is highly uncertain because of rapid technological change. Many of Microsoft's most popular products have replaced similar offerings from other firms that once dominated the market for certain types of software. In addition, Microsoft's products are computer software that does not require expensive production and distribution facilities. Because of the market uncertainties and low level of required operating assets, Microsoft would rely less on operating leverage.

2. Distinguishing Between Operating leverage and Financial Leverage.

   Both operating and financial leverage can be used to increase profit performance of a firm. Financial leverage refers to a firm's capital structure -- specifically, the mix of debt and equity used to finance a firm's assets. Alternatively, operating leverage refers to management's decision about the level of investment in operating assets such as plant and equipment. Specifically, a firm uses operating leverage when managers make decisions that create a high proportion of fixed costs within a firm's total expenses.

   Under the right conditions, both strategies can provide superior earnings for stockholders. They both also provide greater risk for the firm and are more successful when used by firms in stable, predictable markets.

3. Explaining Asset Valuation.

   U.S. GAAP requires that, in general, long-term assets be reported on the balance sheet at book value (cost less accumulated depreciation). Under certain circumstances, investments in securities are valued at market values. For assets such as plant and equipment, if market values are less than book values, market value must be reported. These policies are based on two important GAAP fundamentals: conservatism and objectivity.

4.   Explaining the Effect of Investment Decisions.

Investment decisions affect profitability in several ways. First, large investments in plant and equipment result in high operating leverage and high operating leverage results in more volatile net income. Second, the types of assets acquired may increase or decrease the effectiveness of the business in meeting customer needs. Finally, by reducing or increasing expenses, investments may increase or decrease the efficiency of a business.

5.   Explaining the Value of Information About Long-Term Assets for Creditors.

In order to generate enough cash to repay creditors, a company must invest the resources borrowed in assets that will generate a sufficient cash flow to pay interest and repay the debts. If a borrower is unable to make these debt service payments, creditors may be forced to seize assets that have been pledged as security. In other cases, assets may be sold and the proceeds distributed to creditors. In all cases, when assets decrease in value, the creditors' position becomes more risky. As a result, accounting information about assets is stated very conservatively -- usually at the lower of cost or market value -- to protect creditors.

Chapter Notes

CHAPTER F12: OPERATING ACTIVITIES

Chapter Focus

Major Theme: Operating activities are important steps in the overall transformation process. These activities create and distribute goods and services. This chapter describes accounting issues associated with operating activities and emphasizes the measurement and reporting of transactions with customers, suppliers, employees, other resource providers, and governments.

Important Elements: As you study this chapter, look for the following topics:

Recognition of revenues and accounting for credit sales
Measurement of cost of goods sold and inventories
Reporting issues associated with nonrecurring items and earnings per share.
Differences between accrual and cash flow measures of operating activities

Learning Objectives: After studying this chapter, you should be able to:

Identify: The purpose and major components of an income statement.
Routine and nonroutine transactions that affect a company's income statement.

Explain and Apply: Rules for measuring revenues and receivables and reporting revenue transactions.

Describe and Compare: Reporting rules for inventories and cost of goods sold and reporting of inventories for merchandising and manufacturing companies.

Explain, Apply, and Describe: Rules for measuring cost of goods sold and inventories and the effect of income taxes on the choice of inventory estimation method.

Chapter Review

Introduction. Financing and investing activities acquire the resources necessary for a company to carry on <u>operating activities</u> -- the transformation steps that create and distribute goods and services. The income statement and statement of cash flows report the results of operating activities, and these results also impact a firm's balance sheet.

1. **Basic Operating Activities**. An <u>income statement</u> summarizes operating activities and reports net income for a fiscal period on an accrual basis.

    A. Initial components of an income statement include operating revenues, cost of goods sold, gross profit, operating expenses, and operating income.

    B. Subsequent income statement items include interest revenue and interest expenses, gains and losses on disposal of assets, pretax income and income tax expense, net income, and earnings per share.

2. **Revenues and Receivables**. Operating revenues result from the sale of goods and services to customers. These revenues are the first items listed on the income statement and affect both cash and accounts receivable on the balance sheet.

    A. Most firms recognize revenue when ownership of an item transfers to a customer. For example, retail firms usually recognize revenue when a sale is made and a customer takes possession of the merchandise. Service firms usually recognize revenue when a service is performed.

    B. When a manufacturer or merchandising firm ships goods to a customer, specific terms of the sales contract indicate which party owns the goods while they are in transit.

        1. The phrase <u>free on board (FOB)</u> designates the point at which ownership is transferred.

        2. For example, <u>FOB destination</u> signifies that the seller owns the goods until they arrive at the buyer's location.

        3. <u>FOB shipping point</u> means that ownership passes when the goods leave the seller's business.

C. In general, revenue should be recognized when the following four criteria have been met:

1. Most of the activities necessary to produce and sell the product have been completed.

2. The costs associated with the production and sale of the goods or services have been incurred or can be reasonably measured.

3. The amount of revenue earned can be measured objectively.

4. The collection of cash from the buyer is reasonably assured.

D. For long-term projects that often span several fiscal periods, revenue may be recognized as time passes based on the partial completion of the project. The percentage of completion method recognizes revenue and expenses for a long-term project in proportion to the amount of work completed during each fiscal period.

E. Revenues are reported net of any discounts or returns.

1. A discount represents a reduction in the normal selling price.

a) Many firms grant sales discounts for prompt payment from the customer. For example, a firm may offer its customers a 2% discount if they pay in full within 10 days.

b) Often, firms will recognize a sale at full price and then deduct the discount if a customer pays promptly.

2. Sales returns are also deducted from total sales to calculate operating revenues on the income statement.

F. The matching principle represents an important accounting concept underlying the income statement. Matching revenues and related expenses in the same time period prevents some misstatements of net income. Misstatements can occur when the revenue from a specific transaction and expenses from the same transaction are recognized in two different fiscal periods.

G.   Some accounts receivable may prove uncollectible, and an important matching question arises when sales from one fiscal period prove uncollectible in a subsequent fiscal period.

    1.   In order to recognize the sale and potential uncollectible accounts in the same fiscal period, a firm will estimate the uncollectible amount of accounts receivable at the end of a fiscal period.

        a)   This process also establishes an Allowance for Doubtful Accounts. This allowance reduces the net accounts receivable for the period to the amount of estimated cash received.

        b)   In addition, the Doubtful Accounts Expense is increased during the fiscal period when the accounts receivable originated.

    2.   The level of uncollectible accounts receivable is influenced by a company's credit policies. While sales can be increased by accepting customers with higher credit risk, uncollectible accounts will also rise.

H.   Many firms offer warranties on the goods they produce. They agree to repair or replace a defective good without charge to the customer.

    1.   Warranty costs present another potential challenge to the matching concept.

    2.   Since these warranty costs relate to an initial sale, firms estimate the potential warranty costs associated with a specific sales level and recognize this expense in the fiscal period when that level of sales occurs.

I.   The recognition of sales returns, uncollectible accounts, and warranty costs, therefore, must be timed to coincide with the sales activities that ultimately generated these items. Recognizing a sale and any related returns, uncollectible accounts, or warranty costs within the same fiscal period supports the matching principle.

3.   **Inventories and Cost of Goods Sold**. Merchandising or manufacturing companies generate revenue by selling products. For these firms, sales activity increases the cost of goods sold and decreases inventory.

Therefore, the amount of cost of goods sold on the income statement is linked to the level of inventory on the balance sheet.

A. The reporting of cost of goods sold and inventory activities differs between merchandising firms and manufacturers.

   1. A merchandising firm buys finished goods from manufacturers and resells them to customers.

      a) The Merchandise Inventory account is increased when goods are purchased.

      b) When specific items are sold, Merchandise Inventory is reduced and Cost of Goods Sold is increased to reflect the movement of merchandise.

      c) In addition, merchandising firms also maintain detailed records of specific inventory items, sales patterns, and reorder quantities.

   2. Manufacturing firms fabricate or assemble goods and sell the finished products to merchandising firms or the final users.

      a) The process begins when manufacturers purchase raw materials -- the physical ingredients or components of a product. This activity increases the Raw Materials Inventory.

      b) Once work on the materials begins, these items are transferred to the Work-in-Process Inventory. Two other costs are added to the cost of raw materials during the work-in-process phase.

         (1) Direct labor costs represent the wages and benefits paid to workers who transform the raw material into finished goods.

         (2) Manufacturing overhead costs include items such as supplies, utilities, depreciation, and other indirect costs within the manufacturing process.

c)   When the raw materials have been transformed into completed goods, the costs from Work-in-Process Inventory are transferred to <u>Finished Goods Inventory</u>. These finished goods are products awaiting sale.

d)   Once the finished goods are sold, their costs leave Finished Goods Inventory and are transferred to the Cost of Goods Sold account.

e)   At any time, a manufacturer may have balances in the Raw Materials Inventory, Work-in-Process Inventory, Finished Goods Inventory, and Cost of Goods Sold accounts representing resources or products at various phases of the transformation process.

4.   **Measuring inventory**. Since product costs that begin in inventory on the balance sheet ultimately flow to cost of goods sold on the income statement, measuring the costs associated with inventory transactions is an important part of income determination.

A.   For certain goods -- especially those that are large, easily identified, or expensive -- a firm maintains detailed inventory records that account for the location of each specific unit. In cases such as these, a specific identification process can be used to determine the units that have been sold and the remaining units in inventory

B.   For many other firms, units of inventory are homogeneous and, therefore, not traced individually. In these circumstances, the measurement of inventory costs depends on assumptions about inventory flows.

1.   The <u>first-in first-out (FIFO) method</u> assumes the cost if the first inventory items received are also the first costs transferred to Cost of Goods Sold.

2.   The <u>last-in first-out (LIFO) method</u> assumes the costs of the last inventory items received are the first costs transferred to Cost of Goods Sold.

3.   The <u>weighted average method</u> for valuing inventory uses the average cost of inventory available during the period as the cost of units sold.

**[Important Note: FIFO and LIFO
assumptions are used to determine
the flow of costs from inventory to
cost of goods sold. These assumptions
do not have to match the physical flow
of merchandise through a company.]**

C.   The estimate of inventory value and, therefore, the value of cost of
goods sold has an impact on income taxes.

1.   When the prices of various inventory items change between
inventory purchase dates, FIFO and LIFO assumptions will
transfer different costs to cost of goods sold.

2.   In periods of rising prices, LIFO will transfer higher costs to
cost of goods sold and, therefore, report lower income. This
alternative is attractive for tax reporting since taxes will be
lower.

3.   Tax regulations require that a firm using LIFO for tax
purposes must also use this inventory assumption for
financial reporting purposes.

D.   GAAP requires that firms compare inventory costs with the current
market costs of the products. If the current market cost is below
the recorded costs, the inventory value must be written down to
current market cost. This lower of cost or market valuation process
will recognize a loss during the fiscal period when market costs fell
below recorded costs.

E.   GAAP also requires disclosure of the methods used to value
inventories and costs of goods sold. These disclosures assist in
comparisons among firms.

F.   Companies using just-in-time procedures will carry low inventory
balances since they frequently receive fresh supplies and raw
materials or finished goods are available just before they are
needed.

5.   **Other Operating Activities and Income Statement Items**. In addition to
revenues and cost of goods sold, other categories that appear on an
income statement include operating expenses, other revenues and

expenses, and special items. When all revenue and expense items are considered, the income statement appears as follows:

Sales Revenue
- Cost of Goods Sold
Gross Profit
- Operating Expenses
Operating Income
+ or - Other Revenues and Expenses
Pretax Income
- Income Taxes
Income Before Special Items
+ or - Special Items
Net Income

A.   Operating expenses include nonproduction costs such as marketing, research and development, and general administration activities. Subtracting operating expenses from gross profit determines operating income.

B.   Other revenues and expenses include revenue associated with short or long-term investments or expenses associated with interest on short or long-term debt. These amounts are accrued and recognized even if cash has not been received or paid. Other possible items in this category include dividends received and realized gains or losses from the sale of stock or bond investments.

C.   The income statement reports income tax expense equal to pretax income multiplied by the company's tax rate.

1.   The income tax expense reported might not be the amount of income taxes actually paid on the income.

2.   GAAP and tax regulations sometimes differ on the recognition of various revenues and expenses.

3.   As discussed in prior chapters, these differences often result in a deferred tax liability.

6.   **Special Items**. Special items on the income statement include discontinued operations, extraordinary items, and accounting changes.

A.   A company must report separately revenue and expenses associated with operations it no longer owns. Accounting for these discontinued operations includes reporting both the income (or loss) generated by the operation and the gain (or loss) earned in disposing of the operation.

B.   Gains and losses associated with events that are both unusual and infrequent are reported as extraordinary items.

C.   Net income is determined by deducting the impact of special items from a firm's operating income. Deducting preferred stock dividends from net income determines the net income available for common stockholders.

7.   **Other Topics**. At times, firms have additional information reported on their income statements or rely on additional foundation concepts in preparing income statement disclosures.

A.   When a firm uses the equity method of accounting for an investment in another firm over which it as significant influence, the firm will report equity income on the income statement. This represents the investing firm's share of the other firm's income.

B.   When a firm reports consolidated income but a minority interest exists for one of the consolidated firms, the consolidated income statement should report a minority interest in income. This minority interest is the amount of subsidiary income attributable to the minority owners. The minority interest in income should be subtracted from consolidated income.

C.   Deferred compensation includes pensions, health care, and other retirement benefits accrued by employees. The detailed impact of these items is disclosed in the notes to the financial statements.

D.   Some firms track inventory with a perpetual system while others use a periodic system to determine cost of goods sold and the ending inventory balance.

1.   In a perpetual tracking system, merchandise is recorded as an increase to inventory when acquired and a decrease to inventory when sold. Inventory records, therefore, should accurately reflect the amounts purchased, in stock, and sold.

2.   Alternatively, a firm may track the level of purchases only. A periodic count of inventory and comparison with the amounts purchased reveals the amount of goods sold. This method does not track products into and out of inventory.

These <u>periodic systems</u> determine cost of goods sold and inventory values only after the inventory count at the end of the fiscal period.

3.   Recent developments in technology such as bar coding and optical scanners have significantly increased the use of perpetual inventory systems.

Review Questions, Exercises, and Short Essays

<u>Multiple Choice Questions</u>: These questions reinforce vocabulary and basic concepts from the chapter. In each case, select the answer you believe to be the *best*.

1.   Revenue should be recognized when:
   a.   Most of the activities necessary to produce and sell the goods or services are complete.
   b.   The costs associated with the goods or services have been incurred or can be measured reasonably.
   c.   The amount of revenue can be measured objectively and the amount of cash to be collected is reasonably assured.
   d.   All of the above are criteria for revenue recognition.

2.   For long-term construction contracts, a company *may* recognize revenue:
   a.   When the contract is begun.
   b.   On a percentage of completion basis as the construction is completed.
   c.   As payments are received on the project.
   d.   None of the above procedures is appropriate for long-term contracts.

3.   The amount of *net operating revenue* reported on an income statement represents:
   a.   The total amount earned before any discounts and returns.
   b.   The amount earned after discounts and returns.
   c.   The amount earned after discounts, returns, and allowance for doubtful accounts.
   d.   Gross revenues less operating expenses.

4. Doubtful accounts *expense* represents:
    a. The total uncollectible accounts on the books.
    b. The amount of uncollectible accounts written off during a period.
    c. An estimate of the credit sales of a period that will become uncollectible.
    d. All of the above are included in doubtful accounts expense.

5. For a manufacturing firm, the cost of goods *in the manufacturing process* is called:
    a. Raw Materials Inventory.
    b. Work-in-Process Inventory.
    c. Finished Goods Inventory.
    d. Cost of Goods Sold.

6. The term *manufacturing overhead costs* describes all of the following *except*:
    a. Wages and benefits paid to supervisory personnel in production departments.
    b. Supplies used in production departments.
    c. Wages and benefits for employees working directly on the product.
    d. Taxes, insurance, and depreciation on facilities used in making the product.

7. An inventory costing method that assigns the cost of the most recently purchased merchandise to cost of goods sold is:
    a. First-in first-out.
    b. Last-in first-out.
    c. Weighted average.
    d. Specific identification.

8. An inventory costing method that assigns the cost of the most recently purchased merchandise to ending inventory is:
    a. First-in first-out.
    b. Last-in first-out.
    c. Weighted average.
    d. Specific identification.

9.   A sand and gravel company sells river sand and gravel for construction purposes. Sand and gravel are delivered to the company by trucks that dump loads of material into large piles. When material is sold, a loader scoops from the top of the pile and dumps the material into a waiting truck. What type of inventory estimation technique may this firm use?
   a.   First-in first-out.
   b.   Last-in first-out.
   c.   Weighted average.
   d.   Any of these estimation techniques is acceptable.

10. In a period of falling prices, which method results in lowest net income?
   a.   First-in first-out.
   b.   Last-in first-out.
   c.   Weighted average.
   d.   Since prices are falling, none of these methods will result in the lowest income.

11. In a period of rising prices, which method results in lowest net income?
   a.   First-in first-out.
   b.   Last-in first-out.
   c.   Weighted average.
   d.   Since prices are rising, any of these methods will result in the lowest income.

12. *Operating income* equals:
   a.   Gross revenue less cost of goods sold.
   b.   Gross profit less operating expenses.
   c.   Gross profit less other revenues and expenses.
   d.   Sales revenue less sales returns and discounts.

13. Net income available for common stockholders is:
   a.   Net Income less taxes payable.
   b.   Net Income less common dividends.
   c.   Gross revenue less cost of goods sold.
   d.   Net Income less preferred dividends.

14. To be classified as an *extraordinary item*, a gain or loss must be:
   a.   Unusual and infrequent.
   b.   Recurring.
   c.   The result of a discontinued operation.
   d.   Any of the above criteria defines an extraordinary item.

15. Amounts that are expected to be paid to employees after retirement are known as:
    a. Projected benefit obligation.
    b. Pension benefits.
    c. Deferred compensation.
    d. Plan assets.

Exercises: These questions require the analysis of economic situations and the application of accounting concepts.

1. Calculating Inventory Balances for a Manufacturer. Green Briar Manufacturing began its first year of operations by acquiring $250,000 of raw materials. During the first month, $75,000 of raw materials entered the production process. Direct labor for the month cost $150,000 and indirect labor cost $50,000. Production supplies and utilities for the month totaled $10,000. At the end of the month, Green Briar had sold products costing $78,000 and had finished goods in inventory costing $30,000.

   a. What were Green Briar's Raw Materials Inventory, Work-in - Process Inventory, and Finished Goods Inventory balances at month's end? (Hint: Text Exhibit 5 provides a helpful example for solving this problem.)

   b. Is Green Briar likely to use a *periodic* or *perpetual* inventory tracking system? (This part of the question relates to a section of the Chapter Appendix.)

2.   <u>Comparing Inventory Costing Methods</u>. The Hood River Kite Shop began
a recent year with an inventory balance of $1,500 representing 150
large, handmade kites in assorted colors. During the year, additional
inventory was obtained as follows:

Date	Number	Total Cost
March 30th	100 kites	$1,100
June 30th	100 kites	$1,200
September 30th	100 kites	$1,300

Ending inventory was 90 kites. What was the Hood River Kite Shop's
cost of ending inventory and cost of goods sold under the LIFO, FIFO,
and weighted average inventory methods?

3. <u>Preparing an Income Statement and Calculating Net Income</u>. The Atlantic Coast Fence Company reported the following information at the end of the most recent fiscal period.

Category	Amount
Operating Expenses	$25,000
Cost of Goods Sold	$90,000
Other Revenue and (Expenses) (Before Tax)	($12,000)
Sales Revenue	$150,000
Extraordinary Gain (Before Tax)	$8,000
Tax Rate	35%

Prepare an income statement for the firm and determine net income. (Hint: Follow the basic outline of an income statement included in both the chapter and **Chapter Review** portion of the **Study Guide**. Some of the numbers appear above and the others must be calculated by using the numbers above.)

<u>Short Essays</u>: The following short essay questions not only reinforce important concepts but also give you a chance to practice writing skills. Answer these questions in complete sentences.

1. <u>Recognizing Revenue</u>. The audit of the Rocky Mountain Trading Company raised questions about two orders for merchandise that had been shipped by the firm on December 31st -- the last day of the fiscal period. One sale for $15,000 that cost the firm $10,000 was shipped to San Francisco -- FOB destination. The other sale for $5,000 order cost the firm $3,000 and was shipped to New Orleans -- FOB shipping point. Inventory remaining on hand at the end of the period totaled $125,000 and the accounting records reported sales totaling $1,075,000 including the two orders in question. From the perspective of the revenue recognition point, how are these two orders different from one another? In which fiscal period should each of these orders be recognized?   What should be the firm's gross sales and ending inventory balances for this fiscal period?

2. <u>Recognizing Extraordinary Items</u>. The Foothills Glass Company recently purchased a new warehouse. Unfortunately, Foothills management failed to notice that part of a major, active, geological fault system ran under the building. Two months after the company moved into the facility, a minor earthquake damaged $15,000 of inventory. Should Foothills report this loss as an extraordinary item? Why or why not?

3.   <u>Reporting Accounting Changes</u>. The Big Bend Civil Engineering
        Company recently changed its method of accounting for long-term
        contracts from the completed contract method to the percentage of
        completion method. How should Big Bend report the financial impact of
        this change?

4.   <u>Describing the Matching Principle</u>. Describe the matching principle and
        explain its importance to the income statement. Give an example of an
        application of the matching principle in the operating portion of the
        income statement.

5.   <u>Explaining Deferred Compensation</u>. Explain why deferred compensation
        should be reported as an expense and liability.

Solutions to Review Questions, Exercises, and Short Essays

<u>Multiple Choice</u>:

1. (d) Although the specific point of revenue recognition may differ among firms, all of the conditions described must be met.

2. (b) Accounting for long-term construction contracts allows two approaches, but only one of these alternatives appears as a possible answer. The percentage of completion method should be used unless considerable uncertainty exists about the profits or payments associated with the project.

3. (b) Net operating revenue represents all revenues earned less discounts and returns. The allowance for doubtful accounts is a balance sheet account and does not affect the recognition of revenue. The doubtful accounts expense is considered a selling expenses and not a reduction in revenue.

4. (c) Doubtful accounts *expense* represents an estimate of uncollectible credit sales. The total estimated uncollectible accounts is recorded in the allowance for uncollectible accounts. The amount actually written-off (removed from the accounts) reduces both the allowance and the balance of accounts receivable.

5. (b) Goods that have entered production are called Work-in-Process Inventory. Raw Materials Inventory represents resources before any conversion work has been done. Both Finished Goods and Cost of Goods Sold include only completed work.

6. (c) Wages and benefits of employees that work directly on the product are *direct labor*. All the other items represent manufacturing overhead costs.

7. (b) As the name implies, the LIFO method assumes that the costs of the most recently purchased items will be transferred to Cost of Goods Sold first.

8. (a) The FIFO method assumes that the costs of older inventory are transferred to Cost of Goods Sold first. The costs of the more recent purchases remain in inventory.

9. (d) The firm may use any of the methods listed. The assumed flow of costs does not have to follow the flow of the physical inventory. Although the firm's physical inventory will probably move on a last-in first-out basis, the firm could choose to report using LIFO, FIFO, or weighted average costs.

10. (a) When prices fall, the most recent purchases will have the lowest cost. The FIFO method assigns older costs (higher prices) to cost of goods sold, and therefore, this method will result in a lower net income.

11. (b) When prices rise, the most recent purchases will have the highest cost. The LIFO method assigns newer costs (higher prices) to cost of goods sold, and therefore, this method will result in a lower net income.

12. (b) Gross profit less operating expenses equals operating income.

13. (d) Net income available for commons stockholders is net income less the dividends paid to preferred shareholders.

14.   (a) Financial accounting rules require that extraordinary items be segregated on the income statement. The rules also specify that an item must be both *unusual* and *infrequent* to be considered extraordinary.

15.   (c) The projected benefit obligation is a measure of the total pension obligation that a company has. Pension benefits are the payments to retirees. Plan assets represent the amounts set aside for future pensions. In general pension and healthcare benefits provided to retirees are collectively known as deferred compensation.

Exercises:

1.   Calculating Inventory Balances for a Manufacturer. Text Exhibit 5 provides a framework for organizing the cost information and determining inventory and cost of good sold values.

a.   The inventory balances and cost of goods sold can be determined as follows:

Raw Materials Inventory	Amount
Beginning Balance	$0
Materials Purchases	250,000
Less: Materials Used in Production	75,000
Ending Balance	$175,000
Work-in-Process Inventory	
Beginning Balance	$0
Materials Used in Production	75,000
Direct Labor Costs	150,000
Overhead Costs	60,000
Less: Cost of Goods Completed *	108,000
Ending Balance	$177,000
Finished Goods Inventory	
Beginning Balance	$0
Cost of Goods Completed *	108,000
Less: Cost of Goods Sold	78,000
Ending Balance (given)	$30,000
Cost of Goods Sold (given)	$78,000

* A key calculation in completing the schedule of inventory balances is the determination of the Cost of Goods Completed. This can be initially calculated in the Finished Goods Inventory at $108,000 ($0 + $X - $78,000 = $30,000; X = $108,000). This $108,000 can then be used to determine the ending Work-in-Process Inventory balance.

b.   Perpetual or Periodic Inventory Tracking System: As a manufacturing firm, Green Briar likely uses a perpetual inventory system. Raw materials, partially completed units, and finished units are probably tracked through the accounting system as they move from one production step to the next.

2.   <u>Comparing Inventory Costing Methods.</u> Hood River Kite's cost of goods available for sale equals the beginning inventory cost plus the cost of all the kites purchased. The total cost of goods available for sale, therefore, was $5,100 ($1,500 + $1,100 + $1,200 + $1,300 = $5,100). Cost of goods sold and ending inventory under the various inventory estimation techniques are:

Method	Cost of Goods Sold	Ending Inventory
LIFO (The last 360 costs are charged to Cost of Goods Sold.)	100 x $13 = $1,300 100 x $12 = $1,200 100 x $11 = $1,100 60 x $10 = $ 600 360 $4,200 or $5,100 - $900 = $4,200	90 x $10 = $900
FIFO (The first 360 costs are charged to Cost of Goods Sold.)	10 x $13 = $ 130 100 x $12 = $1,200 100 x $11 = $1,100 150 x $10 = $1,500 360 $3,930 or $5,100 - $1,170 = $3,930	90 x $13 = $1,170
Weighted Average (Unit costs are averaged over the period.)	Average Cost = $5,100 ÷ 450 = $11.333 Cost of Goods Sold = 360 x $11.33 = $4,080	90 x $11.333 = $1,020

In each case, the total cost of goods available for sale equals $5,100 for 450 kites. The three inventory valuation methods do, however, give three different values for the 90 units remaining in inventory and the 360 units in cost of goods sold (450 available - 90 remaining = 360 sold). (The cost of goods sold and ending inventory for the weighted average method were rounded to the nearest dollar.)

3   <u>Preparing an Income Statement and Calculating Net Income.</u> Based on examples in the text and in the *Chapter Review* portion of the *Study Guide*, the income statement for the Atlantic Coast Fence Company appears at the top of the next page

The Atlantic Coast Fence Company
Income Statement
For the Most Recent Fiscal Period

Sales Revenue	$150,000
Less: Cost of Goods Sold	90,000
Gross Profit	$60,000
Less: Operating Expenses	25,000
Operating Income	$35,000
Less: Other Revenues and (Expenses)	(12,000)
Pretax Income	$23,000
Less: Income Taxes	8,050
Income Before Extraordinary Item	$14,950
Extraordinary Gain (Net of Tax Impact)	5,200
Net Income	$20,150

Sales revenue, cost of goods sold, operating expenses, and other revenues and expenses were given. Gross profit, operating income, pretax income, income taxes, and net income can be calculated from the information given. The extraordinary gain of $5,200 is presented after taxes of 35% [$8,000 - ($8,000 x 0.35) = $5,200].

Short Essays:

1. Recognizing Revenue.

One of the Rocky Mountain orders shipped on December 31st should be included in current period activity while the other order should be included in the next fiscal period. The order shipped to New Orleans -- FOB shipping point -- should be recognized as a sale in the current period because the title to the goods passed to the customer when the merchandise was shipped. If no significant uncertainties about collection exist, Rocky Mountain Trading can count this as a sale.

The order shipped to San Francisco -- FOB destination -- still belongs to Rocky Mountain and should be counted as inventory until the goods arrive in San Francisco. The order should not be recognized in current period sales revenue.

Since the sale to the San Francisco customer was erroneously included in current sales, the current sales total should be reduced by $15,000, and since the cost of the goods had already been removed from inventory, current year-end inventory should be increased by $10,000. In addition, since the cost of this merchandise had been prematurely transferred to Cost of Goods Sold, this account should be decreased by $10,000. The revised current year sales should be $1,060,000 ($1,075,000 - $15,000 = $1,060,000). The revised ending inventory should be $135,000 ($125,000 + $10,000 = $135,000).

2. Recognizing Extraordinary Items.

Extraordinary items must be both *unusual* and *infrequent*. For many firms, an earthquake would meet these two criteria. In this case, however, this event probably fails to meet the standard because of the location of the building. Foothills would be required to report these losses as operating expenses prior to the provision for income taxes.

3. Reporting Accounting Changes.

The change from the completed contract method to the percentage-of-completion method represents a change in accounting method. As a result, the firm should report the income statement effect of the change as a special item.

4. Describing the Matching Principle.

The matching principle assists in the fair presentation of revenue and expense items on the income statement. Specifically, the matching principle states that revenues and expenses associated with a specific transaction should be reported -- or matched -- on the income statement of the same fiscal period. Matching helps assure that a transaction's revenues are not recognized in one period while expenses from the transaction are reported in another.

Examples of matching include items such as estimating returns, doubtful accounts, and warranty costs. Doubtful accounts provide an important illustration. The losses from uncollectible accounts should be recognized in the same period as the revenue associated with the originating transaction. The related account receivable may not, however, prove uncollectible until some future period. In conformance to the matching principle, doubtful accounts expense should be estimated for sales that occur during a specific period and charged as an expense of that period. An uncollectible account can then be deducted from an Allowance for Doubtful Accounts without creating an expense in a future fiscal period.

5.   <u>Explaining Deferred Compensation</u>.

When a firm obligates itself to make future payments to another party, this obligation meets the definition of a liability: it represents a future economic sacrifice and should be recognized as such in the accounting records. The matching principle requires that revenues be matched with the cost of the resources consumed in the generation of the revenues (expenses). Deferred compensation is in principle not different from Wages Payable; the only difference is that Wages Payable is a current liability, while deferred compensation items may not be paid for many years. Therefore businesses should accrue the cost of deferred benefits as they are earned by working employees.

CHAPTER F13: ANALYSIS OF OPERATING ACTIVITIES

Chapter Focus

Major Theme: Operating decisions and activities are important components of the transformation process that creates value for both customers and stockholders. Using accounting information to analyze a firm's operating strategy and performance provides insight into current profitability, future prospects, and estimates of company value.

Important Elements: As you study this chapter, look for the following topics:

The importance of operating activities for creating company value
Product pricing decisions and their effect on revenue and profit
Using accounting information to evaluate operating activities
A review of the accounting system and its use in making business decisions

Learning Objectives: After studying this chapter, you should be able to:

Explain: The relationship between product pricing and sales volume in creating revenues and profit.
How operating strategy affects return on assets.
Return on equity and how operating, investing, and financing activities are interconnected.

**Define and
Explain:**   Cost leadership and product differentiation and how companies use these strategies to create profits.

Evaluate: Operating performance by using accrual and cash flow measures.

Describe: The primary components of an accounting system and how they are useful for understanding business activities.

Chapter Review

Introduction. Operating activities represent a key component of the transformation process. Overall, this process creates value and can result in both profit and growth opportunities for a company. Operating activities present managers of a firm with opportunities as well as challenges and uncertainties. Accounting information can assist decision makers in analyzing operating decisions and evaluating the results of those decisions.

1.   **Operating Decisions**. Managers make decisions that shape a firm's resulting operating activities. These operating decisions involve managing revenues, expenses, and assets.

   A.   Two important measures of operating performance are net income and return on assets.

   1.   Since <u>net income</u> equals revenues minus expenses, managers' decisions about revenues and costs and the resulting impact on activity levels determine the income of the firm.

   2.   <u>Return on assets</u> -- net income ÷ total assets -- provides an important summary measure of how well managers use assets to generate profits.

   B.   Management's actions should enhance a firm's capacity to provide value for the customer and a satisfactory return for the stockholders.

   C.   One important dimension of management's operating decisions concerns their approach to <u>sales revenue</u>.

   1.   Sales revenue is always the product of the <u>sale volume</u> and <u>sales price</u>.

   2.   Volume and price are often inversely related. Higher prices usually lead to lower volumes, and lower prices usually lead to higher volumes.

   3.   Depending on specific market circumstances, high sales revenues, however, can be associated with both combinations: high prices / low volume and low prices / high volume.

2. **Developing an Operating Strategy**. Operating strategies involve management planning about the desired profit margin and asset turnover.

   A. Remember from a prior chapter that <u>profit margin</u> measures a firm's ability to generate profit from it sales. Therefore, the profit margin formula is:

      Profit Margin = Net Income ÷ Operating Revenues

      The equation is slightly different than the one presented in earlier chapters. The term <u>operating revenues</u> appears instead of <u>sales</u>.

   B. A prior chapter also presented the concept of <u>asset turnover</u>. This ratio measures a firm's ability to use its assets to generate sales. Therefore, the asset turnover formula is:

      Asset Turnover = Operating Revenues ÷ Total Assets

      Just as with profit margin, this equation appears in a slightly different form than it did in a prior chapter. Once again, operating revenues replace sales. In many cases, however, these terms are synonymous.

   C. Once again, the profit margin and asset turnover measures may be combined to form <u>return on assets</u> as follows:

      ROA = (Net Income ÷ Operating Revenues) x
      (Operating Revenues ÷ Total Assets)
      or
      ROA = Profit Margin x Asset Turnover

   D. Operating strategies focus on generating profits through high profit margins and/or high turnovers. In many business situations, however, high profit margins with high turnovers are very hard to achieve and sustain. In many competitive markets, managers must focus on either a high margin or a high turnover approach.

3. **Interpretation of Operating Activities**. Firms that can operate both efficiently and effectively are more valuable than firms that face challenges in either or both of these areas.

   A. <u>Efficiency</u> focuses on cost controls and is measured by profit margin. <u>Effectiveness</u> emphasizes the use of assets to produce operating revenue and is measured by asset turnover.

1.   Even though firms may be quite efficient and effective, they may not all have the same profit margin or asset turnover.

2.   Various combinations of profit margins and asset turnovers create value and generate profits.

3.   To some extent, the successful combination of margin and turnover depends on both the specific market conditions faced by a firm and management's choice of strategy.

B.   Firms usually focus on either a <u>cost leadership</u> or a <u>product differentiation</u> strategy.

1.   <u>Cost leadership</u> firms compete by controlling cost carefully and offering products at low prices. These firms do not usually offer lots of personal service or special features.

2.   <u>Product differentiation</u> firms compete by offering products with special features, brand names, or superior service. These products often carry higher prices.

3.   Successful cost leadership strategies are often characterized by low profit margins and high asset turnovers.

4.   Successful product differentiation strategies are often characterized by high profit margins and low asset turnovers.

C.   Regardless of strategic emphasis, a firm must also convert its profits into cash. A helpful measure of this ability is the ratio of <u>operating cash flow to total assets</u>.

D.   Managers or analysts may use several other ratios to evaluate a firm's operating strategy.

1.   Two ratios represent more-detailed turnover measures.

a)   The <u>inventory turnover</u> measures a firm's ability to convert its inventory into sales. This ratio is the cost of goods sold from the income statement divided by the inventory balance on the balance sheet.

b)   <u>Accounts receivable turnover</u> measures a firm's ability to convert revenues into cash. This ratio is the operating revenues from the income statement divided by the accounts receivable balance from the balance sheet.

2. Two measures represent components of the profit margin.

   a) The gross profit margin measures the efficiency in the production or purchase of goods. This margin is calculated by dividing gross profit (operating revenue – cost of goods sold) by operating revenues.

   b) The operating profit margin measures the ability of a firm to control nonproduct expenses. This margin is calculated by dividing operating income by operating revenues.

E. Operating, investing, and financing activities may be linked together for an overall measure of return for the stockholders.

   1. Return on equity (ROE) provides a summary measure of the success of a company's operating, investing, and financing activities.

   2. Return on equity is the product of a firm's profit margin, asset turnover, and financial leverage. In equation form, this relationship is:

ROE = Profit Margin x Asset Turnover x Financial Leverage

or

**ROE
=
(Net Income ÷ Operating Revenues)
x
(Operating Revenues ÷ Total Assets)
x
(Total Assets ÷ Equity)
or
(Net Income ÷ Equity)**

4. **The Big Picture**. An accounting information system assists managers and investors as they make financing, investing, and operating decisions and assess the impact of those decisions.

A.   A business represents a transformation process that includes the acquisition of financial resources, the investment of financial resources in productive assets, and the operation of those assets to produce and sell goods and services to customers.

B.   An accounting system measures and reports the impact of these various transformation activities.

    1.   <u>Measurement rules</u> determine which attributes of transformation activities will be captured in the accounting system.

        a)   Using monetary standards -- such as dollars -- as the <u>measurement unit</u>, an accounting system captures <u>historical cost</u> information on an <u>accrual basis</u>.

        b)   Revenues and expenses for specific events are <u>matched</u> and associated with specific <u>fiscal periods</u>. This process often requires <u>estimation</u>, and accounting estimates can often be quite <u>conservative</u>.

    2.   <u>Processing and storage procedures</u> determine how information is entered, stored, and summarized within an accounting system.

        a)   A traditional approach -- <u>double-entry bookkeeping</u> -- records transactions in two or more accounts that are grouped into five major categories: assets, liabilities, owners' equity, revenues, and expenses.

        b)   The <u>accounting cycle</u> provides a process for summarizing accounting information related to various steps of the transformation process.

            (1)   Specific aspects of the accounting cycle include: design and use of source documents, entry of data into the accounting database, retrieval of data in various formats, end-of-period adjustments, preparation of financial statements, and closing the books.

            (2)   In most modern accounting systems, many these steps are performed by computer programs.

(3) In both manual and automated accounting systems, <u>internal control</u> procedures assure the reliability of the information in the accounting systems.

3. <u>Reporting rules</u> determine the type, amount, and format of accounting information reported publicly.

a) These rules require companies to report enough information to permit users to be fully informed about the firms' financial activities.

b) <u>Financial statements</u> include the <u>income statement</u>, the <u>balance sheet</u>, the <u>statement of cash flows</u>, and often, the <u>statement of stockholders' equity</u>. These are accompanied by <u>notes to the financial statements</u> and an <u>audit report</u> from an independent auditor.

C. These financial statements provide important information about financing, investing, and operating activities.

1. Information about financing activities includes a firm's capital structure and specific information about various categories of debt and equity. This information helps decision makers determine the extent of the firm's financial leverage as well as the cash flow implications of specific forms of financing.

2. Information about investing activities identifies the types of assets owned by a firm and the changes in those assets over time. From these disclosures, decision makers can determine the degree of operating leverage a firm employs.

3. Information about operating activities provides decision makers with specific data on a firm's operating efficiency and effectiveness. This information is helpful in assessing both profitability and cash flows.

D. Accounting information contributes to an overall understanding of company value. The value of a firm is based on its profitability, revenues and expenses, asset base, and capital structure. All this information is presented in the summary financial statements.

Review Questions, Exercises, and Short Essays

<u>Multiple Choice Questions</u>: These questions reinforce vocabulary and basic concepts from the chapter. In each case, select the answer you believe to be the *best*.

1. What strategy(ies) is (are) available to manage the relationship between product pricing and sales volume?
    a.   A financial leverage strategy.
    b.   A cost leadership strategy.
    c.   A product differentiation strategy.
    d.   Both cost leadership and product differentiation are possible strategies.

2. A cost leadership strategy requires all of the following *except*:
    a.   Close attention to costs.
    b.   A high sales volume.
    c.   A high asset turnover.
    d.   A high profit margin.

3. The *asset turnover ratio* is a measure of:
    a.   The profitability of a company.
    b.   The ability to use assets to generate sales.
    c.   The ability to turn sales transactions into profits.
    d.   The financial leverage of a company.

4. *Effectiveness* and *efficiency* -- in *this* order -- can be measured by:
    a.   Asset turnover and profit margin.
    b.   Profit margin and asset turnover.
    c.   Return on assets and return on equity.
    d.   Return on equity and return on assets.

5. Successful companies will generally pursue strategies of:
    a.   Focusing only on profit margin.
    b.   Focusing only on sales.
    c.   Focusing only on asset turnover.
    d.   Focusing on either a high profit margin or a high asset turnover.

6. Wal-Mart is a very successful retailer known for low prices. Which of the following statements would you expect would describe Wal-Mart's strategy?
    a.   High profit margin; low asset turnover.
    b.   High profit margin; high asset turnover.
    c.   Low profit margin; high asset turnover.
    d.   Low profit margin; low asset turnover.

7. Disney is a very successful entertainment company. One of the company's great assets is the Disney trademark. Which of the following strategies would you expect Disney to use?
   a. Product differentiation.
   b. Cost leadership.
   c. High asset turnover.
   d. Low profit margin.

8. Which measure allows the comparison among firms of cash flows generated by assets that are used to produce and sell goods and services?
   a. Cash flow from operations.
   b. Investing cash flows.
   c. Ratio of operating cash flows to total assets.
   d. Earnings per share.

9. The *return on assets (ROA)* may be calculated by:
   a. Asset turnover divided by profit margin.
   b. Asset turnover times profit margin.
   c. Profit margin divided by asset turnover.
   d. Asset turnover times financial leverage.

10. A measure of the *effectiveness* of a company in selling its inventory is:
    a. Accounts receivable turnover.
    b. Gross profit margin.
    c. Operating profit margin.
    d. Inventory turnover.

11. A measure of the *effectiveness* of a company in converting sales to cash is:
    a. Accounts receivable turnover.
    b. Gross profit margin.
    c. Operating profit margin.
    d. Inventory turnover

12. A measure of the *efficiency* of a company in the production or purchase of goods for sale is:
    a. Accounts receivable turnover.
    b. Gross profit margin.
    c. Operating profit margin.
    d. Inventory turnover

13.   A measure of the *efficiency* of a company in controlling operating costs other than product costs is:
    a.   Accounts receivable turnover.
    b.   Gross profit margin.
    c.   Operating profit margin.
    d.   Inventory turnover

14.   *Return on equity* can be calculated by which of the following equations? :
    a.   Return on Assets x Financial Leverage.
    b.   Profit Margin x Asset Turnover x Financial Leverage.
    c.   Return on Assets x (Assets ÷ Equity).
    d.   All of these equations can be used to determine return on equity.

15.   A company's value is largely determined by:
    a.   Primarily operating activities.
    b.   Primarily investing activities.
    c.   Primarily financing activities.
    d.   The interaction and success of all three activities.

<u>Exercises</u>: These questions require the analysis of economic situations and the application of accounting concepts.

1. <u>Calculating Asset Turnover, Profit Margin, Return on Assets, and Return on Equity</u>. During the most recent fiscal period, the Columbia Basin Corporation had sales of $1,800,000 and incurred expenses of $1,710,000. The firm had total assets of $600,000, and total equity of $400,000.

    a.   Calculate the following performance measures for this fiscal period.

        (1)   Asset Turnover.

        (2)   Profit Margin.

        (3)   Return on Assets.

        (4)   Assets to Equity Ratio.

        (5)   Return on Equity.

    b.   Briefly explain why ROE and ROA results differ.

2.   <u>Analyzing Operating Performance</u>. The following table presents selected 1998 and 1999 financial information for two corporations that are significant participants in the market for computer processors.

- **Intel** is the largest and most significant producer of processors for microcomputers.

- **Motorola** has a significant presence in the microprocessor market but produces a wider line of consumer and industrial electronic devices.

Selected Financial Information
(In $1,000,000's except EPS)

Financial Data	Intel		Motorola	
	1999	**1998**	**1999**	**1998**
Sales	26,273	29,389	30,931	29,398
Operating Income	8,379	9,767	1,097	822
Total Assets	31,471	38,938	37,327	28,728
Shareholders' Equity	23,578	29,443	16,344	12,222
Cost of Sales	12,088	11,836	19,169	18,043
Total Inventories	1,582	1,626	3,422	3,745
Accounts Receivable	3,527	3,494	5,125	5,057
EPS from Operations	2.51	2.94	1.76	1.37

Sources: SEC Form 10-K and company annual financial reports.

a.   Because Motorola reported the effects of a corporate restructuring, net income for 1998 includes a large reduction for costs of the restructuring. So as not to include this in your analysis, use sales to represent operating revenues, and operating income to represent net income and calculate the profit margin, asset turnover, financial leverage (assets ÷ equity), return on equity, and return on assets for the two firms for each year.

Measures	Intel		Motorola	
	1999	**1998**	**1999**	**1998**
Profit Margin				
Asset Turnover				
Financial Leverage				
Return on Equity				
Return on Assets				

b. Use the information about the two firms on the previous page to calculate inventory turnover and accounts receivable turnover for the firms.

Ratio	1999	1998
Intel		
Inventory Turnover		
Accounts Receivable Turnover		
Motorola		
Inventory Turnover		
Accounts Receivable Turnover		

c. What can you conclude about Intel and Motorola based on the information calculated in the previous parts of this exercise?

3. <u>Analyzing Company Attributes</u>. The following table provides summary financial information about American Airlines and Continental Airlines for the 1997-1999 time period. Using this data, analyze and compare these firms based on ROA (asset turnover and profit margin), ROE (ROA and financial leverage), and growth rates.

Company and Specific Measures	1999	1998	1997
American Airlines			
Asset Turnover	0.727	0.861	0.888
Debt to Equity Ratio	2.55	2.33	2.36
Profit Margin	5.6%	6.8%	5.3%
Return on Assets	4.0%	5.9%	4.7%
Return on Equity	14.4%	19.6%	15.8%
Shareholders' Equity ($1,000,000s)	6,858	6,698	6,216
Market Value of Equity ($1,000,000s)*	5,590	7,256	5,143
Outstanding Shares (1,000,000s)	148.2	161.4	173.2
Growth Rates, 1997-1999:			
Revenues	-.2.2%		
Net Income	0.0%		
EPS	52%		
Continental Airlines			
Asset Turnover	1.05	1.12	1.24
Debt to Equity Ratio	4.26	4.94	5.4
Profit Margin	5.6%	4.8%	5.3%
Return on Assets	5.9%	5.4%	6.6%
Return on Equity	30.4%	32.1%	42.0%
Shareholders' Equity ($1,000,000s)	1,593	1,193	916
Market Value of Equity ($1,000,000s)*	2,194	1,912	1,892
Outstanding Shares (1,000,000s)	65.5	64.4	58.9
Growth Rates 1997-1999:			
Revenues	9.4%		
Net Income	12.2%		
EPS	11.4%		

Source: SEC Form 10K

[* The market value of equity is the total market value of all of the companies' common shares. (Number of Shares x Price per Share = Total Market Value of Equity)]

Short Essays: The following short essay questions not only reinforce important concepts but also give you a chance to practice writing skills. Answer these questions in complete sentences.

1.   Linking ROA, Financial Leverage, and ROE. Explain the relationships among ROA, financial leverage, ROE.

2.   Comparing Operating Strategies. Compare an operating strategy that focuses on asset turnover with one that focuses on profit margin. Why might these two strategies be considered opposites?

3.   <u>Discussing the Relationships Among Financing, Investing, and Operating Activities</u>. How are financing, investing, and operating activities interconnected?

4.   <u>Explaining the Use of Accounting Information to Evaluate Company Value</u>. How can accounting information be used to evaluate a firm's value?

5.   <u>Summarizing the Accounting Information System</u>. Identify the major components of an accounting information system and summarize their functions.

Solutions to Review Questions, Exercises, and Short Essays

Multiple Choice:

1.   (d) Depending on the nature of the market, characteristics of the firm, and specific products, management may adopt either a cost leadership strategy or a product differentiation strategy.

2.   (d) A cost leadership strategy depends on a firm's ability to offer lower prices to customers. This approach would not generally include a high profit margin.

3.   (b) The *asset turnover* measures the ability of the company to effectively use its assets to generate sales. Other performance measures capture information on profitability, the link between income and sales, and financial leverage.

4.   (a) The asset turnover measures the *effectiveness* of a firm's operation -- the level of sales that can be generated by a specific level of assets. The profit margin measures *efficiency* of an organization -- the profitability of each sale.

5.   (d) Most successful companies focus on a strategy of either high profit margin -- high prices with low sales volumes -- or a high asset turnover -- low prices and high sales volumes.

6.   (c) According to the information in the text comparing Wal-Mart, K-Mart and McDonald's, Wal-Mart has a high return on assets resulting from a high asset turnover and low profit margin. The company is known for low prices and high volume operations.

7.   (a) Disney has established one of the best know brand names in the world. Disney can use the power of this brand with a product differentiation strategy. The products are differentiated by the name *Disney*. Disney would maintain a relatively high profit margin and relatively low asset turnover.

8.   (c) The assets that are used for production and sales are operating assets. Therefore, cash flow from operations is a good measure of the effectiveness with which these assets are employed. However, to compare firms -- especially those of different sizes, the ratio of operating cash flows to total assets represents the appropriate measure.

9.   (b) The return on assets (ROA) can be determined by multiplying the profit margin times the asset turnover. In equation form: (Net Income ÷ Total Assets) = (Net Income ÷ Operating Revenues) x (Operating Revenues ÷ Total Assets).

10.   (d) The inventory turnover is a measure of a company's ability to move its inventory. The inventory turnover measures how many times a company sold the equivalent of its entire inventory in a year.

11.   (a) The accounts receivable turnover ratio is defined as operating revenues divided by accounts receivable. It measures the ability of a company to collect its revenues.

12.   (b) The gross profit margin is the ratio of gross profit to operating revenues. Therefore, it measures the percentage of sales dollars that remain after deducting the cost of goods sold.

13,   (c) Operating profit margin is a measure of the ability of a company to control selling and administrative costs. It measures the percentage of sales dollars that remain after deducting both cost of goods sold and operating expenses.

14.   (d) Return on equity is a product of return on assets and financial leverage. Return on assets is itself a product of profit margin and asset turnover. Financial leverage can be measured as assets divided by equity.

15.   (d) Company value is determined by complex interactions among operating, investing, and financing activities. Profits, revenues and expenses, asset base, and capital structure determine the value of a company.

Exercises:

1.   Calculating Asset Turnover, Profit Margin, Return on Assets, and Return on Equity. This exercise provides an opportunity to determine and make comments on the basic ratios and performance measures described in the chapter.

      a.   Calculating Measure: Using the Columbia Basin Corporation information, the following performance measures may be calculated:

          (1) Asset Turnover = Operating Revenues ÷ Total Assets:

              $1,800,000 / $600,000 = 3.00

          (2) Profit Margin = Net Income ÷ Operating Revenues:

              Operating Revenues - Expenses = Net Income
              $1,800,000 - $1,710,000 = $90,000

              $90,000 ÷ $1,800,000 = 0.05 or 5%

          (3) Return on Assets = Net Income ÷ Total Assets

              $90,000 ÷ $600,000 = 0.15 or 15%

              or

              Asset Turnover x Profit Margin
              3.00 x 0.05 = 0.15 or 15%

          (4) Asset to Equity Ratio:

              $600,000 ÷ $400,000 = 1.50

          (5) Return on Equity = Net Income ÷ Equity

              $90,000 ÷ $400,000 = 0.225 or 22.5%

              or

              Asset Turnover x Profit Margin x Assets to Equity Ratio
              3.00 x 0.05 x 1.50 = .0225 = 22.5%

b. The ROE differs from the ROA because of the financial leverage. If the firm has $600,000 in assets and only $400,000 in equity, the difference of $200,000 must be debt financing.

2. <u>Analyzing Operating Performance</u>. Performance measures such as asset turnover, profit margin, ROA, and ROE can be used to compare the performance of firms within an industry.

a. Performance Measures for the two Firms: The following equations were used to calculate comparative performance measures for Intel and Motorola.

Profit Margin = Net Income ÷ Sales

Asset Turnover = Sales ÷ Total Assets

Financial Leverage = Asset to Equity Ratio = Total Assets ÷ Equity

Return on Equity = Asset Turnover x Profit Margin x Financial Leverage

or Return on Equity = Operating Income ÷ Equity

Return on Assets = Asset Turnover x Profit Margin

or Return on Assets = Operating Income ÷ Total Assets

The performance results appear in the following table:

Measures	*Intel*		*Motorola*	
	1999	*1998*	*1999*	*1998*
Profit Margin	33.2%	31.9%	3.5%	2.8%
Asset Turnover	0.75	0.83	0.83	1.02
Financial Leverage	1.32	1.33	2.28	2.35
Return on Equity	33.2%	35.5%	6.7%	6.7%
Return on Assets	25.1%	26.6%	2.9%	2.9%

(Note: Some final results have been slightly rounded. In addition, final results may differ depending on the specific formula used and the degree of rounding in component calculations.)

b. Calculating Inventory and Receivables Turnover: The inventory turnover and accounts receivable turnover for the three firms were computed using the following formulas:

Inventory Turnover = Cost of Goods Sold ÷ Inventory

Accounts Receivable Turnover = Operating Revenues ÷ Accounts Receivable

The turnover results appear in the table that follows:

Ratio	1999	1998
Intel		
Inventory Turnover	7.28	7.64
Accounts Receivable Turnover	8.41	7.45
Motorola		
Inventory Turnover	5.60	4.82
Accounts Receivable Turnover	6.04	5.81

c.   Analyzing Company Performance: The information on Intel and Motorola provides some interesting comparisons.

The firms operate in the same or similar markets. However, while Intel specializes in the production of computer microprocessors, Motorola is a more diversified electronics manufacturer. Intel is the market leader in microcomputer processors with a widely recognized brand and well-established patents. Motorola is the third largest producer of semiconductors and was once the leading producer of mobile telephones, a position it has lost to the Finnish firm Nokia.

Asset Turnover: In 1998 Motorola appeared to be generating the most revenue with its assets. In 1999, however, Motorola's asset turnover slipped, because, while sales increased, the total investment in the company increased more.

Profit Margin: Intel has the highest profit margin. The two years reflect a period during which price competition in microprocessors and consumer electronics was fierce. Given this environment, it might be expected that Intel's brand name recognition and dominance of the processor market for personal computers would allow it to generate greater profits. Motorola's profit margin was quite low. Perhaps in response to profitability pressures, Motorola announced in 1998 a restructuring of the firm, reducing the number of employees by 18,000 and reducing costs by an estimated $750 million. Note that Motorola became more profitable in 1999, perhaps reflecting the corporate restructuring.

ROA: ROA is the product of profit margin and asset turnover. ROA declined for Intel reflecting the trends discussed above, while Motorola held its position.

ROE: In 1999, Intel managed a 33% return on equity. Again, the strength of the Pentium brand allowed Intel to maintain a good positive return. Motorola's ROE remained relatively low, 6.7% in both years.

Asset to Equity Ratio: The nature of the firms' operations is reflected in the decisions made about financial leverage. Motorola has the most diversified product line and so should have a more stable revenue stream. It can afford to use more financial leverage. Intel is more dependent on relatively few products, and these products must be frequently adapted to new demands. It is a riskier business, and as a result, one expects more variable revenue streams. Intel has, therefore, chosen not to magnify the variability of revenue with much financial leverage.

Inventory Turnover. One component of asset turnover is inventory turnover. A high inventory turnover indicates high sales relative to inventory and effective use of current assets invested in inventory. Intel had the higher inventory turnover for the two-year period. Motorola improved somewhat, but its performance lagged the other firm.

Accounts Receivable Turnover. Accounts receivable turnover represents another component of asset turnover. High turnover measures in this area indicate that a firm is effective in collecting accounts receivable -- converting sales into cash inflows. Once again, Intel leads with accounts receivable turnovers exceeding 7.0 for both years. Motorola has a lower receivables turnover, but has shown some improvement.

3.   Analyzing Company Attributes and Value. The information on American Airlines and Continental Airlines provides some interesting comparisons. Both firms compete in the same industry, but their strategic approaches and operating performances are different. American is the second largest air carrier in the U.S. Continental is much smaller and has a turbulent history, having declared bankruptcy in the early 1980s and again in the early 1990s. This analysis compares the firms on criteria such as asset turnover, profit margin, ROA, ROE, financial leverage, market value of equity, and growth rates.

Asset Turnover: Continental appears to be using assets more effectively over the three years. The 1998 asset turnovers are 1.05 for Continental and .71 for American.

Profit Margin: Over the three years, the profit margins are similar for both firms. In 1998, American edged slightly ahead of Continental.

ROA: Continental has a higher return on assets, suggesting more efficient utilization of its fleet.

Debt to Equity Ratio: Financial leverage can also be evaluated by comparing the ratio of debt to equity for both firms. The debt to equity ratio for Continental fell over the three-year period, but Continental is still far more leveraged, reflecting a debt burden taken on the early 1980s. This debt burden twice forced the company into bankruptcy reorganization proceedings, but, today, in a more favorable climate, this leverage seems to help the company sustain a higher ROE

ROE: Continental has a significantly higher ROE, but it has decreased. Notice that the debt to equity ratio may account for the higher ROE. Whether the decline in ROE results from interest rate changes or from operating factors requires additional analysis.

Market-to-Book Ratio: The previous performance measures suggest that Continental is riskier but may be attractive to investors because of a higher ROE. The market-to-book ratio shows that the market reached a similar conclusion.

The market-to-book ratio compares the market value of a firm's stock to the book value of the stock. This ratio was discussed in a prior chapter. High ratios -- where total market value significantly exceeds total book value -- indicate that investors place a high value on the firm.

The ratios for American and Continental are:

Market-to-Book Ratio = Total Market Value of Stock ÷ Total Shareholders' Equity
American = $5,590 ÷ $6,858 = 0.81
Continental = $2,194 ÷ $1,593 = 1.38

Continental's ratio is 1.38 compared with 0.81 for American. The factors below provide some additional perspective.

Growth: Continental came out of its bankruptcy reorganization a smaller and nimbler firm. It focused on profitable routes and competed strongly on price. As a result it grew rapidly. This difference in income growth and the resulting difference in the growth of cash flows likely affect investor attitudes and, therefore, the market value to book value ratio. Note, however, that if fuel costs increase and/or interest rates increase, Continental could once again find itself experiencing financial difficulties.

While these historical performance measures provide important information, the key issue facing current and prospective investors focuses on the future performance of these firms and the resulting changes in company value.

Short Essays:

1.   Linking ROA, Financial Leverage, and ROE.

Combining profit margin and asset turnover, return on assets (ROA) measures the efficiency and effectiveness of a company's investing and operating activities. Alternatively, financial leverage results from a firm's financing activities. The use of debt in a company's capital structure will increase the return on equity when the profit margin and return on assets are positive. If profit margin and return on assets are negative, however, financial leverage will result in an even greater negative return on equity. ROE is the product of profit margin, asset turnover, and financial leverage, and thus, this measure summarizes the impact of financing, investing, and operating activities.

2.   Comparing Operating Strategies.

Management approaches that focus on high asset turnover are often considered the opposite of those that focus on high profit margins. A company focusing on high asset turnover would accept lower prices in order to generate a larger volume of sales with a given amount of assets. These firms often follow a cost leadership strategy. Alternatively, a firm focusing on profit margin would concentrate on product differentiation strategy and higher pricing policies. Since firms must often lower prices to achieve a higher turnover or sacrifice turnover to achieve higher profit margin, the two approaches are often considered opposites.

3.   Discussing the Relationships Among Financing, Investing, and Operating Activities.

Financing activities provide the resources with which to invest and operate. Financing activities involving debt and equity transactions build the liabilities and owners' equity sections of a firm's balance sheet. These resources are subsequently invested in long-term assets, and these investing activities build the long-term asset portion of the balance sheet and the productive assets an organization will use in operations. Once the assets are in place, operating activities provide value for customers and ultimately for stockholders as well. Operating activities are summarized on a firm's income statement.

One formula for return on equity expresses the importance of financing, investing, and operating activities to the success of a company. The equation reminds managers and investors that return on equity is the product of profit margin, asset turnover, and financial leverage.

4.   Explaining the Use of Accounting Information to Evaluate Performance.

Accounting measures summarize the results of the transformation process: a firm's financing. investing, and operating decisions and activities. These activities result in returns to investors in the form of dividends or increases in retained earnings. These returns to investors, their growth, and the associated risk ultimately determine the value of the firm. An accounting system measures and reports these returns to managers as well as current and potential investors. Properly understood, accounting information provides important information about the decisions and activities that create firm value.

5.   Summarizing the Accounting Information System.

An accounting information system consists of several components: a set of measuring rules, a processing and storage system, reporting rules, and financial reports. The measuring rules determine what, when, and how decisions and activities are recognized in an accounting system. These measurement rules attempt to capture the essence of the firm's underlying economic events. These measurements are stored in the accounting system and reported periodically to users according to a set of reporting rules that determine what, when, and how summaries are presented. This summary information influences managers" and investors' decisions that are made about future financing, investing, and operating activities.

CHAPTER 1
ACCOUNTING AND ORGANIZATIONS

EXERCISES

E1-2

Transaction	Amount of Check	Amount of Deposit	Balance
Balance on August 1			$400
a.			
b.			
c.			
d.			
e.			

Freddy's Checking Account Summary of Deposits and Payments For August			
Beginning cash balance			
Cash deposits:			
Cash payments:			
Excess of payments over deposits			
Ending cash balance			

E1-8

Mario's Restaurant Profit Earned For February		

E1-9

The Quick Stop Profit Earned For March		

E1-10

Pam Lucas's Paper Route Profit Earned For May		

E1-19

Activity	Ford	Wal-Mart	Humana

PROBLEMS

P1-2   A.

Date	Check Number	Checks Issued, Withdrawals, and Deposits	Amount of Deposit	Amount of Check/ Withdrawal	Balance
May 1		Opening balance			784

P1-2 (continued)

B.

Computer Consultant Company Summary of Cash Deposits and Payments For May 2002			
Beginning cash balance			
Add Deposits:			
Deduct Cash payments			
Increase in cash during May			
Ending cash balance			

C. _____

_____

_____

_____

_____

_____

_____

_____

_____

_____

_____

_____

_____

_____

_____

P1-2 (concluded)

D.

P1-3   A.

T. Edison Summary of Deposits and Payments For September			
Beginning cash balance			
Cash deposits:			
Total cash deposited			
Cash payments			
Total cash paid			
Excess of deposits over payments			
Ending cash balance			

P1-3 (concluded)

B.

C.

D.

P1-6   A.

Date	Check Number	Checks Issued, Withdrawals, and Deposits	Amount of Deposit	Amount of Check/ Withdrawal	Balance
Oct 1		Opening balance			387

P1-6 (concluded)

B.

Buildings-R-Us Summary of Cash Deposits and Payments For October 2001			
Beginning cash balance			
Add Deposits:			
Deduct Cash payments			
Increase in cash during October			
Ending cash balance			

C.

P1-9

Harry Honda Car Dealership Profit Earned For July		

P1-11   A.

Tender Sender Company Profit Earned For February 2002		

B.

P1-13

A.

_____

_____

_____

_____

_____

_____

_____

_____

_____

_____

_____

_____

_____

_____

_____

_____

_____

_____

_____

_____

_____

B.

CHECK REGISTER
BETSY'S FLAG CO.

Date	Check Number	Check Issued/ Deposit Received	Amount of Deposit	Amount of Check	Balance

P1-17

A. _____

_____

_____

_____

_____

_____

_____

B. _____

_____

_____

_____

_____

_____

C.

Surf-The-Net.com Schedule of Cash Received and Paid For October		

CHAPTER 2

INFORMATION IN ORGANIZATIONS

EXERCISES

E2-9

a. Decision to buy new production machinery.	
b. Decision to change the mix in a chemical compound used to produce a synthetic fiber to reduce the cost of the product.	
c. Decision to replace a factory that is no longer efficient.	
d. Decision to retrain workers to enhance long-run productivity.	
e. Decision to open retail stores in a foreign country.	
f. Decision to count goods for sale to verify inventory records.	
g. Decision to sell a production plant that is no longer profitable.	
h. Decision to survey customers to determine their satisfaction with a company's products.	

E2-11

Activity	Component

E2-14

a.	Accounts Receivable		i.	Cost of Goods Sold	
b.	Accounts Payable		j.	Interest Expense	
c.	Sales		k.	Notes Payable	
d.	Cash		l.	Retained Earnings	
e.	Merchandise		m.	Supplies Expense	
f.	Display Equipment		n.	Utilities Expense	
g.	Leather (materials)		o.	Wages Expense	
h.	Common Stock		p.	Wages Payable	

E2-15

Assets =		Liabilities + Owner's Equity	

E2-16

Christmas Cookie Company Income Statement For December		

Schedule of Resources Acquired and Resources Consumed		

E2-17

RESOURCES:		OPERATIONS:	
Assets Acquired:		Revenues:	
		Expenses:	
Assets Consumed:			
Total Assets		Net Income	
FINANCES:			
Creditors:			
Owner's Investment:			
Retained Earnings:			
Total Finances			

E2-18

Item	Account	Cash	+ Other Assets	= Liabilities	+ Equity	+ Revenues	− Expenses
		Balance Sheet Accounts				Income Statement Accounts	
	Beginning balances	0	0	0	0	0	0
a.	Cash	10,000					
	Owner's Investment				10,000		
b.							
c.							
d.							
e.							
f.							
g.							

E2-21

(1)

Item	Account	Cash	+ Other Assets	= Liabilities	+ Equity	+ Revenues	– Expenses
a.							
b.							
c.							
d.							
e.							
f.							
g.							
h.							
i.							
j.							

Table header spanning: **Balance Sheet Accounts** (Cash, + Other Assets, = Liabilities, + Equity) | **Income Statement Accounts** (+ Revenues, – Expenses)

E2-21 (concluded)

(2)

Amelio's Law Firm Income Statement For the First Week of February		

E2-22

(1)

Item	Account	Balance Sheet Accounts				Income Statement Accounts	
		Cash	+ Other Assets	= Liabilities	+ Equity	+ Revenues	− Expenses
	Beginning balances	26,800	37,500	19,200	45,100	0	0
a.							
b.							
c.							
d.							
e.							
f.							
g.							
h.							
i.							

E2-22 (concluded)

Item	Account	Balance Sheet Accounts				Income Statement Accounts	
		Cash	+ Other Assets	= Liabilities	+ Equity	+ Revenues	– Expenses
j.							
	Ending balances						

(2)

Larissa Enterprises Income Statement First Week of June		

(3)

Larissa Enterprises Balance Sheet End of First Week in June			

PROBLEMS

P2-8

A.

Date: Jan 12 Product	(a) Today's sales	(b) Expected sales tomorrow	(c) Current Inventory System count	(d) Current Inventory Hand count	(e) Units to be Ordered System order	(f) Units to be Ordered Revised order
Milk: Whole, gallon	282	310	27	26	315	
Whole, ½ gallon	455	486	41	40	490	
Whole, quart	188	166	23	23	160	
2%, gallon	389	413	38	40	415	
2%, ½ gallon	533	545	46	5	510	
2%, quart	202	164	18	18	160	
Skim, gallon	330	376	45	46	365	
Skim, ½ gallon	501	538	64	62	520	
Skim, quart	175	146	22	84	140	
Buttermilk, quart	133	140	20	21	135	
Chocolate milk, qt.	119	122	15	15	120	

B.

P2-8 (concluded)

C.
_____

_____

_____

_____

_____

_____

_____

_____

_____

_____

_____

_____

_____

_____

D.
_____

_____

_____

_____

_____

P2-11

A.

Date	Account	Balance Sheet Accounts				Income Statement Accounts	
		Cash	+ Other Assets	= Liabilities	+ Equity	+ Revenues	− Expenses
	Beginning Balance	0	0	0	0	0	0
6/1							
6/2							
6/7							
6/12							
6/26							
6/30							
	Ending Balance						

P2-11 (continued)

B.

Davidson Enterprises Income Statement Month of June		

C.

Davidson Enterprises Balance Sheet June 30			

P2-11 (concluded)
D.

Date	Account	Balance Sheet Accounts				Income Statement Accounts	
		Cash	+ Other Assets	= Liabilities	+ Equity	+ Revenues	– Expenses
	Balances before closing entry						
	Ending balances after closing entry						

P2-12
A.

_____
_____
_____
_____
_____

B.

_____
_____
_____
_____
_____
_____
_____
_____
_____
_____
_____
_____
_____

P2-12 (concluded)

C.

Van de Hay Farm Store Income Statement Month of January		

D.

Van de Hay Farm Store Balance Sheet January 31, 2002			

P2-14

A.

P2-14 (concluded)

		Balance Sheet Accounts				Income Statement Accounts	
Item	Account	Cash	+ Other Assets	= Liabilities	+ Equity	+ Revenues	− Expenses
	Beginning balances	0	0	0	0	0	0
1.	Cash	2,150					
	Investment by Owner				2,150		
2.							
3.							
4.							
5.							
6.							
7.							
8.							

P2-15

A.

Date	Account	Balance Sheet Accounts				Income Statement Accounts	
		Cash	+ Other Assets	= Liabilities	+ Equity	+ Revenues	– Expenses
	Beginning balances	0	0	0	0	0	0
6/1	Cash	650					
	Note Payable—Dad			450			
	Investment by Owner				200		
6/2							
6/3							
6/16							
6/18							
6/23							
6/30							
6/30							
6/30							

P2-15 (concluded)

B.

Randi's Lawnmowing Service Income Statement For June		

C.

Randi's Lawnmowing Service Balance Sheet June 30			

D.

P2-19

A.

Item	Account	Balance Sheet				Income Statement	
		Cash	+ Other Assets	= Liabilities	+ Equity	+ Revenues	– Expenses
1.							
2.							
3.							
4.							
5.							
6.							
7.							
8.							
9.							
10.							

P2-19 (concluded)

B.

Your Business Income Statement For the First Month		

C.

Your Business Balance Sheet End of the First Month			

CHAPTER 3
ACCOUNTING MEASUREMENT

EXERCISES

E3-7

	Cash Flow for September	Cash Flow in Future	Sales Revenue for September
Cash from prior sales			
Cash from September sales			
Total cash received in September			

E3-8

	Cash Flow for June	Cash Flow in July	Wages Expense for June
Cash paid for prior wages			
Cash paid for June wages			
Total cash paid in June for wages			

E3-10

	January	February	March	Total for Quarter
Cash paid for interest				
Interest expense				

E3-11

	2001	2002	2003	Total for 3 Years
Cash paid for equipment				
Depreciation expense				

E3-12

	April	May	June	Total for 3 Months
Cash paid for utilities				
Utilities expense				

E3-13

	Past Cash Flow	April Cash Flow	Future Cash Flow	April Revenues/ Expenses
Cash received for April sales		$180,000	$50,000	$230,000
Cash paid for resources consumed in April: Merchandise Wages Equipment	−$30,000 −40,000	−$60,000 −20,000 0	−$10,000 −6,000 0	
Net cash increase in April				
Net income for April				

E3-13 (concluded)

_____

_____

_____

_____

_____

_____

_____

_____

_____

_____

_____

E3-14

a.

	Past	September	Future	Total
Revenues				
Expenses				
Cash received				
Cash paid				

b.

	Past	September	Future	Total
Revenues				
Expenses				
Cash received				
Cash paid				

c.

	Past	September	Future	Total
Revenues				
Expenses				
Cash received				
Cash paid				

E3-14 (concluded

d.

	Past	September	Future	Total
Revenues				
Expenses				
Cash received				
Cash paid				

e.

	Past	September	Future	Total
Revenues				
Expenses				
Cash received				
Cash paid				

E3-15

	Company A	Company B	Company C
Cash received from customers during 2001	$300,000	$625,000	
Sales revenue for 2001	$352,500	$580,000	$260,000
Accounts receivable at beginning of 2001	$31,000		$35,000
Accounts receivable at end of 2001		$85,000	$53,000

E3-16

a. Advertising expenses	
b. Wages for factory workers	
c. Wages for management	
d. Commissions for sales staff	
e. Depreciation on factory equipment	
f. Depreciation on office equipment	
g. Materials used in production	
h. Merchandise purchased for resale	
i. Utilities used by management facilities	
j. Utilities used by a factory	

E3-18

Item	Account	Balance Sheet Accounts				Income Statement Accounts	
		Cash	+ Other Assets	= Liabilities	+ Equity	+ Revenues	− Expenses
	Beginning Balances	0	0	0	0	0	0
A.							
B.							
C.							
D.							
E.							
F.							
G.							
	Ending Balances						

E3-20

_____ Buildings

_____ Supplies

_____ Cash

_____ Equipment

_____ Accounts Receivable

_____ Patents

_____ Inventory

E3-21

_____ Notes Payable

_____ Wages Payable

_____ Unearned Revenues

_____ Interest Payable

_____ Accounts Payable

_____ Bonds Payable

_____ Rent Payable

_____ Insurance Payable

PROBLEMS

P3-1

A.

		Balance Sheet Accounts				Income Statement Accounts	
Date	Account	Cash	+ Other Assets	= Liabilities	+ Equity	+ Revenues	– Expenses
	Beginning Balance	0	0	0	0	0	0
5/20	CASH	3,000					
	OWNERS, EQUITY				3,000		
5/30	LICENSE EXPENSE						-1,000
	CASH	-1,000					
6/15	RENT EXP.						-900
	CASH	-300					
	RENT PAYABLE			600			
8/1	RENT PAYABLE			-600			
	CASH	-600					
Oct	CASH	22,400					
	SALES REVENUE					22,400	
	SIGN EXPENSE						-5,179
	CASH	-5,179					
	Ending Balance	17,521	0	0	3,000	22,400	-7,079

P3-1 (continued)

B.

Yummy Dogs Company Income Statement May 20 through October 31		

C.

Yummy Dogs Company Net cash Flow From Operations May 20 through October 31		

P3-1 (concluded)

D.

E.

P3-2

A.

Peaceful Rest Funeral Home Balance Sheet at April 30			

Peaceful Rest Funeral Home Income Statement For the Month of April		

B.

P3-2 (concluded)

C.

_____
_____
_____
_____
_____
_____
_____
_____

D.

_____
_____
_____
_____
_____
_____
_____
_____
_____
_____
_____

P3-4

A.

Caldwell Furniture Repair Income Statement For March		

P3-4 (concluded)

B.

C.

P3-7

A.

Event	Revenue, Expense, or Cash Flow?	Month of February	Month of March	Month of April	Month of May	Month of June
1.	Expense Cash Flow	-0- -0-	$1,200 -0-	$1,200 3,600	$1,200 -0-	-0- -0-
2.						
3.						
4.						
5.						

B.

_____
_____
_____
_____
_____
_____
_____
_____
_____

C.

_____
_____
_____
_____
_____
_____
_____
_____
_____

P3-9

A.

The Water Fun Store Net Cash Flow from Operating Activities For August		

B.

The Water Fun Store Acrual Basis Income Statement For August		

C.

P3-11

Khim Lee Company Income Statement For the First Year		

P3-13

A. _____

_____

_____

_____

_____

_____

_____

_____

_____

_____

_____

_____

B. _____

_____

_____

_____

_____

_____

P3-13 (concluded)

Tinker, Evers, and Chance Income Statement For Fiscal 2001		

P3-14

Computer Den Income Statement For April		

P3-17

A.

Desert Harbor Inn Income Statement For the Year Ended December 31, 2001		

Desert Harbor Inn Statement of Cash Flows For the Year Ended December 31, 2001		

P3-17 (concluded)

Desert Harbor Inn Balance Sheet December 31, 2001			

B.

P3-18

A. and B.

	Type of Account					Financial Statement	
	Asset	Liability	Equity	Revenue	Expense	Income Statement	Balance Sheet
1. Wages Payable							
2. Accounts Receivable							
3. Retained Earnings							
4. Buildings							
5. Supplies Used							
6. Inventory on Hand							
7. Cash Sales							
8. Accumulated Depreciation							
9. Loan from Bank							
10. Land							
11. Owners' Investment							
12. Supplies on Hand							
13. Credit Sales							
14. Bonds Payable							
15. Unearned Revenue							
16. Wages Earned by Employees							
17. Utilities Consumed							

P3-19

Item	Account	Balance Sheet Accounts				Income Statement Accounts	
		Cash	+ Other Assets	= Liabilities	+ Equity	+ Revenues	− Expenses
	Beginning Balances	3,200	119,000	52,800	69,400	0	0
	Cash	7,100					
	Accounts Receivable		200				
	Service Revenues					7,300	
	Ending Balances						

P3-20

A.

Zorditch.com Income Statement End of the First Year		

B.

P3-20 (concluded)

C.

_____

_____

_____

_____

_____

_____

_____

_____

_____

_____

_____

_____

_____

CASES

C3-3

FORM 1

C3-3 (continued)

FORM 2

FORM 3

C3-3 (concluded)
FORM 4

FORM 5

CHAPTER 4
PROCESSING ACCOUNTING INFORMATION

EXERCISES

E4-5

	Debit	Credit
a. To increase a liability account		
b. To decrease an equity account		
c. To increase a revenue account		
d. To increase an expense account		
e. To decrease an asset account		
f. To decrease a liability account		
g. To increase an equity account		
h. To increase an asset account		
i. To close a revenue account		
j. To close an expense account		

E4-6

	Debit	Credit
a. Increase in cash		
b. Decrease in accounts payable		
c. Increase in sales revenues		
d. Decrease in equipment		
e. Increase in cost of goods sold		
f. Decrease in accounts receivable		
g. Increase in notes payable		
h. Decrease in owners' investment		
i. Increase in inventory		
j. Decrease in cash		
k. Increase in wages expense		
l. Decrease in inventory		

E4-7

	Debit	Credit
a. Cash		
b. Accounts payable		
c. Sales revenue		
d. Owners' investment		
e. Inventory		
f. Equipment		
g. Cost of goods sold		
h. Notes payable		
i. Wages expense		
j. Wages payable		
k. Buildings		
l. Accounts receivable		

E4-9

	Date	Accounts	Debit	Credit
a.	July 1			
b.	July 5			
c.	July 8			
d.	July 9			
e.	July 10			
f.	July 14			
g.	July 18			

E4-10

	Date	Account	Balance Sheet Accounts				Income Statement Accounts	
			Cash	+ Other Assets	= Liabilities	+ Equity	+ Revenues	− Expenses
a.	Jul 1							
b.	Jul 5							
c.	Jul 8							
d.	Jul 9							
e.	Jul 10							
f.	Jul 14							
g.	Jul 18							

E4-11

	Date	Accounts	Debit	Credit
a.	Oct. 1			
b.	Oct. 3			
c.	Oct. 6			
d.	Oct. 7			
e.	Oct. 9			
f.	Oct. 10			
g.	Oct. 16			

E4-12

	Date	Account	Balance Sheet Accounts				Income Statement Accounts	
			Cash	+ Other Assets	= Liabilities	+ Equity	+ Revenues	– Expenses
a.	Oct 1							
b.	Oct 3							
c.	Oct 6							
d.	Oct 7							
e.	Oct 9							
f.	Oct 10							
g.	Oct 16							

E4-13

	Date	Accounts	Debit	Credit
a.	Mar. 1			
b.	Mar. 4			
c.	Mar. 9			
d.	Mar. 10			
e.	Mar. 13			
f.	Mar. 17			
g.	Mar. 27			

E4-14

	Date	Accounts	Debit	Credit
a.	May 1			
b.	May 3			
c.	May 6			
d.	May 7			
e.	May 9			
f.	May 10			
g.	May 12			

E4-15

Culpepper Manufacturing Computation of Sales Revenue and Merchandise Inventory		
	Sales Revenue	Merchandise Inventory

E4-16

(a)

	Date	Accounts	Debit	Credit
(a)	3/10			
(b)	3/13			
(c)	3/31			

E4-17

(a)

Account	Balance Sheet Accounts				Income Statement Accounts	
	Cash	+ Other Assets	= Liabilities	+ Equity	+ Revenues	− Expenses

(b)

Account	Balance Sheet Accounts				Income Statement Accounts	
	Cash	+ Other Assets	= Liabilities	+ Equity	+ Revenues	− Expenses

(c)

Account	Balance Sheet Accounts				Income Statement Accounts	
	Cash	+ Other Assets	= Liabilities	+ Equity	+ Revenues	− Expenses

E4-18

	Assets	Liabilities	Equity	Net Income
Year-end amounts before correction				
Adjusting entry (a):				
Adjusting entry (b):				
Year-end corrected amounts				

E4-19

	Account	Balance Sheet Accounts				Income Statement Accounts	
		Cash	+ Other Assets	= Liabilities	+ Equity	+ Revenues	− Expenses
a.							
b.							
c.							
d.							

E4-20

(a)

	Account	Balance Sheet Accounts				Income Statement Accounts	
		Cash	+ Other Assets	= Liabilities	+ Equity	+ Revenues	− Expenses
1.							
2.							
3.							
4.							
5.							

(b)

E4-21

Journal			
Entry	Accounts	Debit	Credit
1.			
2.			
3.			
4.			

E4-22

a.

_____

_____

_____

_____

_____

_____

b.

Date	Accounts	Debit	Credit

E4-22 (concluded)

c.

E4-23

a.

b.

Accounts	Debit	Credit

c.

PROBLEMS

P4-2

A.

B.

P4-2 (concluded)
C.

	Account	Balance Sheet Accounts				Income Statement Accounts	
		Cash	+ Other Assets	= Liabilities	+ Equity	+ Revenues	– Expenses
1.							
2.							
3.							
4.							
5.							
6.							
7.							

D. _____

_____

_____

_____

_____

P4-4

	(a) Account Type	(b) Increase	(c) Closed at end of year?
A. Prepaid Insurance			
B. Retained Earnings			
C. Accumulated Depreciation			
D. Wages Expense			
E. Commissions Revenue			
F. Interest Payable			
G. Supplies			
H. Insurance Expense			
I. Unearned Rent			
J. Prepaid Advertising			
K. Notes Payable			
L. Cost of Goods Sold			
M. Machinery			
N. Owners' Capital			
O. Accounts Receivable			
P. Bonds Payable			
Q. Supplies Expense			
R. Depreciation Expense			

P4-7   A

Item	Accounts	Debit	Credit
1.			
2.			
3.			
4.			
5.			
6.			
7.			
8.			
9.			
10.			
11.			
12.			

P4-7 (continued)

B.

Item	Accounts	Debit	Credit
3.			
4.			

C.

Appliance Doctor Company Cash Account Balance April 30, 2002		

P4-7 (concluded)

D.

Appliance Doctor Company Income Statement For the Month of April 2002		

P4-8 A

		Balance Sheet				Income Statement	
	Account	Cash	+ Other Assets	= Liabilities	+ Equity	+ Revenues	– Expenses
1.							
2.							
3.							
4.							
5.							
6.							
7.							
8.							
9.							
10.							
11.							
12.							

P4-8 (continued)

B.

	Account	Balance Sheet				Income Statement	
		Cash	+ Other Assets	= Liabilities	+ Equity	+ Revenues	− Expenses
3.							
4.							

C.

Appliance Doctor Company Cash Account Balance April 30, 2002		

P4-8 (concluded)

D.

Appliance Doctor Company Income Statement For the Month of April 2002		

P4-9

A.

Date	Account	Balance Sheet				Income Statement	
		Cash	+ Other Assets	= Liabilities	+ Equity	+ Revenues	– Expenses
Aug. 1							
Aug. 3							
Aug. 5							
Aug. 6							
Aug. 7							
Aug. 12							
Aug. 23							
Aug. 31							
Aug. 31							
Aug. 31							

P4-9 (concluded)

B.

P4-10

A.

Date	Accounts	Debit	Credit
Aug. 1			
Aug. 3			
Aug. 5			
Aug. 6			
Aug. 7			
Aug. 12			
Aug. 23			
Aug. 31			
Aug. 31			
Aug. 31			

P4-10 (concluded)

B.

P4-11

A.

Item	Account	Balance Sheet Accounts				Income Statement Accounts	
		Cash	+ Other Assets	= Liabilities	+ Equity	+ Revenues	– Expenses
1.							
2.							
3.							
4.							
5.							

B.

Swindle Company Income Statement For the Year Ended December 31, 2002		

P4-14

A. and B.

	Account Balance Before Adjustment	Adjustments		Account Balance After Adjustment
Cash	$52,500			
Accounts receivable	35,250			
Supplies	19,200			
Prepaid insurance	4,050			
Equipment	468,000			
Accumulated depreciation—equipment	(129,000)			
Buildings	649,500			
Accumulated depreciation—buildings	(85,500)			
Land	58,500			
Total assets	$1,072,500			
Unearned revenues	$36,000			
Accounts payable	27,900			
Interest payable	6,000			
Wages payable	0	(1)	+4,350	4,350
Notes payable	420,000			
Common stock	300,000			
Retained earnings *(a)*	224,100			
Total liabilities & stockholders' equity	$1,014,000			
Rent revenues	$100,500			
Wages expense	(36,000)	(1)	−4,350	(40,350)
Supplies expense	0			
Insurance expense	0			
Interest expense	(6,000)			
Depreciation expense	0			
Net income	$58,500			
(a) net income has not been added for the current year.				

P4-14 (concluded)

C.

D.

E.

P4-15

A.

	Date	Accounts	Debit	Credit
1.	Dec. 31			
2.	Dec. 31			
3.	Dec. 31			
4.	Dec. 31			

B.

_____
_____
_____
_____
_____
_____
_____
_____
_____
_____
_____

P4-15 (concluded)

C.

_____

_____

_____

_____

_____

_____

_____

_____

CASES

C4-1

A.

_____

_____

_____

_____

_____

_____

_____

B.

_____

_____

_____

_____

_____

_____

_____

_____

_____

_____

C4-1 (concluded)

C.

Date	Accounts	Debit	Credit

REPORTING ACCOUNTING INFORMATION

EXERCISES

E5-2

a. Wages expense	
b. Wages payable	
c. Cost of goods sold	
d. Common stock	
e. Current assets	
f. Accounts receivable	
g. Sales revenue	
h. Gross profit	
i. Earnings per share	
j. Inventory	
k. Net income	
l. Retained earnings	
m. Contributed capital	
n. Operating income	
o. Common stock issued during the year	

E5-3

a. Changes in a corporation's stockholders' equity for a fiscal period	
b. The dollar amount of the resources available at a particular date	
c. The amount of credit sales not yet collected	
d. Accrual-based operating results for a fiscal period	
e. The cost of resources consumed in producing revenues for a period	
f. The sources of finances used to acquire resources	
g. The effect of issuing stock on the amount of contributed capital during a period	
h. The amount of profit earned by each share of stock	
i. Revenues generated during a fiscal period	

E5-10

Valentine Company Income Statement For the Month of September 2001	

E5-11

Crane Pool Corporation Statement of Stockholders' Equity For the Year Ended June 30, 2001	Contributed Capital	Retained Earnings	Total

E5-12

1.

Moonbeam Enterprises Income Statement For the Month Ended April 30		

2.

Moonbeam Enterprises Statement of Stockholders' Equity For the Month Ended April 30			
	Contributed Capital	Retained Earnings	Total

E5-14

Styles Unlimited Balance Sheet January 31		

E5-15

Moonbeam Enterprises Balance Sheet April 30		

E5-18

Item	Financial Statement	Information Provided
1. Accounts receivable		
2. Rent payable		
3. Retained earnings		
4. Cost of sales		
5. Prepaid rent		
6. Supplies expense		
7. Equipment		
8. Dividends		
9. Depreciation expense		
10. Copyrights		
11. Accrued liabilities		
12. Wages payable		
13. Land		
14. Notes payable		
15. Service revenue		
16. Inventory		
17. Advertising expense		
18. Treasury stock		
19. Common stock		

P5-2

A1.

Income Statements		
	High Flyer Company	**Conservative Company**

A2.

Income Statements		
	High Flyer Company	**Conservative Company**

P5-2 (concluded)

A3.

Income Statements		
	High Flyer Company	**Conservative Company**

B.

C.

P5-3

A.

B.

Parrot Company Income Statement For Year Ending December 31, 2002		

P5-5

A.

B.

C.

P5-6

A.

B.

The Lo Company Income Statement	

P5-6 (concluded)

Statement of Comprehensive Income	

P5-9

A.

B.

Ceramics Inc. Balance Sheet As of December 31, 2001	

P5-10

A.

Argyle Company Income Statement For the Year Ended December 31, 2001		

P5-10 (concluded)

B.

Argyle Company Balance Sheet December 31, 2001		

P5-11

A.

Rustic Company Income Statement For the Year Ended December 31, 2001		

P5-11 (concluded)
B.

Rustic Company Balance Sheet December 31, 2001			

P5-16

	First Month	Second Month	Third Month
Sales revenues	$ 7,500		
Cost of goods sold	(4,000)		
Gross profit	3,500		
Depreciation	(200)		
Other operating expenses	(1,000)		
Income from operations	2,300		
Interest expense	(125)		
Net income	$ 2,175		
Cash	$ 5,275		
Accounts receivable	2,500		
Inventory	1,000		
Plant assets, net of depreciation	22,300		
Total assets	$31,075		
Accounts payable	5,000		
Notes payable	9,900		
Investment by owner	15,000		
Retained earnings	1,175		
Total liabilities and owners' equity	$31,075		

P5-19

A.

ABC, Inc. Income Statement For the Year Ended December 31, 2001		

B.

ABC, Inc. Statement of Stockholders' Equity For the Year Ended December 31, 2001			
	Contributed Capital	Retained Earnings	Total

P5-19 (continued)

C.

ABC, Inc. Balance Sheet December 31, 2001		

P5-19 (concluded)

D.

FINANCIAL REPORTING: THE STATEMENT OF CASH FLOWS

EXERCISES

E6-3

Item		Type of Activity	Add or Subtract
a.	Purchase of plant assets		
b.	Cash paid to suppliers		
c.	Cash collected from customers		
d.	Payment of long-term debt		
e.	Net income		
f.	Depreciation expense		
g.	Payment of dividends		
h.	Issuing stock		
i.	Cash paid to employees		
j.	Cash paid for income taxes		
k.	Disposal of plant assets		

E6-7

_____ a. The amount of cash received from customers is listed.

_____ b. A purpose of the statement is to reconcile the amount of cash generated by operating activities to the amount of net income generated by operating activities.

_____ c. The amount by which cash receipts from customers differed from sales is reported.

_____ d. Certain revenues and expenses that did not generate or consume cash are listed.

_____ e. The amount of net income is listed on the face of the statement.

_____ f. The amount of cash paid to suppliers of inventory is included.

_____ g. The amount of cash paid for taxes is reported.

_____ h. The amount of cash raised from selling bonds to investors is listed on the face of the statement.

_____ i. The purpose of the statement is to reveal the amount of cash received from or paid out for specific operating activities.

j. The amount of cash paid to acquire land and buildings is included.

E6-8

	Statement Section	Statement Format	Added or Subtracted?
1. Decrease in taxes payable			
2. Cash paid to suppliers of inventory			
3. Dividends declared and paid			
4. Depreciation expense			
5. Sale of stock			
6. Increase in accounts receivable			
7. Cash collected from customers			
8. Purchase of plant assets			
9. Payments on long-term debt			
10. Cash paid for taxes			
11. Increase in wages payable			
12. Purchase of treasury stock			

E6-9

Item	Type of Activity	Add or Subtract
a. Purchase of plant assets		
b. Increase in accounts payable		
c. Decrease in accounts receivable		
d. Payment of long-term debt		
e. Net income		
f. Depreciation expense		
g. Payment of dividends		
h. Issuing stock		
i. Increase in inventory		
j. Decrease in taxes payable		
k. Disposal of plant assets		

E6-13

	Account Balance	Adjustment and Reason
a.	Accounts receivable increased $10,000	Subtract $10,000 from net income because cash collected from customers was $10,000 less than sales for the period.
b.	Accounts payable increased $7,500	
c.	Inventory decreased $50,000	
d.	Notes payable increased $100,000	
e.	Equipment decreased $80,000	
f.	Prepaid insurance decreased $22,000	
g.	Wages payable decreased $8,000	
h.	Unearned revenue increased $13,000	

E6-20

Account and Balance	Anticipated Future Event and Cash Flow
a. Accounts Receivable, $12,000	$12,000 of cash should be received from customers during the next fiscal year. Operating activities section..
b. Prepaid Insurance, $22,000	
c. Merchandise, $50,000	
d. Treasury Stock, $33,000	
e. Accounts payable, $6,500	
f. Machinery, $92,000	
g. Notes Payable, Long-Term, $88,000	

E6-20 (concluded)

Account and Balance	Anticipated Future Event and Cash Flow
h. Unearned Revenue, $10,000	
i. Taxes payable, $7,800	
j. Retained Earnings, $56,000	

PROBLEMS

P6-1

San Garza Properties Statement of Cash Flows (direct format) For the Month of January 2002		

P6-2

A.

B.

C.

P6-2 (concluded)

D.

Planet Accessories Company Statement of Cash Flows (direct format) Year Ended December 31, 2002		

P6-3

A.

B.

P6-3 (concluded)

C.

Dollar Sine Enterprises Statement of Cash Flows (operating activities only—indirect format) For the Year Just Ended		

P6-4

Reuben Corporation Statement of Cash Flows (indirect format) For the Year Ended December 31, 2001		

P6-5

A.

B.

C.

P6-5 (concluded)

D.

Planet Accessories Company Statement of Cash Flows (indirect format) Year Ended December 31, 2002		

P6-7

A.

B.

Starkovich Architects, Inc. Operating Activities (direct format) Year Ending December 31, 2002		

P6-11

Office Decor Company Statement of Cash Flows For the Year Ended December 31, 2001 (in thousands)		

P6-17

A. & B.

Event	Type of Activity	Effect on March's Net Income	Effect on March's Cash Flow
1. Sold $18,000 of gods on credit to customers. Received a 25% down payment with the balance on account.			
2. Purchased $500 of office supplies for cash that will be used during April.			
3. Received $3,000 from a customer in full payment of her account balance.			
4. Borrowed $80,000 from a local bank to be repaid in monthly installments plus interest starting in April.			
5. Paid rent on the office space ($1,200 per month) for the months of February, March, and April.			
6. Distributed monthly paychecks to employees totaling $13,300. 30% was for work performed in February and the balance for work performed in March.			
7. Purchased new Internet server equipment at a cost of $50,000.			
8. Purchased a 3-year fire insurance policy at a total cost of $10,800. Its coverage began on March 1.			
9. Purchased merchandise from suppliers on account at a cost of $70,000.			
10. Collected $22,000 from customers in payment of their accounts. 80% of this amount was from sales recorded in February and the balance from March sales.			
11. Collected four months rent in advance (at $700 per month) from a tenant who will move in on April 1.			
12. Paid $45,000 to suppliers in partial payment of goods purchased in #9 above.			
13. Sold $33,000 of merchandise to customers on credit.			
14. Sold an investment in stocks and bonds for $28,000; the same amount that had been paid for it. A 3-year, 9% note receivable was accepted in full payment.			
Totals for March			

P6-17 (concluded)

C.

P6-21

A.

Beltway Distributors, Inc. Statement of Cash Flows For the Year Ended January 30, 2002 (in thousands)	

P6-21 (concluded)

B.

_____

_____

_____

_____

_____

_____

_____

_____

_____

_____

_____

P6-22

A.

Pro-Forma Income Statement	First Month	Second Month	Third Month
Sales revenues	$22,500		
Cost of goods sold	(12,000)		
Gross profit	10,500		
Depreciation	600		
Other operating expenses	3,500		
Income from operations	6,400		
Interest expense	425		
Net income	$5,975		

Pro-Forma Balance Sheet (at end of)	First Month	Second Month	Third Month
Cash	$15,075		
Accounts receivable	7,500		
Inventory	3,000		
Plant assets, net of depreciation	66,900		
Total assets	$92,475		
Accounts payable	15,000		
Notes payable	44,500		
Investment by owner	30,000		
Retained earnings	2,975		
Total liabilities & owners' equity	$92,475		

P6-22 (concluded)

Pro-Forma Cash Flow Statement	First Month	Second Month	Third Month
Cash collected from customers	$15,000		
Cash paid to suppliers	0		
Cash paid for operating expenses	(3,500)		
Cash paid for interest	(425)		
Cash paid for plant assets	(67,500)		
Cash received from bank	45,000		
Cash received from owner	30,000		
Cash paid to repay loan	(500)		
Cash paid to owner	(3,000)		
Net change in cash	$15,075		

B.

CHAPTER 7
THE TIME VALUE OF MONEY

EXERCISES

E7-17

a.

Amount	Rate	Time	Compounding Frequency	Interest Factor	Future Value
$1,000	12%	2 years	Annual		
$1,000	12%	2 years	Semiannual		
$1,000		2 years	Quarterly		
$1,000	12%	2 years	Monthly		

b.

_____

_____

_____

_____

_____

c.

_____

_____

_____

_____

_____

d.

Amount	Rate	Time	Compounding Frequency	Interest Factor	Present Value
$1,000	12%	2 years	Annual		
$1,000	12%	2 years	Semiannual		
$1,000	12%	2 years	Quarterly		
$1,000	12%	2 years	Monthly		

e.

_____

_____

_____

_____

_____

E7-17 (concluded)

f.

_____

_____

_____

_____

_____

E7-22

a.

_____

_____

_____

_____

_____

_____

b.

_____

_____

_____

_____

_____

_____

	Date	Accounts	Debit	Credit
c.				
d.				

E7-23

a.

_____

_____

_____

_____

_____

_____

_____

b.

Date	Accounts	Debit	Credit

PROBLEMS

P7-7

A.

_____

_____

_____

_____

_____

_____

_____

_____

_____

B.

_____

_____

_____

_____

_____

_____

_____

_____

_____

_____

C.

Date	Accounts	Debit	Credit

P7-9

Single Amounts	Interest Rate	Number of Periods	Present Value	Future Value	Annuity Payment
a.	6%		$558.39	$1,000	
b.	12%	15		$7,000	
c.		5	$3,402.90	$5,000	
d.	10%	20	$2972.80		

Annuities	Interest Rate	Number of Periods	Present Value	Future Value	Annuity Payment
e.	7%		$205.01	$287.54	$50
f.	10%	7		$948.72	$100
g.		6	$4,485.92	$7523.33	$1,000
h.	11%	8	$10,292.24		$2,000
i.	12%	10	$5,650.22	$17,548.74	

P7-10

A.

Month	Present Value (Beg.)	Interest Expense	Total Payment	Principal Payment	Present Value (End)
May					
June					
July					
August					
September					
October					
November					
December					
January					
February					
March					
April					

P7-10 (concluded)

B.

_____

_____

_____

_____

_____

C.

_____

_____

_____

_____

_____

D.

_____

_____

_____

_____

_____

E.

_____

_____

_____

_____

_____

P7-12

A.

B.

Period	Present Value at Beginning of Period	Interest at 10%	Payment	Payment of Principal	Value at End of Period
Year 2001					
Year 2002					
Year 2003					
Year 2004					
Year 2005					

C.

P7-13

A.

_____
_____
_____
_____
_____
_____

B.

_____
_____
_____
_____
_____
_____

C.

Date	Accounts	Debit	Credit

EXERCISES

E8-6

	Date	Accounts	Debit	Credit
a.				
b.				
c.				

E8-7

a.

b.

E8-7 (concluded)

c.

Date	Accounts	Debit	Credit
1/1/97			
12/31/97			
12/31/02			

E8-9

	Date	Accounts	Debit	Credit
a.				
b.				

E8-11

	1.	Obligations expected to be discharged within one year
	2.	A financial instrument that promises to repay principal at maturity and to pay interest each period until then
	3.	An obligation to convey resources to another entity in the future
	4.	Debt that is backed up by specific assets of the debtor company
	5.	A bond backed only by the general creditworthiness of the issuing company
	6.	Bonds that can be reacquired at the request of the issuing company
	7.	The amount repaid to bondholders at the end of the bond's life
	8.	The rate of interest that determines the amount of cash sent to bondholders each period
	9.	Bonds that mature a portion at a time over the life of the issue
	10.	The actual (or real) rate of return earned by the holder of a bond
	11.	A type of lease that results in a liability being reported on the balance sheet
	12.	An existing condition that may result in an economic effect later
	13.	A promise to engage in some future economic activity
	14.	A lease that does not result in a liability being reported on the balance sheet

E8-14

Quick Chip Company Stockholders' Equity		
	2002	2001

E8-16

a.

_____

_____

_____

_____

_____

b.

Date	Accounts	Debit	Credit

c.

_____

_____

_____

d.

_____

_____

_____

_____

_____

_____

_____

_____

_____

_____

_____

_____

E8-19

Year	Total Dividends Paid	Dividends to Preferred	Dividends to Common	Unpaid Dividends to Preferred
2000	$50,000			
2001	10,000			
2002	45,000			
2003	70,000			

E8-20

	1. Shares of a company's own stock that have been reacquired by the company
	2. Capital resulting from direct investments made by stockholders in the company
	3. Earnings that have not been distributed to owners as dividends
	4. The voting stock in a corporation
	5. Stock that receives a fixed dividend amount
	6. The document granted by a state that gives a corporation the legal right to exist
	7. An arbitrary value assigned to a share of stock (not a meaningful value)
	8. The maximum number of shares that a corporation is permitted to issue
	9. The actual number of shares that have been sold or given to stockholders
	10. The number of shares that are currently in the hands of stockholders
	11. The date on which a corporation announces that a dividend will be paid
	12. The date that determines who will receive a dividend that has been declared
	13. The date on which a dividend is distributed to stockholders
	14. The privilege of existing stockholders to buy a prorata share of any new stock that is offered for sale
	15. A type of dividend in which new share are distributed to existing stockholders

E8-20 (concluded)

	16. A very large stock dividend
	17. A feature that encourages corporations to make up any previously omitted dividends on preferred stock
	18. Preferred stock that will be repurchased by the issuing company at a fixed future date

PROBLEMS

P8-2

A.

_____

_____

_____

_____

_____

_____

_____

_____

_____

_____

_____

_____

_____

_____

_____

_____

_____

_____

_____

_____

_____

B. At date of issuance

Date	Accounts	Debit	Credit

P8-2 (concluded)

At date of first interest payment

Date	Accounts	Debit	Credit

At date of last interest payment

Date	Accounts	Debit	Credit

P8-3

A. _____

_____

_____

_____

_____

_____

_____

_____

P8-3 (concluded)

B.

_____

_____

_____

_____

_____

_____

_____

_____

_____

_____

_____

C.

Date	Accounts	Debit	Credit

P8-4

A.

_____

_____

_____

_____

_____

_____

_____

_____

P8-4 (concluded)

B.

_____

_____

_____

_____

_____

_____

_____

_____

_____

_____

_____

C.

Date	Accounts	Debit	Credit

P8-7

A.

B.

C.

D.

P8-7 (concluded)

E.

Date	Accounts	Debit	Credit

F.

Date	Accounts	Debit	Credit

P8-8

A.

B.

P8-8 (concluded)

C.

Date	Accounts	Debit	Credit

D.

_____

_____

_____

_____

_____

_____

_____

E.

Date	Accounts	Debit	Credit

F.

_____

_____

_____

_____

_____

_____

_____

P8-10

A.

B.

Date	Accounts	Debit	Credit

C.

D.

Date	Accounts	Debit	Credit

P8-10 (concluded)

E.

_____

_____

_____

_____

_____

_____

_____

_____

_____

_____

_____

_____

_____

_____

_____

_____

_____

_____

_____

P8-11

A.

_____

_____

_____

_____

_____

B.

Date	Accounts	Debit	Credit

P8-11 (continued)

C.

D.

E.

Date	Accounts	Debit	Credit

P8-11 (concluded)

F.

_____

_____

_____

_____

_____

_____

_____

_____

_____

_____

_____

_____

_____

_____

_____

P8-13

A.

Bonzai Company Stockholders' Equity December 31, 2002		

B.

_____

_____

_____

_____

_____

_____

P8-14

A.

Boyer Company Stockholders' Equity After the Stock Split		

B.

Boyer Company Stockholders' Equity After the 100% Stock Dividend		

C.

P8-14 (concluded)

D.

_____

_____

_____

_____

_____

_____

_____

P8-16

A.

Ozzy-Guerra Publishing Company Stockholders' Equity Before Conversion		

B.

Ozzy-Guerra Publishing Company Stockholders' Equity After Conversion		

P8-16 (concluded)

C.

D.

P8-17

December 31	2002	2001
Stockholders' Equity		
8.5% preferred stock, $10 par value, 10,000 shares authorized and issued		
Common stock, $2 par value, 300,000 shares authorized, 110, 000 and 90,000 shares issued		
Paid-in capital in excess of par value		
Retained earnings		
Treasury stock (4,500 and 3,100 shares at cost)		
Total stockholders' equity	$1,411,750	$1,037,800

CHAPTER 9
ANALYSIS OF FINANCING ACTIVITIES

EXERCISES

E9-14

		Debt to Equity	Debt to Assets	Financial Leverage	Current Ratio
a.	Sold common stock to investors				
b.	Borrowed cash from a bank on long-term note				
c.	Paid cash dividends on stock				
d.	Sold inventory for cash				
e.	Paid off loan in part b				
f.	Bought stock of another company				
g.	Purchased treasury stock				

PROBLEMS

P9-4

Mount Baker Company Pro Forma Income Statement		
	Equity	Debt

P9-5

A. and B.

Crossroads Company Pro Forma Income Statements		
	Equity Financing	Debt Financing

C.

EXERCISES

E10-2

Iteljack Oil Company Long-Term Assets Section of Balance Sheet At Year-End		

E10-9

a. _____

_____

_____

_____

_____

_____

b. _____

_____

_____

_____

_____

_____

E10-9 (concluded)

c.

	1998	1999	2000	2001

d. _____

_____

_____

_____

_____

_____

_____

_____

_____

E10-12

	Date	Accounts	Debit	Credit
a.				
b.				
c.				

E10-13

	Date	Accounts	Debit	Credit
a.				
b.				
c.				

E10-14

	Date	Accounts	Debit	Credit
a.				
b.				
c.				

E10-15

a.

Date	Accounts	Debit	Credit

b.

_____

_____

_____

_____

_____

_____

c.

_____

_____

_____

_____

_____

E10-16

1.

Date	Accounts	Debit	Credit
5/15/99			
9/12/99			
12/31/99			
9/12/00			
12/31/00			
1/6/01			

E10-16 (concluded)

2.

E10-21

Zirconium Graphics Company Partial Statement of Cash Flows For the Year Ended December 31, 2001		

E10-22

a.
_____

_____

_____

_____

_____

b.

Date	Accounts	Debit	Credit
Jan. 1			
Dec. 31			
Dec. 31			

E10-22 (concluded)

c. _____

_____

_____

_____

_____

_____

PROBLEMS

P10-1

A.

Depreciation Schedule

Year	Straight-Line Method		Declining-Balance Method		Units-of-Production Method	
	Depreciation Expense	Book Value	Depreciation Expense	Book Value	Depreciation Expense	Book Value
0						
1						
2						
3						
4						
Totals						

B.

_____

_____

_____

_____

_____

_____

_____

_____

_____

_____

_____

_____

_____

_____

_____

P10-1 (concluded)

C.

_____

_____

_____

_____

_____

_____

_____

_____

_____

_____

_____

_____

_____

_____

_____

_____

_____

_____

_____

P10-2

A.

Year	Book Value at Beginning of Year	Usual Double-Declining-Balance Method (2/6 × Book Value)
2001		
2002		
2003		
2004		
2005		
2006		
Total		

B.

Book Value at Beginning of Year	Modified Double-Declining-Balance Method

P10-2 (concluded)

C.

Year	1 Modified Double-Declining-Balance Method	2 Straight-Line Depreciation (Cost ÷ 6 years)	3 Difference in Income (Column 1 − Column 2)	4 Difference in Taxes (Column 3 × 35%)
2001				
2002				
2003				
2004				
2005				
2006				
Total				

D.

P10-5

A.

	Straight-Line Depreciation			
Year	Beginning Book Value	Depreciation Expense	Accumulated Depreciation	Ending Book Value
1				
2				
3				
4				
5				
Total				

	Double-Declining-Balance Depreciation			
Year	Beginning Book Value (BBV)	Depreciation Expense (BBV × .4)	Accumulated Depreciation	Ending Book Value
1				
2				
3				
4				
5				
Total				

B.

	Units-of-Production Depreciation			
Year	Beginning Book Value	Depreciation Expense	Accumulated Depreciation	Ending Book Value
1				
2				
3				
4				
5				
Total				

P10-5 (continued)

_____
_____
_____
_____
_____
_____
_____
_____
_____

C. _____
_____
_____
_____
_____
_____
_____
_____
_____
_____
_____
_____
_____
_____
_____
_____
_____
_____
_____
_____

P10-5 (concluded)

D.

_____

_____

_____

_____

_____

_____

_____

_____

_____

_____

_____

_____

_____

_____

_____

_____

_____

_____

P10-6

A.

_____

_____

_____

_____

_____

B.

	Straight-Line Method		Double-Declining Method	
Year	Depreciation Expense	End-of-Year Book Value	Depreciation Expense	End-of-Year Book Value
0				
1				
2				
3				
4				
5				
6				

P10-6 (concluded)

C.

Income statements: Straight-line depreciation	All years are the same

D.

Income statements: Double-declining balance	Year 1	Year 2	Year 3	Year 4	Year 5	Year 6

E.

_____
_____
_____
_____
_____
_____
_____
_____
_____
_____
_____
_____
_____
_____

P10-7

A.

Straight-Line Depreciation				
Year	Beginning Book Value	Depreciation Expense	Accumulated Depreciation	Ending Book Value
1999				
2000				
2001				
2002				
2003				
Total				

Double-Declining-Balance Depreciation				
Year	Beginning Book Value	Depreciation Expense	Accumulated Depreciation	Ending Book Value
1999				
2000				
2001				
2002				
2003				
Total				

B.

_____

_____

_____

_____

_____

_____

_____

_____

P10-7 (concluded)

C.

D.

E.

P10-8

A.

Straight-Line Depreciation				
Year	Beginning Book Value	Depreciation Expense	Accumulated Depreciation	Ending Book Value
2001				
2002				
2003				
2004				
Total				

Double-Declining-Balance Depreciation				
Year	Beginning Book Value	Depreciation Expense	Accumulated Depreciation	Ending Book Value
2001				
2002				
2003				
2004				
Total				

B.

_____

_____

_____

_____

_____

_____

C.

_____

_____

_____

_____

_____

_____

_____

_____

_____

_____

P10-8 (concluded)

D.

P10-10

A.

B.

2000	Leonardo	Shylock	Total

2001	Leonardo	Balthasar	Total

C.

Effect on income in 2000:	

Effect on income in 2001:	

P10-12

A. _____

_____

_____

_____

_____

_____

B.

1 Period	2 Present Value at Beginning of Period	3 Interest Revenue	4 Cash Interest Received	5 Amortization of Premium	6 Value at End of Period
1					
2					
3					
4					

C.

Date	Accounts	Debit	Credit
4/1/01			
9/30/01			
3/31/02			
9/30/02			

P10-12 (concluded)

Date	Accounts	Debit	Credit
3/31/03			
3/31/03			

D.

E.

P10-13

	Date	Accounts	Debit	Credit
A.				
B.				
C.				
D.				
E.				
F.				
G.				
H.				

P10-13 (concluded)

I.

	Original Cost	Amortization of Premium	Market Value Adjustment	Carrying Value (Book Value) at End of Year 1
C.				
D.				
G.				
H.				

J.

1	2	3	4	5	6
Year	Present Value at Beginning of Year	Interest Revenue	Cash Received	Amortization of Premium	Value at End of Year
1					
2					
3					
4					
5					
Totals					

P10-14

A.

Date	Accounts	Debit	Credit
Jan. 1			
Dec. 31			

B.

	If the bonds are?		
	Held-to-Maturity Securities	Trading Securities	Available-for-Sale Securities
Accounting method to be used			
Amount of unrealized holding gain (loss) to be reported on the income statement			
Amount of unrealized holding gain (loss) to be reported on the balance sheet			
Amount of discount amortized during 2001			
Balance of investment account on balance sheet			

P10-15

A.

Date	Accounts	Debit	Credit
Aug. 22			

B.

	If the total number of Radius common shares outstanding totals		
	1 million	80,000	30,000
Accounting method to be used			
Amount of unrealized holding gain (loss) to be reported on the income statement			
Amount of unrealized holding gain (loss) to be reported on the balance sheet			
Balance of investment account on balance sheet			

C.

Date	Accounts	Debit	Credit
Jan. 23			

P10-16

A.

	Date	Accounts	Debit	Credit
1.				
2.				
3.				

B.

P10-17

A.

Date	Accounts	Debit	Credit

B.

C.

D.

_____
_____
_____
_____
_____
_____
_____
_____
_____
_____
_____
_____
_____

E.

Date	Accounts	Debit	Credit

P10-18

A.

Date	Accounts	Debit	Credit
7/1/98			
12/31/98			
12/31/99			
12/31/00			
6/30/01			
6/30/01			

B.

P10-18 (concluded)

C.

P10-20

A.

Date	Accounts	Debit	Credit
Jan. 1			
Dec. 31			
Dec. 31			

P10-20 (concluded)

B.

	Question	Solution
1.	In which section of the balance sheet will this investment be reported? Be specific.	
2.	What amount will be reported on the balance sheet for this investment? Show your work.	
3.	What amount of income will be reported on the income statement related to this investment? Explain.	
4.	What information will be reported about any unrealized holding gain or loss? Explain.	

CHAPTER 11
ANALYSIS OF INVESTING ACTIVITIES

EXERCISES

E11-2

a.

b.

c.

E11-6
The effect of the sales on the company's accounts would be as follows:

Account	Balance Sheet Accounts				Income Statement Accounts	
	Cash	+ Other Assets	= Liabilities	+ Equity	+ Revenues	− Expenses

The financial statements would report the following:

	No Sale	Sale of A	Sale of B

PROBLEMS

P11-3
A.

	County Residents Only	County Residents Plus Two Towns	County Residents Plus Four Towns
Revenues			
Fixed expenses			
Variable expenses			
Net income			

P11-3 (concluded)

B.

	County Residents Only	County Residents Plus Two Towns	County Residents Plus Four Towns
Revenues			
Fixed expenses			
Variable expenses			
Net income			

C.

P11-15

A.

	Current Operations	Expansion of Current Operations	Addition of Dragons	Addition of Games

B.

_____

_____

_____

_____

_____

_____

_____

C.

_____

_____

_____

_____

_____

_____

_____

_____

_____

_____

_____

_____

_____

_____

CASES

C11-2
Pro forma income statement

	Before Acquisition	Effect of Acquisition	After Acquisition

Pro forma statement of cash flows

	Before Acquisition	Effect of Acquisition	After Acquisition

C11-2 (concluded)

EXERCISES

E12-2

Trailer City, Inc. Income Statement Year Ending December 31, 2001	

E12-6

a.

Date	Accounts	Debit	Credit

b.

E12-11

Date	Accounts	Debit	Credit

E12-12

a.

Event	Date	Accounts	Debit	Credit
1				
2				
3				
4				
5				
6				
7				
8				
9				

E12-12 (concluded)

b.

_____

_____

_____

_____

_____

_____

_____

_____

_____

_____

_____

_____

_____

_____

_____

_____

_____

_____

_____

_____

_____

E12-23

a.

E12-23 (concluded)
b.

_____

_____

_____

_____

_____

_____

_____

_____

PROBLEMS

P12-1

Veggies, Inc. Income Statement For the Month of January 2001		

P12-5

Computation of Manufacturing Inventory Costs:

Raw materials inventory:	
Balance on 1/1/01	
Materials purchased in 2001	
Materials used in production	
Balance on 12/31/01	
Work-in-Process Inventory:	
Balance on 1/1/01	
Materials used in production	
Labor costs	
Overhead costs	
Cost of goods completed	
Balance on 12/31/01	
Finished Goods Inventory:	
Balance on 1/1/01	
Cost of goods completed	
Cost of goods sold	
Balance on 12/31/01	

P12-8

A.

Event	Date	Accounts	Debit	Credit
1				
2				
3				
4				
5				
6				
7				
8				

P12-8 (continued)

Event	Date	Accounts	Debit	Credit
9				
10				

B.

Noise and Abuse Recording Company Income Statement For the Month of October		

P12-8 (concluded)

C.

D.

P12-9

A.

Event	Date	Accounts	Debit	Credit
1				
2				
3				
4				
5				
6				
7				

P12-9 (concluded)

B.

P12-12

A.

	Current Methods	Alternate Methods

B. _____

_____

_____

_____

_____

_____

P12-13

SCHRIVER Company Income Statement For the Year Ended December 31, 2002 (in millions)	

P12-15

A.

Pelican Enterprises Income Statement (in 000s) Year Ended June 30, 2002	

B.

P12-15 (concluded)

C.

D.

P12-16

	A. Minimum Net Income	B. Maximum Net Income

C.

CHAPTER 13
ANALYSIS OF OPERATING ACTIVITIES

EXERCISES

E13-2

	Strategy A	Strategy B	Strategy C
Unit price			
Estimated sales in units			
Sales revenue			
Variable expenses			
Fixed expenses			
Additional advertising			
Total expenses			
Pro forma operating profit			

E13-21

Attribute	Magnitude of Attribute	Expected Company Value
Asset growth	High	
Debt to assets	Low	
Dividend payout	Low	
Equity growth	Low	
Investing cash outflow	High	
Operating cash inflow	Low	
Research and development expenditure	High	
Return on assets	Low	
Return on equity	High	
Sales growth	High	

PROBLEMS

P13-3

A.

	Strategy 1	Strategy 2	Strategy 3
Selling price per case			
Estimated monthly sales (cases)			
Sales revenue			
Expenses:			
Fixed, per month			
Advertising, per month			
Variable per case			
Total monthly expenses			
Pro forma monthly profit			
Pro forma annual profit			
% return on $3 million investment			

P13-3 (continued)

B.

P13-3 (concluded)

C.

_____

_____

_____

_____

_____

_____

_____

_____

_____

_____

_____

_____

_____

_____

_____

_____

_____

P13-9

A.

_____

_____

_____

_____

_____

_____

P13-9 (continued)

B.

Year ended December 31	1998	1997	1996
Net sales			
Cost of products sold			
Gross income			
Selling, general, and administrative expenses			
Trade names and goodwill amortization			
Operating income			
Nonoperating (income) expenses:			
Interest expense			
Other, net			
Income before taxes			
Income taxes			
Net income			

C.

P13-9 (concluded)

D.

_____

_____

_____

_____

_____

_____

_____

_____

_____

_____

_____

_____

CASES

C13-3

A.

	Expected	Minimum

C13-3 (continued)

B.

C.

C13-3 (continued)

D.

Cash flow from operating activities	Expected	Minimum

C13-3 (concluded)

E.

F.